For my grandchildren:
Shenna, Nicole, Joshua, Breeana, Vincent,
Justin, Camille, Kennie & Chrystie

From Kansas to Kalimantan
A Humble Missionary Journey

Arny Humble

Published by UCS PRESS
P.O. Box 12797
Prescott, Arizona 86304-2797

Publisher web site:
www.marjimbooks.com

Cover design by Rob Herman

ISBN 978-0-943247-55-7

First edition printed in June 2012

Contents

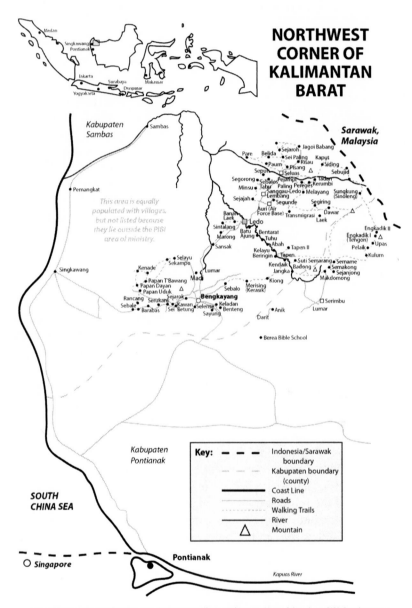

NORTHWEST CORNER OF KALIMANTAN BARAT

Medan
Singkawang
Pontianak
Jakarta
Surabaya
Makassar
Yogyakarta
Denpasar

Kabupaten Sambas
Sambas
Sarawak, Malaysia

Pare · Belida · Sejaroh · Jagoi Babang
· Sei Paling · Risau · Kaput
· Paum · Pisang · Siding
Sepun · Seluas · Sebujid
Segorong · Sebalo · Pejampi · Tadan
Minsu · Tabu · Paling Pereges · Kerumbi
Pemangkat · Sanggau-Ledo · Melayang · Sungkung (Sinoleng)
Sejajah · Lembang · Segunde · Segiring
Auri (Air Force Base) · Transmigrasi · Dawar
Banan Laek · Ledo · Laek
Sintalang · Bentarat · Engkadik II
Batu Ajung · Tuhu · Engkadik I (Tengon) · Upas
Marong · Abah · Pelaik
Sansak · Kelayu · Tapen II · Kulum
Beringin · Tapen
Selayu · Kendaik · Suti Semarang · Semame
Kenade · Sekampo · Badong · Semakong
Lumar · Jangka · Sejanjong
Papan T'Bawang · Madi · Makdomong
Papan Dayan · Kiong
Papan Uduk · Sebalo · Merising (Kerasik)
Rancang · Sejarok · Bengkayang
Sebale · Serukam · Kawan · Keladan · Serimbu
· Barabas · Sei Betung · Selemet · Benteng · Lumar
Sayung · Anik
Darit

This area is equally populated with villages, but not listed because they lie outside the PIBI area of ministry.

Pemangkat

Singkawang

· Berea Bible School

Kabupaten Pontianak

SOUTH CHINA SEA

Key:

– – –	Indonesia/Sarawak boundary
· · · · ·	Kabupaten boundary (county)
▬▬▬	Coast Line
·········	Roads
– – –	Walking Trails
———	River
△	Mountain

Pontianak
○ Singapore
Kapuas River

The author has slept and preached in almost every village on this map. Most of them have PIBI churches (1984).

ACKNOWLEDGEMENTS

It was primarily my children who first urged me to put my life story into print. I found it a "humbling task" (no pun intended), to share my thoughts and actions on paper. Only their encouragement, as they read the first few chapters, encouraged me to continue writing. They believed that the life lessons and the core beliefs God has instilled in me through the years should be recorded, especially for their own children.

I have been most inspired in life by my wife, Wanda. The reader will discern that it has been my attempt throughout the book to make her the heroine – which indeed she was. Apart from Christ Himself, I owe the most to her for the spiritual formation of my character. I acknowledge that, humanly speaking, her belief in me has, for the past fifty-five years, been the strongest encouragement for me to believe in myself. Her faithful writing of letters to family and supporters for more than half a century provided me with dates and facts that would have otherwise slipped into oblivion.

Fortunately, I have had professional editorial help from a former co-laborer in Kalimantan Barat. Grey and Mary Ann Jeffreys served alongside us for more than a decade during the time our Indonesian Baptist church was in a fruitful growth stage. Since returning to America in 1987, Mary Ann has edited the books of many well-known authors. For mine, she allowed that her effort was a "labor of love." I am most grateful for her generosity. She often reminded me of the big picture with statements like, "Arny, you can't write everything" – thus keeping me from writing a five hundred page book! At the local level I have had grammatical help from a former fifth grade teacher, and present librarian from my church, El Camino Baptist of Tucson, Arizona. Phyllis Quesnel, who followed the missionary work of Wanda and myself for nearly five decades, has spent many hours poring over each revision of my manuscript. I acknowledge the immense help of Phyllis and Mary Ann, while I hold myself solely responsible for the contents and the accuracy of language and grammar.

Finally, I acknowledge my grandchildren, for being the reason for this writing. If it were not for them, my story would never be recorded. Breeana Humble created the book cover.

FOREWORD

It is an honor for me to write the introduction to this amazing Humble missionary journey, "From Kansas to Kalimantan." I have been serving with WorldVenture, formerly CBFMS, for over thirty years. The last twenty have been as the President. During these years, I have had the amazing opportunity to visit our missionary family in action in over sixty countries of the world. Visiting Indonesia has been a special treat along the journey, and seeing the lasting imprint of Arny and Wanda has been so obvious everywhere I traveled.

In my position I can't have favorites, but I always say that Arny and Wanda Humble set the standard of what missionaries should be. *Being* is actually of greater consequence than *doing* in God's economy. This book is an amazing description of a journey from the humble beginnings in Kansas to one of the most strategic international missionary impacts that I have personally witnessed. Arny and Wanda Humble truly embodied the incarnation of Christ as they became Indonesian. I have watched them in action with national Indonesian leaders and have seen the enormous respect as those leaders look to Arny as a father figure. Many missionaries never achieve that status. How did they do it? Read and enjoy.

God's choice chosen servants, Arny and Wanda Humble, are the very kind of people that have made it such a joy for me to serve in leadership in missions. I do what I do so they can do what they do. Here are two lives well lived in their lifelong commitment to the evangelization and discipleship of the people of Indonesia. This is a great read which you will thoroughly enjoy.

Hans Finzel
President of WorldVenture

INTRODUCTION

I awoke with the whole house swaying under me, unable to remember exactly where I was or what was happening. Could it be an earthquake, or was I possibly suffering from vertigo? It was nearly pitch black so at first my eyes adjusted to nothing. In those first few seconds between being awake and asleep, there was a definite sense of anxiety bordering on fear. Then I could at least see that I was under my mosquito net. I could also make out the flicker of two smoky kerosene lamp wicks burning faintly on each side of a large, open room. The one-half-inch-thick sleeping pad under me was stretched across the bamboo slat floor, leaving ribbed marks where I had been lying on it. Then I heard the grunt of a large pig below me, as he rubbed himself vigorously against the pole directly under my makeshift bed. He must have found the pole that stabilized the rest of the smaller stilts that elevated the house six feet off the ground. Now it came back to me where I had gone to sleep the night before. I was in a Dyak tribal village, far back in the jungle of Kalimantan Barat. Soon the rhythmic thudding of mortar and pestle rice- pounding started up just a few feet from my head. The whole floor shook with the impact. Dyak women start their workday at four o'clock in the morning. I knew my night of sleep was over.

Most of you reading these words have, at one time or another, awakened in a strange place and wondered: *Where am I, and how did I get here?* This book is my humble attempt to explain how I got from Kansas to Kalimantan. As my grandchildren were growing up, they often asked me to tell them stories of my youth on the farm. I began to think how great it would be to know up close the history of my own grandpa or great-grandpa. I decided to write my life story for my grandchildren. I have been a missionary working with WorldVenture (formerly Conservative Baptist Foreign Mission Society) for more than forty years. So, there was a missionary story to be told as well. At one time my wife and I were supported by forty-four churches and twenty-six individuals. Many friends among this supporting constituency also urged me to tell my story of pioneering two mission fields under the auspices of WorldVenture. It is my earnest prayer that God will be glorified as I attempt to relate some of the high and low points of this life venture.

PART 1 – THE EARLY YEARS

"Give me a child until he is seven and I will give you the man" is a quote attributed to St. Francis Xavier, co-founder of the Jesuit Order. The obvious meaning is that the soul of a child is most moldable in his or her earliest years. Fortunate indeed is the country boy who spends his early years under the tutelage of a mother such as I had. In spite of my wanderings in later years, God "began a good work in" me through her influence. Once the mold of my sensitive conscience was set, it was a force to be reckoned with, whether or not my conduct always showed the result of it.

The rigors of farm life in southeastern Kansas also played a part in my spiritual formation. Today most children know about animals only as house pets to be coddled and spoiled. In the thirties and forties every farm animal had a use. Dogs were for herding cows or sheep. Cats caught mice in the barn. None of the farm animals got inside the house! It was a different world. It was my world. The animals were all expected to work for their keep, and so was the farm boy. It wasn't all work, though it seemed to me to be that way at times. Not many people appear in the early part of this story. That's because any farmhouse we lived in was usually at least a quarter of a mile from the closest neighbor. The people closest to me were very special people. I will start by telling about my mom.

Chapter 1 – Mom – the "Golden Thread"

I am mindful of the sincere faith within you,
which first dwelt in your grandmother Lois.
(2 Timothy 1:5)

It was my mother who was named Lois, not my grandmother, but sincere faith it certainly was, and it was indeed passed on to me. In the small town of Humboldt, Kansas, Lois Olive Humble was about to give birth to her first child. Her petite five-foot-two frame promised it would not be an easy delivery. Then came the exquisite anguish of becoming a mother. A few drops of ether from Dr. Chambers helped quell the pain of childbirth. Like every other obstacle Lois had faced in life, her practical nature won out over emotion as she bore down and looked forward to her new joy. Coming out of the fog of anesthesia, Lois was flooded with happiness at having birthed a baby boy. Her first thoughts might have been of her own receding birth pangs, or of how happy and relieved it felt to have a new son, but that was not on her mind. Her initial joy collapsed into one single thought, *I have borne a child who has an unbelieving father. I must do everything in my power to be sure this child follows the Lord.*

In Lois's soul was a *golden thread* of faith. She was a "born again" Christian in the days before that terminology had lost much of its meaning. When she married my dad, she knew she was out of God's will, because Charles was not a believer. Charles was a handsome, brown-eyed man, five years older and eight inches taller than Mom. They met one summer when my dad boarded in the Gray home during haying season. Albert Gray, my grandpa, was running a haying crew, and my dad was one of the hired hands. Mom helped Grandma Gray prepare meals for the haying hands, and there she met Charles. For Lois, it was apparently love at first sight. Much later, when her curious granddaughters would ask her why she married an unbeliever, Lois would only say, "It had to be Charles. He was the man for me."

Just eleven months after my older brother, Marvin, was born, Mom informed Dad that she was pregnant again. She said Dad was quite disappointed. Apparently he thought one child was enough. In a little house, just a few blocks away from where Marvin was born, Lois gave birth to an almost-ten-pound baby boy, with about five pounds of the weight owing to an overly large head. That was me, Arnold Leon Humble, born on October 24, 1934. My brother and I were the only two children she bore, and she never wavered from her earliest pledge to do her best to see that we follow the Lord.

By default I ended up spending a lot of time around the house with Mom. I think it was because Marvin was twenty months older and more useful doing outside work with Dad on the farm. Not long after I was born, we moved to a farm close to Rose, Kansas. Farm wives in the midthirties did not have it easy. No plumbing, no electricity, and no labor-saving devices were available. Clothes had to be washed in a tub with a scrub board. Every meal was cooked from scratch. In the late summer and fall there was canning to be done, which meant boiling pint and quart Mason jars full of garden products in a pressurized canner. That was very hot, steamy work in temperatures that often topped 100 degrees. Canning could be done only when food had been thoroughly processed by hand. Even butter had to be churned by hand.

Mom was small but strong. I can see her even now, vigorously beating up a cake in a crock bowl, with a little frown on her brow that almost made her look like she was mad at the batter. I believe she made biscuits for breakfast all but about ten mornings while we lived on the farm. Maybe a slight exaggeration, but Dad loved biscuits, and she enjoyed pleasing him in her cooking. She never seemed to sit down and rest during the daytime.

Mom's domain was mainly the house, the garden, and the chickens. We often bought the fuzzy baby chicks in town, and Dad would contrive a homemade brooder house, using kerosene lanterns for warmth. Mom fed and cared for the growing chickens and eventually gathered their eggs when they became laying hens. She not only cooked the young frying chickens, she also wrung their necks, scalded, plucked, and then singed them to get off the little pinfeathers from their skins. She would take a fryer's head in her right hand and whip the body of the chicken around fast like she was cranking a Model-T Ford. It only took a couple of turns before the chicken was flopping around on the ground "like a chicken with its head cut off." Later I liked to stand up to the counter and watch while she gutted it and cleaned out the entrails. I would gag and gag as she got to certain yucky parts of it, and she would always tell me to go away if it made me sick, but I had to stand there and see it all.

When I think of my mom's determination to put God first in her life, I think of it somehow as the beginning of that *golden thread* that started with her and carried on through many of her children and grandchildren. I am not speaking of her personhood as being the *golden thread*. The thread was her absolute commitment to seeking the will of God for herself and her family. Nothing else would do. There was a right path and a wrong path, and only surrender to God would take you down the straight path. She believed we boys should have the influence of church and Sunday school, so it was church every Sunday for us, rain or shine. There was a little Methodist church close by our home when we lived near Rose, Kansas, but somehow it did not seem to meet her ideals of a place to meet God. So, dressed in her Sunday best, she herded us into the '36 Ford sedan and drove a few miles farther east, sometimes over muddy, rutted roads, to Ridge Baptist Church. There the gospel was clearly preached. A preacher from town would show up from time to time, but often it was just Sunday school that was offered. I did not care much for the preaching, so she would spread a small handkerchief on her lap and let me put my head down to sleep and sweat during what seemed to be long sermons, especially in the summertime.

I embarrassed her a couple of times at church, and she reminded me of it later. Sunday school classes were divided by only a thin curtain hanging between them, so individual voices were easy to hear on the other side. One Sunday morning she heard me telling my Sunday school teacher in a rather loud voice: "I've tasted beer before, I've tasted whiskey before, I've tasted wine before, I've tasted brandy before..." and so on down the beverage list. Actually my dad often gave us just a sip of whatever he was drinking, so it was not totally a lie, just not a good place to be bragging about such information. Another time as Mom exited the church, she saw a group of people gathered around a couple of boys fighting. They were really kicking up the dust in the churchyard as they thrashed around on the ground. When she got through the circle, it was Marvin and me that she witnessed in one of our usual vigorous combats, but this time in our best church clothes. She was pretty upset and got us straight into the car without bidding folks good-bye. I can't remember what she said to us, just how she looked as she laced us down on the way home. She had no problem showing anger that bordered on wrath when the occasion demanded it.

It was usually Dad's job to do the spanking (more about that later), but she did not always wait to turn us over to him for discipline. Direct disobedience or defiance could earn a spanking before Dad got home. Dad always used switches from the elm tree. Mom used the butter paddle. That's a fairly heavy piece of wood about ten inches long and a half-inch thick, perfectly shaped to be grasped by the handle and applied with rapid-fire motion to the "seat of learning." She always draped me over her knees where I was upended with overalls stretched tight. It was not two or three good whacks as a gentle reminder, but a staccato warming up that gradually turned to white-hot heat by the time she was finished. I won't say she wasn't angry. I don't know of any parents in those days who didn't spank when they were angry. But it was never brutal or overdone. She seemingly could detect when the pitch of my wailing showed the point of my full repentance was reached, and then she would stop. She never apologized for spankings but once, and that was when I had kept hitting at, and finally hitting, her while she was telling my uncles some embarrassing little thing I had done. She spanked me especially hard that time, but I could tell somehow by her later words and actions that she felt bad for punishing me when I'd just reacted because of her embarrassing me.

I made my first public decision to follow Christ at Ridge Baptist Church when I was about ten years old. An evangelist from a nearby town came out to preach a week of revival meetings. We went every night, and I was getting some of the meaning of what he was saying about following the Lord. What I remember mainly today is his emotional fervor, zeal, and sweat when he preached. Every night there was an invitation to "go forward" to accept the Lord as one's Savior. After several nights of this urging, Mom spoke to Marvin and me, asking if we thought we should go forward and accept Christ. Toward the end of the week we did go forward. As I approached the altar, the preacher took my hand, leaned down close to my face, and, looking very serious, asked, "Son, are you really sure you know what you are doing?" Thinking back later I realized I was a bit embarrassed and may have even had a little smile on my face that belied my sincerity. In fact, I was not absolutely sure what I was doing, but I was earnest about it, whatever it was. I cannot remember any surge of joy or peace, but I can remember my mom's satisfaction that we had done the right thing. We were told to tell someone about our decision, so I talked to my teacher, Mrs. Peck. She was a serious Christian, and she also asked me, "Did you really mean it?" I believe questions like that drove the decision a bit deeper than it might have been otherwise.

A week later we were baptized at a Southern Baptist church in Yates Center since we had no baptismal tank at our church. Some other country boys were baptized with us. My clearest memory of that day was the Stoll boy panicking and thrashing both of his feet above the water while his head was briefly immersed. Not the most pious memory that should be held after such an event. My public confession and baptism were just the first step toward a surrender to God that would be truly meaningful.

Mom's church life was exemplary, but her home life of devotion engraved far more lasting impressions on my young mind. She was a long ways from perfect, but she had a great passion for God. I was three years old or younger when prayer before bedtime started. She had us down on our knees at our beds beside her every night before going to sleep, saying the "Now I Lay Me Down to Sleep" prayer. Then she started adding other little prayers to our routine. I can't remember when we first started praying for Dad to get saved. I am not even sure it was said exactly like that, so directly. I just know we learned from her prayers with us that Dad was not right with God and needed to be. Somehow she did that without showing disrespect for him or making us feel judgmental toward his person.

Mom was a woman of prayer. She used to say, "I must be the meanest woman in the world. If I don't pray forty-five minutes to an hour a day, I am not fit to live with." She often went to her bedroom during the daytime, letting us know she was not to be bothered during her hour of prayer. It sometimes irritated me because I would want to ask her something and was not supposed to disturb her. By this time I was in junior high or high school, and my needs were not that pressing; she never did that while we were younger. She loved to sing old hymns around the house, and while her voice was not solo quality, there was pathos in it, a yearning for God that was palpable to my young mind. One of her favorites was "In the Garden":

I come to the garden alone, while the dew is still on the
roses;
and the voice I hear falling on my ear,
the Son of God discloses.
And He walks with me and He talks with me
and He tells me I am His own.
And the joy we share as we tarry there,
none other has ever known.
I'd stay in the garden with Him,
though the night around me be falling...

The tenderness and intimacy in her voice almost raised uneasiness in my mind as a young child. In my immature thinking I had a feeling like, *Does my dad know about this relationship?* I had the sense that she was really expressing her heart, not just practicing her singing or filling a quiet farmhouse with noise.

She also loved to read the Bible and did it faithfully, probably more in later years, but also when we were young. She believed The Book from cover to cover, never doubted a line of it. And she never wavered from that position until the day of her death. Her complete confidence in the Bible gave her a strong assurance of salvation, and she would take His Word over anybody's word any day. In retrospect I can see how much she depended on the Word for strength when she had an unbelieving husband and how much comfort she got from it. A hymn she often sang was "Precious Book":

There's a dear and precious Book,
 though it's worn and faded now,
That recalls the happy days of long ago.
As I sat on mother's knee with her hand upon my brow,
And it told at last of that bright home above.
Precious Book, Holy Book,
on thy dear old tearstained leaves I love to look.
Thou art sweeter day by day as I walk the narrow way.
And it leads at last to that bright home above.

Her strong confidence in the Word was what also gave her absolute hope toward the end of her life. She never wavered as to whether she would go to heaven when she died. More than once, she would assure me during her last days of terminal cancer, "Oh, I know where I'm going, I know where I'm going..." But I'm getting ahead of my story here in talking about her death.

Mom was also very discerning in matters of what I call "the powers." She had good discernment in areas of recognizing the spirit world. Before Peter Wagner and others ever wrote about "spiritual warfare," my mom was already practicing it. She had a very real concept of a real Devil and was aware of his devices. I often heard her say, "You don't fool me, 'old boy,' I know who you are." She was referring to Satan's attempt to seduce her thought life. She admitted there was a time when he could have fooled her, but she had learned by experience to detect when he was trying to influence her, and she addressed him directly to cut him off.

Perhaps the most meaningful thing to me was my mom's nonjudgmental spirit and tender treatment of people who did something wrong. We used to have testimonies on prayer-meeting night at church, and it could be a temptation for some people to boast a bit by name-dropping. I recall one deacon who liked to talk about such things as "some big shots from DC that I met on my job this week…" As a high school kid I saw this as hypocrisy and told her how disgusted I was. She knew the man was a full-fledged braggart, but she just said, "Well, Arny, haven't you ever said things in public and then gone home and wished you hadn't said them?" She gave him the benefit of the doubt. It was just her natural tendency to treat people like that, believing the best about them. She was especially tolerant of preachers, their conduct, and their preaching. A preacher would have to be a real scoundrel to draw a word of criticism from her.

She treated me the same way. When I was in the fifth grade, the Connor family with their two boys moved into a house across the gravel road from us. They had been living in the city and come back to the farm. In those days there was a huge difference between "city kids" and "country kids." Bill and Jim were a couple of years older than Marvin and I, and they lost no time bringing us up to speed on the facts relating to the birds and the bees. We had been taught, even by our dad who did cuss, that it was not right for us boys to cuss and swear. But these guys were determined to enlarge our vocabularies to include all the words we'd been missing out on. And so after their badgering and cajoling for several weeks, I also started using those words when we were around them, so as not to feel left out. They were immensely pleased and showed how proud they were of my new courage to cuss. But it was not long before God just gripped my conscience, and I began to feel ugly inside. One night at dusk, talking with Mom outside the farmhouse, I could stand it no longer and confessed to her: "Mom, I've been cussin' a little bit." I didn't know what she would say, but I knew I had to get it off my chest, as it seemed to be crushing me. She was surprisingly gentle and understanding. She even said it was not unusual for boys to say some of those words, but that I should be very careful not to use Jesus' or God's name in vain. She wasn't exactly giving me permission to keep using the lesser cuss words, but she seemed to be taking it easy on me so I would not feel like dirt. It was kind of her, but it did not salve my burning conscience. I lay in bed that night unable to sleep, and finally around 10:30, from the upstairs bedroom I yelled, "MOM!" She came up and asked me why I couldn't sleep. Was it because of the bad words I'd been using? I admitted it was. Then she said something that stuck in my mind forever. She said, "God likes to forgive little boys when they have done wrong, so we need to ask for His forgiveness." I can't remember if she or I or both of us prayed the prayer of confession, but I remember the wash of relief that came from feeling forgiven when it was over. It was probably my first real spiritual experience in an existential sense. The ritual would always be with me for the rest of my life: you sin, you feel miserable, and you ask for forgiveness. It's that simple. That principle carried me through the teenage years when some people looking at my life from the outside could probably only tell I was a Christian because I showed up at church on Sunday. They didn't know that every night, wherever I'd been, or whatever I'd done, I'd have a painful confession session with God before going to bed. The relief on the other side was always worth it. It may have been the most helpful truth I ever learned: God loves to forgive little boys, and big boys, and old gray-haired men.

In closing this section regarding my mom, I have to go back and pick up my earlier thought regarding the *golden thread*. I have said that the *golden thread* was her total commitment to the will of God for her life. I call it golden because it was precious and it was pure. Like gold, it did not tarnish with time. It was consistent and it was prized above all else in her life. It is just not normal for a human being to sacrifice his or her own will for the will of *anyone* else. But living near her heart, I learned that she would rather I have God's will than anything else in the world. She had found hope and peace, and she wanted that for me, too. Like a thread, it could be stretched out over time, binding together generation after generation. I saw it in her and wanted it for myself. I pray my children saw it in me and want it for themselves. I pray that my grandchildren will see it in their parents and want to be bound by this *golden thread*. I will forever be indebted for my mom's example and for her being the starting point of the *golden thread*. My life would never have taken the God-directed turns it did without her influence on me.

Chapter 2 – Farm Life

What does man gain from all his labor...under the sun?
(Ecclesiastes 1:3)

It was common information in the sixties that 80 percent of foreign missionaries in those days came from rural backgrounds. I never verified the statistic, but I can see how it was not a very far jump from farm life in America to jungle life in the Third World as far as roughing it was concerned. Farmers across the central United States in the thirties and early forties seemed to have very similar living conditions as those in less developed countries. They usually lived in wood-frame houses that were poorly insulated, if at all. Double-paned windows had not been invented yet. The kitchen range was wood powered, and women sweated over it a lot in the summer. The potbellied stove in the living room used wood or coal. Houses were hot in the summer and cold in the winter.

In one house we lived in, the kids' bedroom was in a far-back corner of the house. We had to cross a cold linoleum floor through the kitchen and pantry in our bare feet to get to it. The potbellied stove in the living room kept things warm within about ten feet of it, and it got really hot up close. Marvin and I would stand near it when it was red-hot and try to get our pajamas heated up enough to get us to that far-back bedroom before the cold penetrated. We would nearly singe ourselves and then tear across the cold linoleum floor, through the kitchen and pantry room, to the bedroom. There we jumped under several heavy comforters. Occasionally our folks would heat a couple of bricks and wrap them in newspapers to put at the foot of our beds to put our cold feet against. That was a rare treat.

There was a well with an old-fashioned pump just a few feet from the kitchen screen door (which was banged shut by a long coil spring every time it was opened). An enamel bucket and washpan stood handy on the washstand by the kitchen door. A long-handled dipper was used by anyone who was thirsty. It was absolutely forbidden to dump water back into the bucket if you didn't finish your dipperful. The remainder of what you didn't drink got poured into the washpan for hand washing later. Neighbors who came to our house and did not understand this etiquette were considered pretty uncivilized. I don't remember our ever varying this routine of drinking from the same dipper, even when one member of the family fell sick.

The chicken house stood between our house and the pig lot. There was a pig wallow right next to the fence before getting to the pig shed. Any chicken that wandered across the fence and got mired in the muddy wallow soon became hog food if it did not extract itself by furious flapping. The chickens seemed to gain a lot of frantic energy just before the pigs got to them and usually escaped. There was the open-faced toolshed where Dad stored hand tools and sometimes worked in its shade. Outside it was a big, foot-pedaled grindstone. The granary stored burlap bags of chicken, pig, and cow feed in the front section. Harvested corn was piled high in the back. Marvin and I discovered by trial and error which kinds of grain would do for a snack. Cotton cake (cotton seed), bran, and "shorts" (whatever that was) seemed pretty tasty if we got hungry enough between meals. The outhouse was not far from the chicken house: a "two-holer" equipped with the thick Sears or Wards catalogue used for toilet paper. Having two holes was convenient to allow more than one client to occupy it at one time. The other advantage was it also kept us from having to go to the toilet alone at night, which was a bit scary. Sometimes serious personal problems were discussed in this small building, and the darkness made it a modest experience. Nobody seemed to notice that it rarely got cleaned out.

The barn is a special place on the farm. It is especially nice when it seems to get too crowded in the house where you aren't allowed to be rambunctious and throw things around. There was a section on one side of the barn for the draft horses. The other side was reserved for the cows when they came in to be milked. They had stanchions waiting to lock their heads in when they came in from the pasture. A bait of grain would be waiting for them in a trough just in front of the stanchion. With their heads locked in, the milking could be done without the cow's wandering around. A couple of cows liked to kick, so a pair of "kickers" locked their hind legs together. A short chain kept them from kicking more than a few inches. Nothing, however, seemed to keep the bony, ever-swinging tail from clobbering us on the sides of our heads as we nestled into the cow's flank for milking. That warm flank felt good in the wintertime but could be pretty disgusting in the summertime. Dad did most of the milking, but Marvin and I had our turns at it also. The barn cats came around begging for their treat, and we would squirt milk from the cow's teat into the cats' mouths five feet away while they stood up on hind legs and tried to catch the whole stream. It was most comical to see, as they seemed not to want to lose a drop of it. Dad did not like us to waste the milk this way, but it was irresistible to do a bit of it from time to time.

Then there was the hayloft and the hundreds of hay bales stored in the barn. Prairie hay has a nice smell, and we spent a lot of time there, often with neighbor boys who were visiting at the time, just talking and playing. It was also the place where the cats gave birth to their kittens, so on rainy days we would spend hours playing with them. Joker was there, too, in a little stall beside the cows. He was a half-Shetland pony my uncle Tom bought for us. He had two "glass eyes" that looked translucent blue. One half of his face was white and the other half brown. His coat fuzzed up in the winter like a little bear, and then he shed it all in the summer, looking sleek again.

Joker and I had a love-hate relationship going. He was both smart and naughty. In the cold winter he would bite my fingers through my leather mittens if I gave him half a chance. He also learned just where my feet, shod in brogans, were planted and he would step on my nearly frozen toes, seemingly on purpose and then lean against me. It was hard to push him off my foot since he was already standing on it. When mounting him, I was too short to jump astride him with one leap. I had to lie across his back for a second, my head hanging down on one side and my feet on the other. Before I could swing my right foot over his back, he would grab me by the seat of my overalls and drag me back off of him. A routine punch in the nose helped break him of this habit, eventually. He could open the barn door that was hooked securely, hardly pausing as he lifted the hook with his teeth to make his exit. We had to get a special lock for it to keep him in. But Joker was also my faithful transportation to the far pasture to get the cows each evening for milking. It would have been a long, lonesome walk on foot. Or if the fences went down after a storm and the cows wandered off a few miles, he and I would follow their muddy tracks and bring them back to our own pasture.

Even more comforting was Joker's apparent empathy when I was sad. I was sometimes a melancholy kid, and he seemed a good listener. He was fat and therefore wide, almost flat, across the back and rump. If I'd just been disciplined in some way I thought unfair, I would go out to the barn and lie down backward on him with my head toward his tail. Resting my head on his rump, I would sometimes snivel and tell him at length what I was thinking about it all, or sometimes I'd just lie there grieving quietly. At those times, he seemed gentle and understanding, an ear cocked back with what in my boyish imagination I perceived as sympathy. Joker was destined to take a long journey with me later, where he would again be useful, but in a very different way.

I may have been a lazy kid. I am not sure. My dad seemed to think so, but I don't remember his ever saying it directly to me. In retrospect, I can't tell if I was really lazy or just did not like the division of labor. Some work projects didn't bother me at all. For instance, holding down the half-grown boar pigs while Dad used his freshly sharpened pocket knife to castrate them and then put rings in their noses did not really bother me. It did leave me half deaf for several minutes afterward, from being so near their ear-piercing squeals during the painful operation. Anything that had to do with the horses and cows was also duty I could accept. But when it came to hoeing the garden or the cornfields, it was a different thing. It was suffocating to be deep in a patch of corn with not a breath of air stirring. It was humid and the air even smelled thick somehow. The rows of corn seemed a mile long, and the offer of a penny a row for wages did not increase my ambition. I would have much preferred to be driving the tractor or doing something that seemed important. Marvin was twenty months older than I was and a very responsible kid, so it seemed to me that he got all the good jobs. I never felt I measured up to what my dad hoped for when it came to hard work. I can't remember his ever saying I did a good job on anything, but that could well be because I didn't! Anyway, parents didn't praise their children much in those days. Kids could get spoiled with too much praise, I suppose was their thinking.

Though hard work was required of us, the tasks on our farm shifted for us as different seasons rolled in. In the big garden beside the barn we would pick up the potatoes Dad dug with a special potato fork. Sometimes we plucked bugs off of potato and tomato plants, dropping them into a bit of kerosene in a tin can. Their instant death brought us a touch of satisfaction. With Mom out there directing us, we would help harvest the garden products such as beans, peas, carrots, and beets when they were ready for picking or pulling. Sometimes we would help shell the fresh peas, which seemed a never-ending task.

In the fields Marvin and I often just rode around on the farm implements being pulled by the tractor, for instance, watching wheat or oats or flaxseeds flow out of the combine chute and pour into the bin as we circled the field. We often sampled them ourselves. Flaxseed tasted the best, slick going down after being well chewed. We would ride on the back of the drill, watching it drop the grains into soft ground and then cover them over with a length of log chain dragged behind it. I liked riding on a fender of the tractor with Dad driving, my leg slung over the headlight to keep on my perch, while he pulled a cultivator, a plow, a drill, or a disc. If my rump got too far to the outside, the tractor tire would give me a rub with its big rubber tread, reminding me to pull it in. Riding with Dad on a harrow pulled by horses required careful balancing while standing on a plank. I would get preoccupied, lose my balance, and my foot would go under the harrow, turning my foot back so the instep was dragging painfully in the soft earth.

(Harrowing was the very last thing done after plowing and disking to make the ground powdery soft for planting, so it was not as though my foot was going to get broken.) If it happened more than once in a morning, Dad would cuss and tell me to get off of the thing. Then in the fall there was the husking of corn. Every ear had to be shucked and then tossed into the horse-drawn wagon.

Haying season was the really big event of the summer because Dad had his own stationary hay baler. It took quite a crew to run it. The tall prairie grass had to be mowed, dried where it lay, sulky-raked into windrows, and then collected with a buck rake, which then pushed a big pile of hay up to the baler. Two hay pitchers forked the hay into the hopper where it was first packed down and then plunged through the back of the baler to be tied and ejected out the end. There was a rhythm to it and a lot of sweating going on. Some of the guys pitching hay seemed to get what people today might call "endorphins" from their work. In the heat of the afternoon, sweat soaking their shirts and glistening on their chests, one of them would throw back his head and yell, "Yehaw, pitch hay!" Then he would let out a big belly laugh. I didn't think it was that much fun, but it did lighten up the day considerably to hear them yell.

My job was to buck rake, using a team of draft horses named Bill and Dan. They were so strong that they could have easily been pulling a plow rather than pushing a light load of hay. One day when I had collected about a half buck rake of hay, a couple of the long tongues of the buck rake rammed into a clump of Kansas prairie sod and the horses plunged forward, straining into their collars instead of stopping and backing up like they were supposed to do. The result was that I, sitting far on the back of the rake, was vaulted high in the air, landing mercifully in part of the pile of hay. Somehow it panicked the horses and they each ran off in separate directions, splitting the rake between them. Bill took just the tongue with him, but Dan, who weighed around 1400 pounds, loped off with the rest of the buck rake trailing behind him, knocking off a few of its two-by-four teeth as he galloped by the mowing machine. I got a pretty good knot on my head from having had the rake dragged over me. When my dad caught up with Dan, it was horse discipline time.

When haying season was over the folks would take us to the carnival in Chanute or Iola, where we could blow the money we'd earned for the summer on things like Ferris-wheel rides and cotton candy. It wasn't much, but just looking forward to the carnival all summer long made sweating in the hayfield seem a little more bearable.

Evenings on the farm were usually very quiet times. During summers, work went on until late, and there was nothing left to do but go to bed. But in wintertime the nights often seemed to drag on and on. Our house was lit by two kerosene lamps, one of which did not give out much light from its wick because the chimney was smoke blackened. The other lamp was an Aladdin, with its fragile mantle that glowed brightly from the kerosene flame beneath it. It was probably as good as or better than a twenty-five-watt bulb, and we got near it to do our homework. No entertainment was available. At one point the folks started reading books checked out of the town library. Marvin, Mom, and Dad got totally engrossed in their books, sometimes chuckling to themselves, or making exclamations about what they were quietly reading to themselves. I was too young to get involved in books, and I would sometimes sit for what seemed hours in total silence, just listening to their occasional murmurings and the ticking of the clock. The boredom seemed excruciating, and my complaints about my boredom in a very quiet farmhouse may have broken their evening reading habit to some extent. Anyway, it was a great day when Dad brought home a brand-new battery-powered radio. Marvin and I would hurry home from school to listen to *Terry and the Pirates, Hop Harrigan, the Lone Ranger*, and several other favorite programs. After supper all the family would gather around the radio on certain nights to hear *Fibber McGee and Molly, George Burns and Gracie Allen,* and *Lux Radio Theatre.* World War II stories were a favorite since the war was going on at the time. We shared the moments of humor and pathos, looking into one another's eyes while we collectively either laughed or nearly cried. So different from having one's eyes glued to the television set as we do today.

Did I love the solitude of farm life? I am not sure. I just know my bent often seemed to be toward doing things that required being alone. Once I rode a plug horse ten miles into town without thinking much about it. The poor old nag was destined for the glue factory, I suppose, too old for further use. It plodded along, not even trotting the whole way. I just sat there and persevered through the ride. It was a rather big deal in those days since nobody rode that far on a horse just to get it to town! I also, as mentioned earlier, was alone in bringing in the cows in the evenings, spending time in the green pastures on horseback at dusk. There was a lot of time to think, but I am not implying my thinking was deep or profound at that point. When I was too young to work in the hayfield, I would still go and just hang out under the wagon all by myself for hours. Perhaps this was why more missionaries came from rural areas than urban in those days—it was a kind of preparation for the independent living and solitude one often experienced in foreign lands in those days.

Chapter 3 – Dad and Brother Marvin

Take what is yours and go. I want to give this last man the same as I gave to you. (Matthew 20:14)

Dad and Marvin, in my earliest memories, belong in the same chapter. I heard later from Mom how proud Dad was of his eldest son when he was born. Dad had been quite a rounder in his day, but when he got married and had his first son, he became a real family man, proud of his child. Mom says he carried Marvin around town, to the pool halls, or wherever he went, to show him off. To me, they seemed always close together. Marvin talked early and could sing all the pop songs on the radio, right on key, by the time he was two years old, even if he could not yet pronounce all the words correctly. He was a precocious child, skipping a grade in elementary school because the teacher could not keep him busy. Even after moving up a grade he had a lot of spare time. The teacher often asked him to help the younger children practice their reading while the teacher was busy with other duties. As far back as I can remember, he brought home straight A's on his report card. My grades had a bit more variety to them!

My earliest memories of Dad were from the farming days in Kansas. We lived in four different farmhouses that I can remember—none of which had indoor plumbing or electricity, but each one was a bit upgraded from the previous. The last one had natural gas piped in and an outdoor toilet built so tight that snow did not sift in on the seat in the winter. That was a major improvement over the others. Dad never owned a farm, just rented. Those were the days of transitioning from horse power to tractor power, so we used both, raising multiple crops of corn, wheat, oats, barley, maize, etc. to feed the cows, horses, pigs, and chickens. We never seemed to have much "spending money," but there was homegrown meat on the table three times a day besides all the other good garden stuff, either fresh from the garden or from Mom's canning for winter. Dad was a good provider, working hard; he seemed tired a lot of the time. We always made the Saturday-night foray into town, Yates Center, which nominated itself "The Prairie Hay Capital of the World." Marvin and I would watch a movie and have chocolate malt at the drugstore. It was served in a huge stainless-steel container with contents so thick you could barely suck it through a straw. Looking forward to Saturday night kept us alive the rest of the week, especially during the hot summers when hay baling was going on. Money for these things came from somewhere, certainly not from my earnings, so Dad must have been generous in this. He got a little cash from selling eggs and cream in town, so perhaps that was the source of income. While we were at the movies, Dad would put one foot up on the bumper of the 1936 Ford and talk for hours to other farmers who were also gathered in the Town Square to visit and grocery shop. Occasionally they would attend the movie with us or, even more rarely, see a movie preview they liked and take us to the theater on a weeknight—that was really rare!

Dad was never what you would call "warm" toward us boys, nor were any of the other dads I knew of in those days. But he could be compassionate when we needed it most. In wintertime when Marvin or I had the flu, measles, or chicken pox, he would come in and lay a cool hand on our forehead and say, "How are ya, boy?" He would say it looking you right in the eye so you knew he cared how you really were. It was a soothing thing to have two parents who had some empathy. From the time we were very young, we got into the habit of exchanging kisses on the cheek with him before we went to bed every night. Mom joked, "You boys kissed your dad good night until you were fifteen years old." That's a slight exaggeration but not too far off. One night when I was about ten years old, Dad and I had a disagreement of some kind, and I stormed off to bed in a huff without the routine kiss. I am not sure how it happened (probably Mom did some urging), but somehow he was the one to take the initiative and come in and give me the little peck on the cheek so I could go to sleep. That gave me a warm feeling of hope that I can remember to this day.

A couple of times when Mom went off to an overnight "church convention" meeting, Marvin and I got to sleep with Dad, one on each side of him, which we thought was a great treat. In the years before underarm deodorant, B.O. might have been offensive to some people, but we thought it smelled great on our dad. He smelled like a real man!

With an array of different kinds of animals to deal with, Dad needed a lot of patience, which as a matter of fact he did not have. Especially with cows or horses, he would totally lose control of everything including his tongue. Red in the face, he would articulately cuss them out with an incredibly diverse and profane vocabulary (but never using the "f" word). Occasionally he would use corporal punishment on them that today would bring down the wrath of the Humane Society. I might add that his approach to child discipline would also bring the Child Protective Agency of today running. Marvin and I would often fight and bicker over insignificant things. Dad would warn us for several days that it was coming. Occasionally he would catch us in the yard beating each other up and would go to the great elm tree, cut a sizeable switch with his pocketknife, and begin to trim the young leaves from it. We would usually start bawling at this point while he was still fifty feet away. He would walk straight toward us and then on past us to the barn, still slapping the switch menacingly against his rubber boot as he went. It was fair warning, but we couldn't seem to hold the point in our minds. A couple of days later I would be running around and around him as he held my left arm and whaled my bottom. I would arch my back as much as possible to put some slack in my overalls and yell, "I'll never do it again, I'll never do it again, I'll never do it again…" (But of course I did!) Slack overalls or not, the pain still got through with welts to prove it. Later, Marvin and I would go to the outhouse to count who had the most red streaks on our posteriors. When it was over, it was over. Dad never stayed angry and never apologized to us later. We never held it against him, and in fact we tried to get physically close to him after a good spanking. He had a problem with parents who, he said, "just spanked their kids enough to make them mad." I'll testify that we were always more broken than angry when the discipline was over. I will always attribute my ability to "fear God" in the right sense to an appropriate fear and respect for my dad.

It is hard to figure out why Marvin and I fought so much as kids. I got one of my hardest spankings on a birthday for biting him in the middle of the back before we got out of bed in the morning. We have talked about it now that we are older, and neither of us can explain it. We were together virtually all the time, so maybe it was partly to pass the time. I can't remember many events in early life where we both were not present. We were inseparable on Saturday-night trips to town when we sometimes had to defend ourselves against city kids. If someone wanted to beat me up, Marvin was always protective, feeling that was his call in life, not somebody else's. We slept in the same bedroom and in the same bed. We even got in trouble for peeing out the same upstairs window when we lived on the Connor place. Even Dad thought that was pretty gross since it rusted the screen and ran down the roof into the eaves trough that emptied into our drinking water cistern. But there were some times I felt I got left behind. Marvin was older and more responsible and therefore treated more like an adult. I remember when our neighbor lady committed suicide by drowning, taking her delightful, curly-haired two-year-old daughter with her. Dad and Marvin went down to visit the awful scene, the bodies still lying beside the pond. I was not allowed to go, and I never let them forget it. Sometimes we both would theoretically be taking a nap in the afternoon, and I would get up to find Marvin and Dad had gone off to an auction. I would make a pretty big ruckus about such things. Then during our teenage years Dad and Marvin took the truck off to follow the harvest for several weeks, leaving me with Mom in Yates Center. So I tended to feel that Dad and Marvin had something of a unique relationship and that Mom tended to give me some special attention as the younger sibling—to say she babied me would be carrying it a bit too far!

Some rather humorous events took place from time to time. Once we were loading the pigs for market and had a difficult time getting one of them up to the pen and into the chute leading into the trailer. Most of them were compliant and moved in the right direction, but there was one shoat that was determined not to leave the farm. We could get him right up to the chute, and then he would whirl and run between us, back into the huge pig lot. We would have to go back again and again to drive him back up to the loader. Finally we closed in on him, and he had nowhere to go but through us. He chose to head for Marvin and ran right at him. Marvin straddled his legs, and the pig ran through them, but not before Marvin closed quickly on him just behind the front shoulders. It was a good-sized pig, and suddenly Marvin was on a wild ride, literally going backward piggyback at breakneck speed. It looked to me like he was on a bucking bronco the way he was gyrating with each leap of the pig. His eyes bugged out and he looked excited but not scared. He fell off to the side unhurt after quite a few healthy strides, and I was howling so hard with laughter that I almost fell down in the pig dirt myself. I'm not sure how we got the pig loaded because my vivid memory of Marvin's pig ride blots out such a detail.

My dad had his own experience later that was also somewhat comical. At a Yates Center auction he once bought a horse that was completely an unknown. Trying him out on the corn planter, he found that the horse just "dogged" along. Dad finally tired of his snail's pace and popped him on the rump with the end of one of the heavy leather lines. The horse went from a slow walk to a dead run in three jumps, inciting the other horse beside him to try to outrun him. Marvin and I, sitting under the hedge trees while Dad planted, looked up to see what appeared to be a one-man chariot race. The broad wheels of the corn planter were sending two geysers of soft earth high, high into the air as the team raced around the field. With his feet braced against the planter, Dad pulled back on the reins so hard that the tugs went slack. The horses were literally pulling the corn planter with their mouths. Under that kind of stress one of the old leather lines broke, and Dad did a clean flip over the back of the seat, landing on his rump in the soft earth. We laughed to see the acrobatics once we saw

Dad was not hurt. This time he did not get angry but just sat there in the dirt looking slightly amused, watching the runaway team as the remaining line slowly wound around the axle to pull them into a tighter and tighter circle. When it was completely taut, they could not move another step. They stood still panting and trembling, with their mouths pulled all the way around to one side. He straightened them out, unhooked them, and took them back to the barn. No horse discipline took place that day. Marvin and I had that action scene engraved on our retinas forever—it was better than going to the Saturday-night movies.

In spite of Dad's temper toward the farm animals, he was basically good-natured with our mom, with the extended family, with neighbors, and even with strangers. I never saw him threaten Mom in any way or even curse at her (like he did us a few times). Psychologists say the best thing you can do for your kids is to love your wife. Dad didn't know that important bit of advice, but he certainly lived it out as far as we could see. Mom would smooch on him in front of us, reaching up high to wrap her arms around his neck, as he was six inches taller. He seemed happy for the affection. Meanwhile, Marvin and I would pretend to be gagging. His humor came out strong when we went into town and he would "act the fool" with our uncles, Clifford, Harold, and Virgil. They loved to laugh and goof off together. He also seemed congenial with all of his six brothers and five sisters along with their respective spouses and children. As far as we knew, there was nothing but good feelings between him and the others, which seems quite a feat with so many siblings to relate to.

Dad was anything but religious, but he never kept Mom from taking us to Sunday school and church—even during World War II when gas rationing was in place. He would occasionally go to country church with us at Ridge Baptist for some special revival meetings or a Children's Day program but rarely if ever to a regular Sunday service. Mom was a really strong Christian, and Dad seemed to be a really strong pagan, and I loved them both just as they were. (I probably didn't know I really loved my dad until many years later because he seemed so tough on the outside.) It was a huge advantage to see no hypocrisy in the home.

I wonder how many sons and daughters in this world wish their dads had lived long enough for them to gain a maturity to understand them at the deeper level. I really never knew what was going on inside of him. What did he think about when he habitually got up at 4:30 a.m. and smoked for an hour or so, just resting there quietly in his rocker? Or in later years, after our move to the Southwest, he would be sitting in the backyard at night as the Arizona sun went down, sometimes alone but usually with Mom. By then he'd changed his occupation from farming to carpentry work. He would be wearing just the perennial khaki pants and an undershirt, usually smoking, saying nothing, or maybe making an occasional comment to my mom. He spent almost every evening out there in a lawn chair, enjoying the passing of the day's heat and resting his bones from a long day of carpentry work. He certainly wasn't into meditation, but he seemed to need that alone time every day. Today I value his sweat and sacrifice to make us a decent living. He didn't much share his private thoughts, but he had a kind of worldly wisdom or good horse sense that we were aware of. He had an absolute distrust of politicians and was in general a good judge of character. His own youth had been pretty immoral, by his own testimony, and he did not offer us much encouragement to stay out of trouble in that area. Somehow Mom's prayers and a faithful God kept me straight anyway. But he did offer advice along the line of his own evaluation of women. One thing he said was never to have a fight over a girl. (The only shiner I ever brought home happened because of a fight over a girl, and it was not even my girl!) Also, when discussing women, he categorized them into the kinds that were just for dating, and those just for marrying. He had certainly followed his own advice on that point and obviously was happy with the way he had married.

No doubt my dad shed tears on several occasions, but only three times in my life did I see him cry. The first was at his own mother's funeral. He was struggling hard to hold it back, but big tears welled up and ran down his cheeks, and his face looked truly stricken. It was such a rare and moving sight; I was more overwhelmed by my dad's sorrow than by the death of my grandmother. The second time I saw him cry was when I went off to Biola Bible College at the age of seventeen. A few days earlier he and I had talked late into the night as he tried to talk me out of going to that d--- Bible college. We never raised our voices, but it was a very tense time for me, and it seemed so for him too. His reasoning was primarily that "preachers don't make nothin'." He offered to try to help finance me in any secular college I might choose if I would forget this d---- foolishness. When I persisted that I thought I ought to go, he finally gave up and we both went to bed feeling bad. The afternoon I left home was a hot Arizona day in late August. My ride across the scorching desert was waiting out front, and I had put my suitcase in the car as I said good-bye to Mom and some neighbors gathered around the car. I made an excuse to go back inside and get one last cold drink from the refrigerator. Dad was sitting there at the supper table in his undershirt. As I was leaving, I just put my hand on his bare shoulder and said, "Good-bye, Dad." He did say good-bye, and big tears rolled down his cheeks, and his shoulders shook a bit as he got that tremor he always seemed to have when he was emotionally shaken. I should have begun to understand then that he was a lot softer on the inside than I had ever thought him to be. I later learned that, at seventeen, I was the same age he was when he ran away from his own home in Oklahoma to work in the Texas oil fields.

By 1961, I was leaving, along with my little family, for the mission field of Kalimantan Barat (then called Borneo). Wanda and I, along with Cheryl, were staying with the folks when departure day arrived. This time I guess I was really dreading to say good-bye to my dad. Mom supported our mission fully, but Dad still did not want to see his kid and family go overseas. It was just beginning to get light when Dad came into our bedroom to say good-bye before going off to do some carpentry work at the mines. It seemed a bit strange to say good-bye while lying prostrate on my back in bed, but I stuck my hand up to shake his. After shaking hands and saying good-bye to me, he reached across me to give Wanda a little kiss and hug. He was leaning low when he passed back over me, and spontaneously I threw my arms around his neck and gave him a big hug and a kiss on the cheek. This was the third time I saw him cry. He just collapsed on my chest and sobbed for quite a while. I rubbed his back and kept saying, "It's okay, Dad, it's okay." Then he walked over to the door and before leaving said, "Well, I shore didn't want to do that. I want you kids to know that I wish you all the success and happiness in the world in the work you are going out there to do." That was long before all the talk about "affirmation" started coming out in circles like ours, but affirm us he did. I think the impact of that moment on my life carried me through a lot of tough times, and I didn't even realize how it had affected my life until many, many years later.

As time went on, Mom said Dad began to talk more positively about our missionary work overseas. Mom told us he even boasted a bit about it to some people. When we were back home on furlough in 1971–72, we had some time with him, but somehow I could not really express my heart to him. It was part of the generation thing in those days perhaps. We were about a week from returning to Indonesia when Dad took Marvin and me on a little fishing trip to a lake just south of Tucson. At the end of the time he showed us a nodule that had come up right beside his clavicle. He said he had to have it checked and that he felt "all used up inside." We were terribly concerned and put our departure off a week to find out how the lump tested out. I took him to the doctor's office one day, and as we were driving back, I tried to talk to him about his need of accepting the good news of what Christ had done for him. He listened politely enough, but at any age I never lost the fear of my dad, so I was pretty nervous and got so shook I nearly missed turning into our own driveway. He pointed that out rather tersely. The subject kind of dropped as we got to the house, and I never directly tried to "convert" him again. Anyway, back to the cancer. He told us his test turned out negative for cancer and that we should not worry about him. He said we had our work to do and should go back over there and do it. In fact he turned out to have fatal lymphosarcoma, and I will never know if the test itself was faulty or if he was just trying to relieve us of any worries by falsifying the medical report.

The cancer took its toll on him for the next couple of years, and finally he started going down pretty fast. On one occasion in 1974, Missionary Aviation Fellowship had flown me out to a village called Suti Semarang where I was helping with an annual conference and training church leaders. The next day, when the plane came to bring supplies, there was an empty seat available, so Wanda came on it, bearing a very special letter for me. She said it would be better to get off alone to read it, so I took the one-page aerogramme off into the jungle and read it by myself. Finding a quiet spot, I read Mom's account of how she and Dad were one day listening to a televangelist who gave a clear presentation of the gospel. The timing felt right, so Mom said to Dad, "Don't you think you should think about believing in the Lord?" Dad, getting really mellow toward family in those days, responded right away, "Yeah, for your sake and the kids', I suppose I should." So Mom encouraged him to go ahead and believe in the Lord right then and there. He said, "I can't believe. I don't know how to believe." She invited him to pray, but he answered, "I don't know how to pray." It was as though after rejecting God for a lifetime, it was impossible to start believing now. What is "believing" anyway? But when Mom moved over and took his hand in both of hers and asked him, "Would you just pray after me?" he agreed to try that. She started with just two words, "O God." Dad repeated, "O God" and then spontaneously began to weep. He went on to confess he was a sinner and ask Jesus to come into his heart to take away the sins of a lifetime. Afterward he said, "I shoulda done that a long time ago." I sat there in the jungle with only the chirping birds to witness my tears. It was one of the happiest days of my life. I had gone around the world to reach the former headhunters of Borneo, leaving behind a dad who might not share a glorious eternity with me. And now he was on the way. Mom said that after that experience Dad always wanted people to pray with him when they came to visit and that his attitude toward the things of God was totally changed. He often repeated that same phrase in the last few weeks of his life, "I shoulda done that a long time ago." Mom's testimony was: "I prayed for Charles forty-three years...and it didn't seem like a very long time once he accepted the Lord." When I finally got news of Dad's death, it was sad, but the hope of meeting him again was now so strong that it took away most of the grief.

It probably sounds strange to many ears that a man who lived his life in rejection of Christ at the very end gets "grace" (a freebie) to be accepted into heaven. But here is a little story to back up the fact that it really can happen this way. Early one morning in a small town square a group of Mexican migrants were gathered in the fall morning chill, hoping someone would come along and hire them for the day. A wealthy landowner living not far away came by about 6:00 a.m. to get a pickup load of them, taking them off to work his orchards. He came back around noon and got a few more and took them out to the same field. Funny thing was that he came back again at 3:00 and 6:00 p.m. to get a few more workers since there were still a few hours of daylight for them to work. The sun was setting when he called them all in to pay them. He took the ones who came latest to pay first and handed them sixty dollars each. There was an immediate buzz of excitement among the others, thinking they were going to get really big money for their long day of work...but he gave them all the same amount, sixty dollars each. They began to complain and said, "We worked through the heat of the day; how come these guys who came in at the end of the day got the same amount as we did? That's not fair!" The owner told them that it was his money and he was paying them the wage they had agreed upon. Was it their business if he wanted to be generous with the ones who came late? It wasn't costing them anything for him to give the same amount to the latecomers, was it? Couldn't he be generous if he wanted to be? That was his point—and indeed he could, since he was the owner of the field and a generous man. I'll bet those guys were glad they hung around the square until evening time. They nearly got left out!

When I read the above story in Matthew 20 (well, it's pretty close to the same story!), I thought *Wow, that's just like the grace extended to my dad*. God's grace just doesn't fit in with our legalistic ways of thinking. Jesus told this story to let people know that it's never too late...never too late. One word of repentance toward God, and God comes running to make Himself known, and to shower us with His grace.

There are a number of other things I could mention regarding Dad's life. For instance, he had a lot of humorous sayings I would like to list for you, but every one of them had just one little word in there that does not quite meet publishing standards—or at least not in any book I would write. (I'm sure they would go fine on TV in today's programming.) He loved to take naps, around three of them a day after he had retired. He loved sweets like hard candy, especially at Christmastime. He was a silly old grandpa, loving to play on the floor with the little ones. (I inherited that trait from him for sure.) He let me have the Oldsmobile every Friday and Saturday night during my last couple of years in high school. He offered logical advice when it was needed. All in all, I am most grateful for the dad I had and, as I said above, I only wish he had lived long enough for me to really understand him better. But I have no doubt that I will meet him in heaven some day. One of the first things I think I'll ask him is, "What on earth did you used to think about for an hour in the morning before anyone else was up?"

Chapter 4 – School Days

*I instruct you in the way of wisdom
and lead you along straight paths.
(Proverbs 4:11)*

My first schoolhouse was a little white one made of wood. Harmony School, about a half mile from our house, was where I spent my first two and a half years of school. There were no kindergartens in rural areas in those days. I was not quite six years old when I started the first grade and was small for my age, but I was raring to go to school. Marvin had been coming home for a whole year telling good stories of exciting things happening at school while I was housebound, just waiting for him to get home every day. He would tell of Miss Ling's tapping her heel on the floor in staccato fashion when she got really frustrated with one of the big eighth-grade boys, or even slapping him once in a while. Schoolboys brushed their teeth, so I finally got a toothbrush about then, which was a big thing to make me feel more important. Before that I'd just been allowed to have Mom rub my teeth with a rag with some tooth powder or baking soda sprinkled on it to imitate teeth brushing. We weren't encouraged to brush more than once a day because the tooth powder cost money.

There were about ten students in the one-room schoolhouse. In my grade there was a cute little fat-cheeked girl whom I tried hard to stay away from. I don't know why, but I did not like her at all, mostly because she was a girl, I think. My first teacher was Miss Turner, a brand-new college graduate from Ohio or Iowa—they both sounded the same to me in those days. She boarded at the Chandler home a half mile to the south of our farm, walking by our home every day to get to school. I thought she was beautiful and treated her a bit too casually. She once kindly took us on a little field trip down to the reservoir behind the school, and I took the occasion to playfully try to push her into the pond. Somebody reported this to my parents who did not think it was humorous in any way. The only thing I can remember about the school lessons was how difficult I found penmanship. I learned to read and do the math, but it was impossible to make my pen go where it was supposed to in forming cursive letters. The frustrating thing was that I really tried hard and just could not make the letters look straight or pretty. That is something that has never changed for me to this day! Miss Turner only stayed a year. I hoped it was not because I tried to push her into the pond. Mrs. Ratts replaced her for my second year of school. She was a very strict-looking lady who demanded perfect order in the classroom. She usually looked unpleasant, and in my young mind I felt she was appropriately named. So I was not too sorry when Dad decided to rent a farm in another school district. In the middle of my third year of school we moved from "the old Gray place" to the "Estel Mackenzie" place. Every farm seemed to need to be identified by the name of someone who had lived on it previously.

Rose School really was the traditional red-brick schoolhouse. Rose itself was a whistle-stop with a tiny general store, a post office inside it, and a dozen or so houses surrounding it. Our house was a mile or more away from this little community, and we walked to school every day. In winter we wrapped up good and even put a newspaper in under our coat sometimes when the wind was especially strong. The school was quite modern by the standards of its day. Several steps led up to the entryway where there was a cloakroom and a water fountain, fed by a crock container that had to be filled by hand. A makeshift apartment in the basement provided a place where the teacher could live. A coal-burning furnace down there heated the whole building. Our live-in teacher seemed always to have the building toasty warm by the time we arrived, chilled to the bone from our walk in the snow. It contrasted wonderfully with the farmhouse that always seemed cold. A bank of windows filled the whole west wall of the large schoolroom. We overlooked a little slough, with railroad tracks visible in the distance. Passing freight trains occasionally broke the monotony for anyone staring out the window. Lighting seemed perfect for reading, even on a cloudy day. New-looking school benches were also up-to-date, quite different from the old style used at Harmony. There was even a little stage where plays could be performed. The library was in another room where you could close the door and be separate from where the teaching was going on. Unfortunately it also provided a place where the Connor boys could initiate our sex education by finding some kind of a picture even in an old encyclopedia that seemed to them to be a bit revealing. By the time I finished sixth grade at Rose, I'd read every reading book in the library. We only got a handful of new books each year, and these were quickly devoured.

Every day began with the flag salute and singing at least one patriotic song. In fact, we sang a lot of patriotic songs. Before opening our lessons for the day, we would always gather around Mrs. Peck at the piano and sing through the old songbooks she kept handy. It was during the years of World War II, and her husband was in the army overseas. We learned just about every popular war song in those days, and there were a lot of them such as: "When Johnny Comes Marching Home Again," "Victory Polka," "Bell Bottom Trousers," "Johnny Got a Zero"...and many more. We also memorized all the words to all the verses of the Navy, Caisson, Marine, Army Air Corps, and Marine anthems. We were really into the war and had a club called WAFC that privileged us to Write A Fighter Corps military person. A colorful badge was given to several of the older students who participated in this. I was not quite old enough to get into it but still wrote the letters anyway.

Mrs. Peck rarely lectured all of us from the front of the class since there were six different levels to be taught. The school went through eighth grade, but with more than one student in some grades, she could get by with supervising the ten students in only six of those grades. I had two others in my class, Myrtle Mackenzie and Paul Cash. We studied independently, much like homeschooling is done today, each with our own workbooks and assignments to complete. There were times when Mrs. Peck took the three of us off to one side to practice our spelling words. Myrtle and I could usually spell our words, but spelling was especially hard for Paul. To help him out, I often sat by him and drew each letter on his back with my finger to speed up his progress a bit. I suspect Mrs. Peck knew what I was doing since my arm was moving all the time, but she was perhaps as bored as I was with his long pauses between letters. There were few discipline problems, and no bullies to contend with. Once the girls got caught smoking in the girls' outhouse, and that was considered major drama. We were all horrified, and they were terribly ashamed, all except the oldest one who still faked it that she was. Another time Billy Connor drew a bit of pornography that involved the teacher and got caught with it before he could destroy it. As the teacher sat him down and began to confront him, he leaped up and flew out the door, racing straight home to his parents to avoid the discipline. However, his mother brought him back in the car a few minutes later. There was no spanking, but the shame was pretty big in such a small school.

We played hard at recess, but it was not organized or supervised. Maybe the teacher watched us from the window, but she was rarely outside. If she did look out the window, she saw us either playing some kind of a tag game, or beckon, or hide-and-seek. Otherwise she might have seen Paul and me taking on Marvin and Ross in a tag-team wrestling match. Paul was tall and gangly. Ross was tiny and younger than I was. That made it sort of even since Marvin was stronger than any of us. We spent a lot of time just wrestling. Sometimes we played on the playground equipment that was surprisingly sturdy and complete: a fine set of swings, a sort of merry-go-round we could spin by kid power, and a huge pole planted in the ground with chains hanging down on all sides that had a handgrip at the end of each chain. Several of us would grab the handles and run around and around the pole to get up to speed, then we would take turns swinging up in the air when we got up enough momentum. When we came in sweating from play, Mrs. Peck would read to us for about a half hour as we lay our heads on our desks to cool off. I may have gained my love for hearing stories read out loud from her entertaining us in this way.

Music was emphasized as much as possible with what instruments were available. At one point we were all required to buy "Tonnettes," which looked like little black recorders. We tried to play together in unison, but I think Marvin was the only one who pretty much got all the notes right. If we played well enough, our folks said we could get a musical instrument. Marvin excelled enough to eventually earn a trumpet and took lessons for a while. I apparently didn't make the grade, but not much was said about it. The school rhythm band provided us with practical noisemakers. There were enough instruments to go around, and basically the purpose was to teach us to keep time with the music and understand its beat. There were sticks, bells, jingle clogs, a triangle, tambourines, drums, and cymbals. Played all together, these instruments made a cacophony of sound. I never got to hear us play except when I was in the middle of it, so I could never tell if it sounded musical in any way. But I suppose it did since we played for parents when we had special programs. These programs seemed to be held a couple of times a year, one of them just before we were let out for summer vacation. Farm kids got four months of vacation so they could help their parents during harvest season, so it was a celebration time before that long vacation. Programs consisted of short plays, singing, and the rhythm band. We got accustomed to performing before an audience and always got good feedback from them. Our parents did often praise us for learning our lines and speaking them well.

Big changes were in store for me as I finished sixth grade at Rose School. Uncle Tom had convinced my dad that a better life awaited us as a family if we would just move to Tucson, Arizona. Tom and Aunt Helen had already moved there and were fascinated with the world out west. There seemed to be lots of migration in the lives of Americans in 1946, following the close of World War II, and the new spirit of adventure apparently caught on with my parents as well. So an auction was held in which nearly all our earthly goods were sold. It seemed strange to have an auctioneer right on our property doing his "Ockedy-dok" (that's what my folks called it) over our farm machinery, furniture, and farm animals. It was the only time I remember ever having scores of people traipsing all over our house and yard. But there was an air of excitement about it, too, like something big was about to happen. Indeed, it was bigger than I could have ever imagined. If I had known how big it was, I would not have been so cheerful on the day of the auction.

PART 2 – LIFE TRANSITIONS

Above all else, life transitions mean *change*. The change may be geographical, cultural, or status related. It could be moving across the United States, moving across the ocean, or moving into adulthood, and then moving on into a marriage relationship. Major changes require major adjustments. Major adjustments demand growth, or withdrawal of some sort to try to avoid the growth. I have found my transitions of life to be stretching experiences. None of them came easy for me, but as I just said, they did provide opportunities for growth. They also provided opportunities to experience the gracious hand of God in my life.

Chapter 5 – From the Farm to the Desert

He found him in a desert land...he instructed him...he kept him as the apple of his eye. (Deuteronomy 32:10)

We left Kansas in August 1946, driving a one-and-a-half-ton 1936 Ford truck. It was loaded with our remaining belongings after the auction. Mom had refused to part with her wedding set of walnut-colored bedroom furniture, which caused a bit of tension for a moment, but Dad finally relented and reluctantly loaded it on the truck. The rest of our stuff was mostly clothing and kitchen utensils. When everything had been tied down and a canvas thrown over it, there was still room for a set of bedsprings with a mattress laid out on top of it, positioned near the tail of the truck bed. The canvas was held high by a center pole running the full length of the center of the truck bed, making it feel like we were traveling in an airy tent. Marvin and I reclined on the mattress, listening to the whine of the knobby truck tires on the asphalt as the miles rolled by. Sometimes we preferred sitting up and dangling our feet off the back of the truck bed, eating watermelon, and waving at all the people passing us. The first overnight out we spent with an uncle and cousins in Oklahoma City. There we found an alley and unloaded Joker from his trailer that had been pulled all day behind Uncle Tom's Pontiac. These relatives lived in a poor section of the city, and the neighborhood kids quickly gathered around to see a horse up close, even touch him gingerly. Our entrepreneurial cousins decided to charge the town kids twenty-five cents for a ride on him, but money must have been scarce, as we didn't get many takers. From there on we camped out along the way, where the mattress and springs came in even handier. There were no rest stops, but we managed to find open places out in the country that were not in use, sometimes just a few feet from the road. Once we got to Tucson, Tom had a horse pen and shed all ready for Joker. In some ways he seemingly fared better than we did. He had a little shed all to himself, while the four of us lived in one room.

Our first home in Tucson was a garage with adobe walls eighteen inches thick. Adobe was a lot cooler than cement block or wood structures. The garage had a couple of small windows on three sides of it and was cooled by evaporative cooler. We all slept in the same bedroom, with Mom and Dad's bed just a couple of feet from ours. The kitchen and dining rooms were all in there with the bedroom. It truly was a one-room apartment for four. Our bathroom had only an outside entrance, so we had to go out the back door and around the side of our quarters to get to it. It was still quite a step up from the outhouses of Kansas, and it was the first time we lived in a house with a flush toilet.

The upheaval in my life from the farm to the desert was huge. It was partly just moving from a green area to a dry and, what seemed to me, forsaken one. The desert has its beauty and mystique, but it took some time for me to appreciate that. Cactus of all varieties, mesquite trees, and creosote bushes appeared so very stark and unfriendly at first. Fortunately, I had Joker there to give me some identity in this new Western world. Some neighbor boys, like John Henry, felt attracted to anyone who owned a horse, so they came around to get acquainted. But they were not yet comfortable old friends like the farm kids we'd known in Kansas. Homesickness was already building up like a great green lump in my stomach, and it finally came with a vengeance when I entered the seventh grade at Sunnyside Junior High School. There I found, on the first day, what seemed more like a mob of disorderly people than a school. Instead of eight meek children like there had been at Rose, there were thirty seventh graders in one room, many of whom were not at all intimidated by the teacher. Mr. Stevens, my homeroom teacher, also worked part-time for the sheriff's department. He was a very large man with a red face and a long scar down the side of one cheek. I couldn't figure out why everyone didn't cower as he came into the classroom that first morning. He removed his pistol, tossed it into the steel file drawer, then slammed and locked it. I was certainly trembling inside and not just because of him. My homesickness had turned into nausea, and I became physically ill from the strange surroundings.

Teachers were very nice to me, sometimes offering to let me sit outside for a while to see if I would feel better. But no matter what they did, there were too many strange people around me for me to be comfortable. "Mike," a pretty girl too old for her grade and with a lot of lipstick smeared on, was seated just ahead of me. Almost every day she would turn around with her cool smile and say softly, "I could whip you, Humble." I had no doubt that she could, and if she couldn't, her ninth-grade boyfriend sure could! He was the toughest kid in the school.

This horrible situation seemed to go on for weeks, but perhaps it was only days. One day Mr. Stevens flung a *Prose and Poetry* book and hit Francis, who was sitting in the back row, right in the chest. Francis still did not look intimidated! Another day, a Hispanic boy in the sixth grade, several years too old for his class, decided to slap me around on the basketball court. He would kick at my groin, and when I jumped back, my jaw was leaning forward in just the right place to connect with the flat of his hand. The slapping sound made my ears ring. Fortunately Marvin came along right at that instant and asked him what he thought he was doing. Marvin was not much bigger than the Mexican kid, but he had a couple of his big ninth-grade buddies with him, which gave him a lot of authority. The slapping session was over. Not all the Mexican boys were aggressive toward me. Felix Olivas saw my sadness and depression at other times and more than once helpfully offered to beat up anybody that was giving me trouble. I came home so depressed that Mom began to talk to Dad about the possibility of returning to Kansas, but he was not about to make that move. It came to the point where I became so dysfunctional in my mind and in my studies that I was sent to the principal to see if I should be put back a grade. My mom came to the rescue and faced the principal with me, assuring her that I was mentally capable, just needed time to adjust. I also got strong impetus to stay in my class since I did not want to be put back in the sixth grade with the slapping boy.

Over time, almost imperceptibly, school life started getting better. It might have started the day Mr. Stevens approached my desk. Towering over me, he glared down and said, "Humble, I wish I had thirty students like you." I was stumped for a response, but it seemed like a rather good moment. Spankings were common. Even the girls, if naughty, did not escape the paddle. It was a flat board nearly three feet long and had holes bored in it so it seemed to make a swishing noise just before it hit the seat of the offender. Spankings were done in front of the class, without bothering to get approval from the principal. I was beginning to feel just a little bit at home now, and it seemed important to me that I should join the ranks of those who had been paddled. Mr. Stevens sensed what I wanted and obliged immediately. Once was enough. Whatever I had done to precipitate the discipline, he called me forward one day in his gruff voce. At his order, I bent over and grabbed my knees in front of the whole class, as that was the ritual. The paddle nearly lifted me off the floor, making a considerable racket. It really, really stung, and I could hardly hold back a tear! The only consolation was that the expressions of sympathy on the girls' faces showed they were barely able to bear it that I got spanked. That paddling was enough to put me in favor with the whole class, not just the good kids.

Near Christmas an election was held for king and queen of Sunnyside Junior High School. A couple was chosen from the seventh, eighth, and ninth grades. Miracle of miracles, I was the boy chosen by my own classmates as the candidate from the seventh-grade class. The final election was held on the evening of the school fair. A half-gallon glass jar with a slot cut in its lid was set out for each couple. Parents, family, and students alike were allowed to vote by dropping coins or paper money through the slot. Every penny counted as one vote, and there were a lot of pennies filling the jars. Uncle Tom made it a point to keep checking on the voting jars throughout the evening. Every time one of the other candidates appeared to be pulling ahead in the polls, he would drop a dollar bill into my jar. When the counting was done, Pat Hollis, also a seventh grader and Marvin's girlfriend, was chosen queen. Pat and I were crowned king and queen of the junior high school. It probably mattered only to me that Pat was three inches taller than I was as we paraded across the stage in the auditorium, crowned with aluminum-foil crowns and dragging purple robes behind us. Apparently I was a very solemn-looking king because people kept calling out to me to smile and wave. Finally I did, waving to the smiling people in the full auditorium and savoring the moment greatly. It had been a very long and hard adjustment to this new world, but at last I felt I had arrived!

Outside the classroom I was beginning to enjoy the desert instead of hating it. My two friends, both on full-sized horses, welcomed Joker and me to do a lot of riding across the desert, running short races and raising dust. Joker would jump out at the beginning and be ahead by a couple of lengths, but the instant the larger horses were past us, he would lose all interest in the race and slow to a trot. We could ride for miles, all the way to the Papago Indian reservation, without meeting any fences or obstacles, just dodging the various forms of cactus that grew in abundance. We found that the young ladies our age loved horses, which gave us quite an advantage over guys who were on foot or on bicycles. It was more fun riding double on a horse than on a bike. Joker also helped me on my paper route. Dad's job as a day laborer did not afford him the wherewithal to give us much of an allowance. Marvin and I each took on a paper route to provide us with needed spending money. People who had moved to Arizona from the East and Midwest loved the idea of getting their paper delivered by horseback, so Joker and I got a lot of attention. One customer often came out to offer Joker a swig of beer straight from the bottle he'd been drinking from. Joker never turned him down, though fortunately he could not get much liquid from a bottle neck. Mom trained us to tithe from our paper-route income, a practice begun and never stopped for the rest of my life. I am not sure I was a totally cheerful giver, but neither did I complain about it.

This transition from Kansas to Arizona was my first truly "cultural experience" in life. There were others to come, greater than that one. However, I will always believe that going through this major change in my formative years prepared me in a special way for life experiences still ahead.

There was another aspect of my new life in Arizona that helped me in my adjustments. Emery Park Baptist Church was in its early stages of formation and as yet had no building of its own. The new congregation gathered on Sunday mornings in the auditorium of Sunnyside Junior High School. Many people like us had just come to Tucson and, like my mom, found this Conservative Baptist church to hold hope for them and their children. Even though I did not know the church people, there was not the same strangeness about the church as there was about the school. Familiar songs and prayers were a balm to my spirit on Sundays, even though I still did not much enjoy long sermons. The church was in the process of calling a new pastor and finally settled on an energetic young New Englander named Don Gagnon. He would play a strong role in my life as an example of Christian joy and spirituality. Perhaps the main thing I liked about him was his upbeat spirit and ready smile. Even when he was making serious points in his sermons, he often did it with a smile.

During that era the pastor led the whole worship service and then preached the message. He repeated the same procedure in the Sunday evening service. On Wednesday nights he was expected to bring a fresh Bible study. The Sunday evening services were geared to be much lighter than the morning worship service. Gospel choruses and lively hymns were sung. In this relaxed atmosphere Gagnon would nearly dance as he led the singing with a radiant smile. He also often dramatized the Bible stories by acting out the scenes. This is not to say he always kept our attention since we were often preoccupied with other thoughts during teenage years. He was as great an example of a godly pastor and as consistently good-natured as any spiritual leader I have ever met. On communion Sunday, while the bread and cup were being passed, he would often quote from Scripture. He had a great collection of verses memorized that had to do with the death of Christ on the cross. It made an indelible impression on my spirit, hearing verse piled on verse that had to do only with the sufferings of Jesus. This done in the quietest hour of the service made an even greater impact. It was probably my first taste of what "worship" really meant. I truly felt the presence of God in community with others, something I'd never known in our Kansas church.

I am beginning to sound as though I was really growing spiritually under the care of a godly shepherd. In fact, I was still struggling a lot with "the flesh." There was a constant battle, especially during high school years. It seemed like a continual tug of war where I was being dragged over the line by the wrong things and then pulled back by "getting right with God" on Sunday nights at the invitation. I got tricky in figuring out how to look good to church people whose approval I wanted.

Some Sunday mornings, my friend and I would go to Sunday school, then take off to go cruising in his parents' Buick during worship hour. We would time it to get back at the very end of the service to ask a friend what the basics of the sermon had been. That way I could discuss it with some knowledge if my mom asked me about it. At the same time, I was also open to listening to truth when I heard it presented in an attractive way. The better sermons did get through to me, and I responded to them in my heart. I recall a time of going forward in church to confess I was not living for the Lord as I should. We young people were called upon to surrender everything to Christ. I was moved to tears and shed them before some of the spiritual leaders of the church who were doing the counseling. It was a time of deep conviction of sin and then a wonderful release from pent-up guilt. Afterward my friend and I walked a few miles in the desert, just enjoying the afterglow of that spiritual experience. But walking daily in the Spirit was not yet something I could maintain on a consistent basis. There was still a world out there to be enjoyed, besides the church teachings to be adhered to.

The world did have its attractions, and I had a bent toward enjoying them. My last year of high school I got a dress-up job selling boys' clothing in Jacome's Department Store. It was an upper-class retail clothing store, and I'd gotten the job by taking an advanced sales class as part of my high-school curriculum. I made enough money to be independent in dating and buying gas for Dad's car. The fifties were the heyday of the drive-in theatre, and I had the use of a sleek Oldsmobile 76 on Friday and Saturday nights. Movies were preached against at every series of revival meetings, so there was guilt associated with attending. I still attended the shows regularly and dealt with the guilt later. Dates to drive-in theatres gave plenty of opportunity for accumulating guilt, even for those of us who somehow were protected from crossing the line to committing sexual immorality. Interestingly, preachers often harped on the evils of movie-going but never mentioned making out in the back seat of a car! Then there was also the influence of my non-Baptist buddies. By today's standards they might be considered examples of moral excellence. They bought a case of beer once in a while to share around. Somehow it seemed to foam up in my throat, so I never managed to get it down in quantity. None of them were addicted smokers, drunkards, or carousers. However, they were still so very far from the standard I learned about in church that I knew they were dragging me down. I seemed to be alternating between two worlds: one literally was the "world" and the other was the church. I was always shifting between the two, making the adjustments that felt right for the crowd, but feeling miserable when I offended what I knew to be God's will.

As I neared high school graduation, I knew I was coming to a major crossroad in life. No clear path emerged before me. I did not think of myself as good at any trade or excelling in any discipline. Subjects like physics and advanced algebra I avoided, feeling I could never make the grade in the math area. Because of this I thought trade-school subjects might be more appropriate. I tried wood shop, metal shop, sheet-metal shop, and advanced sales in high school. None of these things clicked for me as something I could devote my life to, nor was I good at any of them. My dad often said, "Boy, whatever you decide to be, be a d-- good one." I now know he spoke out of his own feeling of lack of expertise in life. He was not proud of his expertise as a farmer or rough carpenter. I felt that there was nothing I was good at! There was just one thing in life where I had enjoyed some feelings of significance and that was in the spiritual-leadership realm. With the great lack of leadership in our church youth group, I was selected to be the president of the group. I seemed to be accepted as their natural leader whether I felt like a leader or not.

Pastor Gagnon must have seen things I did not see, because he worked very hard to move me toward ministry. His approach was subtle. Instead of telling me he thought I should become a pastor or missionary, he just kept repeating one theme. His New England accent corrupted my name "Arny" to "Ahnie." He kept playing the same string in his kind and gentle way. He would often say to me, "Ahnie, you really need to discover the Lohd's will for your life." The logic was on his side: "God knows the future, and you don't, so try to find out what He has for you." He also pointed out that if I hung around with my old friends in Tucson, I would probably just keep doing what they were doing. If I was to discover God's will for me, it was important that I leave my present environment and get off to a place where I could hear God's voice. He suggested Biola Bible College in Los Angeles as an ideal spot. It was far enough away from home where I would not be tempted to return to my girlfriend and other old friends on weekends, and close enough not to be too costly for transportation. My mom was also praying fervently for me. Actually, she had been praying for years for me, that God would get a hold of my life. Gagnon told me later how she had agonized in prayer for me, especially during the years when I would come home very late at night or early mornings. Now her prayers were being answered as I began the search for God's will for my life.

The *golden thread* that had started with her was now beginning to weave itself into my life. However, to want to do God's will is one thing, and to perform it is another. Just before going to Biola, I got cold feet and went to Gagnon to tell him I did not think I could do it. Part of my problem was financial; most of it was emotional and spiritual. He reminded me there would always be one more mountain of doubt to overcome, and this was just the first one. So I swallowed my fears temporarily and set my face toward Los Angeles.

A couple of nights before I left home, my mom came out on the front porch where I was sitting in the moonlight. It was already late, and Dad had gone to bed. Dad was really giving her a hard time because he said she had convinced me to go off to Bible school. She wanted assurance that it was not because of her persuasion that I was going. I assured her it was my own choice and not because of her urging. A few days later I was not sure at all why I had volunteered for this radical transition.

Friends from my Emery Park Church, Grace and John Moreshead, picked me up in late afternoon to make the journey from Tucson to Los Angeles. I have already discussed in an earlier chapter the tearful parting with my dad. I could feel the knot growing in my stomach as we left the place where I had spent most of my teenage years and made my formative spiritual decisions. My Tucson roots were deeper than I thought, and there was more parting pain than I had bargained for.

Chapter 6 – From the Desert to the City

I urge you, brothers,...to offer your bodies as living sacrifices.
(Romans 12:1)

We had driven all night across the desert from Tucson to Los Angeles to avoid the heat of the day. We were now in the city, and the sun seemed to be trying to shine through but failing miserably. The smog in Los Angeles measured more dangerous to one's health in the fifties than it does today. As we drove into this vast metropolis, a pall hung over our car that matched the feelings in my heart. The sunshine of the desert contrasted drastically with this drab scene. The smog stung my eyes and made my nose run. John had a professor-friend at Fuller who invited us for a lovely breakfast at his Pasadena home. However, the knot in my stomach had by then consumed so much space, there was no room left for the hot biscuits that were offered me. A serious case of homesickness was again making me literally sick.

The old Biola campus was located on Fifth and Hope Streets in downtown Los Angeles. As we turned onto Hope Street, we saw it dead-ended into the City Library, which stood directly in front of our car. Biola's "campus" was adjacent to it, so there was no through traffic. The campus consisted totally of concrete construction. No trees, grass, or even cactus were visible, except for the lawn of the City Library next door. This was visible only from the men's dormitory. However, looking out in that direction could also be a shocker to a desert boy. On a couple of park benches below our dorm windows we could often observe couples expressing romantic affection without reserve. Some of the couples were same-sex people, making it even more shocking to observe. The great Church of the Open Door with its three-thousand-seat auditorium connected the boys' and girls' dormitories. The dorms on either side of the church were thirteen stories high, towering over the church that arched between them. It made an appealing architectural design for those who had eyes to see it. I didn't have the eyes at the moment. On top of the dorms were two neon JESUS SAVES signs that were at least nine feet tall. These were the highest-profile buildings in downtown Los Angeles when they were built in the early 1900s.

All freshmen students were required to take entry exams to see how we qualified to be placed in Biola's study programs. If we did well on the exam, we were recommended for the four-year bachelor of arts program. If not, it was suggested we take the two-year Bible Institute course. My thoughts were preoccupied the day of the exam. Smog hung heavy inside the large exam room, making everything feel gloomy. I found it impossible to focus on the material before me as depression deepened. Results for my entry exam showed it would be better for me to just sign up for the two-year course, but I rejected their advice and went for the four-year BA in Bible course.

In my heart I was wondering if I would last even another two weeks. It was nearly the same as I had felt when I'd moved to Tucson. Again I was struck with gut-wrenching homesickness. I did not like downtown Los Angeles. Police sirens echoed between tall buildings day and night. Bums panhandled their way along the main streets. The food in the cafeteria was barely edible for those who were hungry, and I was not among those. A creative student, tired of the quality of the fried eggs, thumbtacked one by its brittle edge to the bulletin board in the stairwell of the men's dorm.

My dormitory room was tiny. Biola had built small rooms in the early days, intended to house just one student, but then the school grew, and they had to have us double up. The two study desks touched each other and barely gave room for a dresser at one end of the room and a sink at the other end. Sitting at my desk, I could lean my chair back and fall onto the bottom bunk bed. My roommate was a nice guy but already an old man—twenty-six years old and with a receding hairline. Tall windows reached the ceiling, translucent glass with no curtains to break the glare. Everything about the room was plain and stark. We finally purchased some green plastic drapes to break the monotony a bit.

From Kansas to Kalimantan / 60

Every Biola student had to select a practical work assignment. For some reason I chose the skid-row street team rather than teaching a Sunday school class. I took the assignment without a clear understanding of what skid row meant. Once a week, six of us guys would carry a little pump organ a few blocks from Biola campus to the corner of Fifth and Wall Streets, the seamy section of the city. As we neared this district, we saw that every other shop was a saloon or a liquor store. Men were staggering in and out of them. Painted women were usually sitting at the bars and quite visible from the sidewalk. We set up the little organ on the street and sang a few gospel songs while the homeless gathered. The noise of our singing did not seem to penetrate the din of traffic and rough voices around us. A favorite we often sang was, "He Is Able to Deliver Thee." After singing, we would take turns giving our testimonies and quoting Bible verses. One older man would preach a bit longer, and then we would break up and pass out tracts to people whose breath reeked of stale alcohol and who seemingly had not had a bath for a long time. The scariest part was trying to think what to say to them. Those few minutes of being up front, shouting Bible verses and telling them that Jesus does save, seemed very long. One night a drunk walked up to our semicircle of singers and lifted his wine bottle high, threatening to shatter it against the curb. We all jumped back, to his glee.

The best part of the night was coming back to my wretched little room and realizing what a haven it was compared to what I had just witnessed among the homeless. I would get on my knees by my bed and give heartfelt thanks to God for all the bad things that had *not* happened to me in life.

My sense of "call," if I'd ever had any, was fading fast as I endured those first days at Biola. I decided that it was not "God's will" after all that I be at this school, but how could I just walk out the door and go home? I felt trapped. I nearly did just walk out the door a couple of times. After the first week I tried to look up an uncle who was living in the Los Angeles area, thinking I would just go to his home and then run back to Tucson from there. I had one digit wrong in his street address so could not find him. I will always wonder what I would have done had I been able to contact him at the end of that first week of school. My first letters home must have sounded desperate because both Mom and Dad got on the phone to talk to me. I was surprised to hear Dad's voice on the other end saying, "Don't feel like a quitter, boy, if you decide to come home." I had never heard him talk like that with such a note of empathy in his voice. I was tempted but felt just the opposite of what my dad had said. I would indeed be a quitter if I came home. I told him I could maybe hold out until Christmas. I wondered if I could.

Finally, I hurt so much I decided to let the dean of students know how I felt. Al Sanders was dean at the time. I walked into his office one morning and told him straight out, "I do not feel good here at Biola, and I don't really think it is God's will that I stay here." I thought the "God's will" card would play better than any other reason I could think of. Al was a man of great wisdom and personal charm. He was handsome and suave, with eyes and a smile that showed his inner warmth. Without agreeing or disagreeing with me, he said, "Arny, why don't you pray about it again and try hanging in there for a few more weeks to be sure you are making the right decision?" Then he got me down on my knees beside him in his office to pray that the Lord would make it very clear to me as to what I should do. Just having this kind of attention from a man of his quality lifted my spirits—for a while at least.

The real struggle was not the smog of the city or the size of the dorm room; it was rather an inner one. My friends in Tucson had been left behind. I was now living under conditions that could limit the desires of my flesh, but that did not mean I was growing in spiritual things. There were still areas in my life that I felt were not under God's control. I was discovering that surrender to God is a process, not a one-time event. For a kid of seventeen, I felt like I was praying a lot, but it just wasn't working. There was no peace or joy in my life. I was desperate for some kind of spiritual satisfaction.

One night a missionary from Korea spoke at the Church of the Open Door. He spoke on surrender to God—not a new subject to me, but one that still convicted me more than anything else. That night I went back to my little room, where alone I knelt on my "prayer rug" and prayed: "Oh God, I can't seem to give You my life. If You want it, You will somehow have to take it for Yourself. I am helpless in this matter, and I desperately need You to come and take all of my life to become Yours." At that very moment He did, He really did, and I knew it at the time. There was a spontaneous spiritual relief and release. I had joy for the first time, joy that exceeded the kind of happiness I had known before. For the remainder of that whole freshman year I pretty much forgot about sports and the opposite sex, favorite pastimes I had majored in during high school. I still struggled in the area of total surrender from time to time, because that is a lifetime struggle. But life was never quite the same after that night of surrender. After this somewhat mystical experience I became a bit too "pious." Beside my bed I had a braided rag rug I'd brought from Tucson. I began to prize it as my "prayer rug" and enjoyed a little too much falling down on it and pouring my heart out to God. I had high regard for some of the upperclassmen who were able to talk about the "deeper things" of God and hold forth on spiritual matters. I sometimes enjoyed feeling spiritual more than I enjoyed God! It took awhile for me to see through this sort of superpiety. But maybe I needed it to prop me up for a while.

Bible synthesis with Dr. J. Vernon McGee was the highlight of all my courses at Biola that freshman year. I could depend on him to be entertaining and inspiring in every class. He brought Old Testament stories to life, getting downright emotional at times but never to excess. Not that I made A's in his class, since all final exams were based on rote memorization of his famous outlines of the books of the Bible. Memorizing has never been my strong point. Hearing a man preach like Dr. McGee made me want to try to preach.

Personal-evangelism class required lots of Scripture memorization. We were required to give out evangelistic tracts as part of our assignment. Honor system demanded that we confess on Friday whether or not we had handed out at least one evangelism tract that week. Thursday evenings would find some of us out on the street, offering our tracts to Los Angeles's few late-night window shoppers who had already been offered lots of tracts that night. I felt handicapped in any class that required turning in written assignments. My penmanship was legible, but oh not pretty! When I finally got a typewriter, my grades picked up quite a bit.

Most Biola students worked part-time to pay their tuition and buy books. I worked at Orbach's Department Store four hours a day after school. It was an unchallenging job, just stocking shelves and sweeping floors. Minimum wage barely paid my room and board. Life at Biola eventually became a routine. Hours for meals, school, work, and homework were set. Intramural sports on Saturdays provided exercise and fellowship. Sundays I attended one of the great downtown city churches. It was a stable environment where I was insulated from the world while living in the heart of a worldly city. I was also being detoxified to some extent from the life I had known earlier. Sounds funny, I know, when I think of the toxins that are out there today to corrupt young men.

Before December rolled around, I had written to break up with the girl I'd left behind in Tucson. Pat, the cute little five-foot-tall redhead, was my last tie to the "old life." She had been hinting for an engagement ring just before I left Tucson, and that had scared me. It was especially hard for her since I was the one who was breaking it off. I was again back to using the excuse of "God's will," which in this case happened to be absolutely valid. However, it was very hard on me as well. One should never make light of adolescent love, even if it is heavy on the side of *eros*. Breakups are painful, and this one was no exception.

It was exciting to go home to Tucson that first Christmas. I was able to get my old job back at Jacome's, selling boys' clothing. My folks were happy to have me at home again. Contrary to my earlier pledge, I had a few dates with Pat, realizing at the time I was falling from grace. This was positive proof that I still had a ways to go in conquering the flesh. To celebrate my homecoming, Dad had bought me a twenty-gauge, double-barrel shotgun for a present. He took me quail hunting and acted more warmly to me than I could ever remember. He even casually put his arm around my shoulders one day while I was standing close beside him, making me feel a bit awkward. It was obviously his last-ditch attempt to show I was loved and wanted at home. But the fact is: "You can never go back." At the end of the vacation time I knew I needed to return and finish what I'd started at Biola, even if it meant becoming a pastor or a missionary—God forbid!

Back at Biola the second semester I did serious repentance with tears for any "worldly acts" I'd committed at home. Life was back on an even keel, and I was building strong relationships with some guys in the dorm. Relationships became the essence of life. My practical work assignment that semester was street preaching in another part of the city. This time it was on the famous intersection of Hollywood and Vine. The drunkards were fewer, but the challenge was at least as great as skid row. Instead of trying to convert drunks, we were getting catcalls from the well-dressed yuppies of the fifties hanging out of their convertibles. Among other things, they loved to call out, "Save me, mister." But I was learning a few more verses and yelling my testimony a little bit louder. A Biola bus brought us back to campus after each ministry session on the streets. The huge JESUS SAVES signs on top of Biola were clearly visible from the freeway as we approached. Just as the signs came into view, without fail, our team burst into singing, "We have heard the joyful sound, Jesus saves, Jesus saves..." It was a triumphal ritual that I looked forward to every Friday night.

By my sophomore year, I had bought an old '39 Ford. I'd had a bad summer between school years. There was a costly driving accident, costly for the other driver. I was in the wrong and had to pay the damages or get the car owner sued. Trying to pay it off ate up all I would have saved for the next year, and I had no money to pay tuition for the first semester. It looked as though I would not be able to get back into school. However I went ahead and enrolled anyway, praying that the needed funds would come in to pay off my school debt. A friend, and my new roommate, Bob Blankenbaker, figured out what I needed and left a check for me in my Bible without telling me. It was a generous gift at that time— seventy dollars. It was great to be back in the security of the Biola atmosphere.

While I felt secure, I also felt that I was not experiencing much spiritual formation from attending the many Bible classes. One class on Spiritual Life made me feel even less spiritual than before I took it. Dr. Whiting's classes were the exception. When he taught on grace, I finally began to get the idea of what God's love was all about. My heart swelled up so big I felt like jumping to my feet and shouting "Hallelujah" during his lectures on Ephesians.

Outside of class some spiritually formative things were happening to me. An attempt toward spiritual renewal of the student body was spearheaded by Harvey Lifsey, who was student-body president. Harvey was a Korean War veteran, a few years older than I, and a very pious person. He had a passion for prayer and wanted to stir others up for revival. Several of us started meeting on Friday nights, the same evening all Biola sports events were held. The basketball jocks would be waiting for the bus to take them to the game, and we'd be on the same sidewalk, waiting for a car to take us to an off-campus prayer meeting. I felt they were eyeing me with disdain. Some of the sports enthusiasts began calling us "the holy club." It was obviously not intended as a compliment!

Dr. Arthur Mouw of the Christian and Missionary Alliance hosted some of these prayer meetings in his home in Glendale. He was a man who believed in prayer and told wonderful stories of how God had answered prayer while he did missionary work among the Dyaks of West Borneo, Indonesia. He was an unmatched storyteller. He painted verbal pictures of the Dyak tribespeople living far up the Kapuas River. He spoke of the smoky resin torches used for lighting the longhouses while he preached the gospel far into the night. He told of the turning of whole villages from idolatry to serve the living God. I was glued to every story. Part of it was the power of speech of a godly man. We used to say, "When Dr. Mouw speaks, every word weighs a pound." He enthusiastically joined us in prayer for revival at Biola. It was a first for me—the first time I had ever experienced what it was like to pray an hour with people who had passionate and penitent hearts. The guys and girls prayed separately. After the prayer time we got back together. There seemed to be an inner glow that reflected on everyone's face. Even the "unpretty" Biola girls seemed to be beautiful after these sessions. Not everyone needed this kind of experience, but I guess I needed to hear how people who mean business with God talk to Him.

But a negative side to this "spiritualism" began to develop. Several of Harvey's disciples were trying hard to copy him and go beyond his experience. One of them had a serious swagger to his gait when he clicked down the dormitory hall with steel caps on his shoe heels. He also had a sensual gleam in his eye for the girls when he forgot to act spiritual. He was one of those who started practicing "holy laughter" over in a corner of the prayer room. The sanctity of the sessions seemed to be enjoyed a bit too much, and there were those looking for an emotional peak. Spiritual pride pops up in the strangest places! Some of the prayer clan looked down their noses at the less spiritual students, or at least were thought to do so. I can't describe how subtle is the Enemy when it comes to imitation of the real thing. I only know I could recognize it when I saw it. Harvey himself got strong criticism from some people. An anonymous letter from a fellow student told him his voice sounded *odious* when he prayed in chapel. That hit him hard since he was student-body president that year. Actually, he did have a strong "holy intonation" when he prayed before the student body. In a student-council meeting with then Biola president, Sam Sutherland, Harvey was told to try not to get too far ahead of the other students in his public praying. These things dampened his spirit and ours as well. The prayer meetings died out, but I had already had my taste of extended prayer with some zealous types of men. (At least I thought it was extended until I later participated with Indonesian Christians in holding all-night prayer meetings.) In truth, some of the godliest men I knew at Biola never attended these meetings at all. I needed this experience and they didn't was all I could figure out. Also, I had my introduction to the Dyak tribespeople through the eyes of Dr. Mouw. That was more relevant to my life than I could have understood at the time.

Everything came together during my senior year. In truth, too many good things came together! I'd finally gotten the coveted job as a cashier at Pershing Square underground parking lot. It paid well, and I was furnished a cool-looking blue uniform that I wore to class sometimes. My new job provided a safe and free place to park the 1947 Plymouth I'd upgraded to from the old 1939 Ford— parking was a terrible problem in downtown L. A. Several of my good buddies such as Loren Fischer, Neil Fischer, Cal Bogaard, and others also worked in this place that provided parking for 2,600 cars underground. I still keep close contact with some of these buddies to this day.

I decided to go out for touch football that year since my good friend Lee Rhyne was the substitute coach. (We never won a game all year!) As if school, homework, a part-time job, and sports were not enough to keep me busy, I had been elected as Biola Men President the end of my junior year. This was partly due to my friend Harvey's influence since he was involved in the nomination process. He tried, and failed, to get me elected to the office of either the student-body president or student missionary-union president. He finally had to settle on the third choice as Biola Men President position. Now I had a top leadership position at the school, but I was not quite sure what to do with it!

Finding the "Perfect" Woman

One thing had been conspicuously missing during my Biola days, and that was dating. For the first three years of college I had not had a dozen dates. It was almost obligatory to have a date for the Spring Banquet, so I'd gone to a couple of those. None of the women I invited had created any chemistry that affected me. After the "Pat experience" during high school days I was determined that the next time I got serious with a girl, it was going to be *the* girl. Working on student council in my junior and senior years I had the opportunity to get acquainted with some quality women. There was one in particular who was attractive to me. She had held the highest offices for a woman student: Secretary of Student Body in her junior year, and in her senior year, King's Daughters President. She was a faithful member of the China prayer band that met on Wednesday nights. She was an artist, a hard worker, and an early riser who would eventually be a magna cum laude graduate. She was short in stature, which was high on my list of prerequisites since I was only five feet six inches tall. Most of all, she exuded a happy spirit that never seemed to waver. In the hall, the library, the cafeteria, wherever I met her, she was always wearing that radiant smile. (She later told me that as a missionary kid, she never knew what to say to people, so she just smiled a lot.) The smile seemed genuine, however, as her eyes were always smiling, too, with a special gleam in them. Her nose turned up just a bit, enough to make it cuter than it would have been otherwise. She was not beautiful but very cute and very magnetic in personality. In fact, I figured she might have been just right for me if I were just a little smarter and a lot more disciplined. But there were obstacles to be overcome if I was to build a relationship with her.

First and foremost, she was busy dating other men. Worse than that, they were all high-quality candidates for marriage. Some of them were my good friends, and they would share stories with me about how great she was. Among her many suitors was the man who would later spend twenty-seven years of his life as the president of Biola University. They only dated twice, but he was at least on the list! Some of my friends even shared with me what they talked about on dates with her. I saw how she faithfully wrote clever little notes to one guy in particular. He'd come grinning from his mailbox almost every day, reading his note. I was envious. I could imagine what it might be like to live with someone who showed a man that kind of attention.

Wanda was a year ahead of me at Biola. She had dated a lot her senior year and the summer following it, but none of the relationships had developed into something lasting. I watched from the sidelines, wondering if there would be a break in there between guys dating her where I might sneak in. But I also had the feeling she was out of my class, and I shared that feeling with some of my buddies at Biola. They just looked at me strangely as if they thought I was kidding. I knew my own lack of discipline as an early riser, felt my inadequacies as a leader, and even harbored some feelings of inferiority. I definitely felt Wanda would be an overmatch for me. It helped a bit to be Biola Men President, as that gave me an ascribed status whether I felt like Mr. President or not. In my heart I recognized that this was the kind of girl my dad had spoken of a few years earlier. I am talking about what he said in an earlier chapter, "Boy, there are two kinds of women: the kind you date, and the kind you marry." This was definitely the marrying kind.

Finally the opportunity came. Wanda had just broken up with one of my most respected friends. (He went on to be a seminary professor and pastor.) Another guy had also been standing in line and had jumped in ahead of me to date her a couple of times, but I considered him less competition. The crucial moment came one day as she walked by my friend and me while we were standing in front of the men's dormitory. She was, as usual, flashing that radiant smile. I was with Don Stiver, who later became a sheriff's deputy. I said to Don, "There goes Wanda. I wish I had the guts to ask her for a date." Don's knee-jerk response was not to me but to Wanda. He called out, "Hey, Wanda, come here a minute." Don was friendly enough but just greeted her nicely and then walked away, leaving the two of us standing there looking at each other.

The dean's office where she worked was on the second floor, so I walked her up there and on the way invited her to go to the Friday-night football game. She accepted without the slightest hesitation. In fact, she seemed more eager than I would have expected. Don offered that we double date to the game on this first date since both he and I would be playing in the game anyway. That first date was just before my birthday. Wanda hopped into the back seat of the car with me and immediately produced a large chocolate cupcake with chocolate frosting. She stuck a small candle in it and came up with a match from somewhere to light it. Then she sang "Happy Birthday" to me. Don and Ruth joined in from the front seat. I felt happier than I could ever remember feeling in my whole life! It did not matter that the other team outscored us horribly. I still got to take Wanda home afterward. I could feel that my competitor for her attention was losing ground already. He did get one more date with her, but that was because she had promised him one in advance. I did not like it and told her so, but she salved my feelings by saying repeatedly, "Please ask me out again." I had no intention of doing otherwise.

My whole life took on new hope and meaning as my relationship with Wanda deepened. We laughed a lot when together on dates. She was sweet twenty years old and had never been kissed. I was not planning to break that record for her unless I was sure she was going to be my wife. Sounds pretty weird today, I know. Alone or in a group, it just felt right to be with her. I was not even engaged yet but felt confident of being able to deal with life as long as I had her help. You might think this comfortable assurance was enough, but doubts still plagued me. My youthful obsession with seeking "God's will" for my life almost blew up my new romance. I had this feeling that I had to have a revelation from God that Wanda was the right one. In this case, though, I was even more concerned that I might spoil her life. I often prayed that, if we married, I would never hold her back. I felt that God had great things in store for her in the future. Once or twice a month I would go through what might be called a releasing process. I would literally weep through a prayer session that ended in my telling God once again, "I surrender this relationship to You. Remove her from me if that is best for both of our lives." I wanted to have my doubts before marriage, not afterward. I kept setting dates of when God should let me know for sure, or else I should break it off and let her go. Setting deadlines for God does not work. He didn't say a thing that I could hear. Given this silence, I told her at Spring Banquet that year that I really was having doubts and could not get a clear answer from God. Perhaps we should call it quits. That evening depressed me even more. I had no peace that she was definitely the right person, and I had even less peace when I thought of walking away from her. Even though God had not met my deadline for knowing His will, we continued our relationship with regular dates on weekends. It seemed a good idea to get a second opinion on Wanda from my family in Arizona. Perhaps that would shed more light on God's will for me.

At Thanksgiving vacation I took Wanda to Tucson to meet my parents. For Dad and Wanda it was love at first sight. Dad was a smoker, but so were some of Wanda's uncles. Wearing her bright yellow dress with a light yellow choker, she would perch on the edge of his overstuffed chair and talk to him whether he was smoking or not. He also was as charmed as I was by her smile. I asked Mom if Dad liked her. She said, "I think you better take her back to California or your dad is going to make you marry her before you leave here." She got along fine with Mom, too, and indeed Mom was surprised that I did not pop the question while we were in Arizona. We headed back to Los Angeles, happy but not yet certain of the future. Somehow, I still had my doubts that seemed impossible to shake.

Then one day it happened during a prayer time in my Biola dorm room. One minute I was struggling away, and the next I was certain that I should ask her to marry me. I was so sure of that fact that I got up from my knees at that moment and headed down to the little office where she worked. I said to myself that I would close and lock the office door and tell her how I felt, right then and there. I got to her office door with my heart pounding, partly from running down the steps, mostly from anticipation. But when I walked into her office, I found that she had unexpectedly gone home for the day, saying she was not feeling well. This was not the day I would get deterred. I ran a few blocks to pick up my car at Pershing Square garage and drove straight to the studio apartment she shared with a girlfriend. At my knock Wanda's tear-stained face appeared at the door. I was not used to seeing this side of her. I asked her what was wrong. She said she'd left work because she was emotionally upset. "About what?" I wanted to know. "I was thinking about us," she answered. "I just feel so uncertain as to where this relationship is going." That was good news to me because that is what I'd come to tell her. She invited me in and welcomed the old "I love you and want to marry you" words from me as though they had never been said to anybody else in all of history. (She later told me she wondered how I could have waited so long to affirm the love I knew I already had for her.) Into the late afternoon we sat on the couch talking about the future. At one point she jumped up and grabbed a small mirror plaque off the wall that had a Scripture verse etched into its glass. She read it aloud: "The Lord hath done great things for us, whereof we are glad." She thought it was perfect for such a time as this, and so did I. We laughed like silly kids. She could no longer say she had never been kissed, admitting at the same time she needed more practice at it. She was definitely right about not knowing how to kiss, but I told her I did not think that practicing a lot would be a problem.

I made a down payment on a set of rings at the Biola poor boys' shopping spot. It was a little second-floor jeweler's shop that wasted no money on display windows. The man selling me the diamond looked like the same guy who might be cutting them. The diamonds I could afford were small but of good quality. We wanted to announce our engagement to close friends before college was over, but I couldn't afford to pay the final installment on the rings that early. The current dean of students, Chet Burwell, and his wife, Bonnie, offered to host our engagement party. This couple had already been good friends to Wanda, and they took me in as well. Chet had even trusted me so far as to say I could use his name on the Biola sign-in sheet if I was ever dating Wanda and got back to the dorm after curfew hours. At the reception, donuts were served, perhaps because we thought donuts were some kind of a "ring." Inside each of them was a piece of paper with the names "Arny and Wanda" printed on it. Some of our close friends were astonished that we had made the commitment, and that made our day. One skeptical fellow kept asking, "Wanda, won't you reconsider?"

Beginnings of Ministry

Approaching graduation I was in correspondence with Don Gagnon regarding further training. He was sure I should go on to the Conservative Baptist Theological Seminary in Denver but wanted me to assist him for a summer in Tucson before going on to Colorado. Uncle Tom's comfortable three-bedroom house in Tucson was empty, and I had the run of it for just doing some irrigation of his plants and trees. I was to organize a summer youth program and also preach the four Sundays when Don Gagnon was on vacation. This was my first experience at "full-time ministry." Fortunately a very giving couple, Carl and Lova Snider, were sponsors of the young people. They had me over for supper almost every night and sacrificially gave of themselves to plan and show up for all youth retreats. We soon had twenty-plus young people meeting for prayer meeting on Wednesday nights, more than the adult attendance. Many of them were unchurched youth. Often after prayer meeting we would hit a local swimming pool. Honestly, I don't recall that many of them made serious life commitments as a result of the flurry of activities we held that summer. However, it was a training time for me. I learned a lot about the fickleness of youth, especially female youth. A planned retreat at beautiful Mt. Lemmon could suddenly be threatened with missing five girls because somebody got upset at somebody, who in turn had her own set of miffed friends.

I agonized over message preparation, whether it was for speaking to young people or adults. I always felt I had to have "a message" from God before I could stand before people. When I could not get "the feeling" for it, I felt panicky inside right up until the time I had to speak. Usually the panic would subside just before I had to get up and deliver the message. By then I was so wired that I definitely spoke with enthusiasm. There were few resources that seemed practical for what I wanted to preach. I had not had enough life experience to preach with relevance to adults.

The time came for Gagnon to go on his vacation, and I was to fill the pulpit four Sundays in a row. With the help of a little book given me by Deacon Tom Gillespie, I managed to pull together some outlines. Fortunately the whole congregation was pulling for me. I was the homegrown kid and got nothing but affirmative nods, smiles, and handshakes all around. Nevertheless, I could not visualize preaching for a full half hour or more as was Gagnon's custom. That first Sunday I was to preach I kept signaling the young pianist to play a few more introductory hymns that would consume more of my preaching time. After one extra song, she nodded "no" to me, and I realized it was all mine. Leading the opening service was no problem. I could carry a tune and do the announcements. Filling the preaching time was another story. I usually made it to twenty or twenty-five minutes. One Sunday I closed after just seventeen minutes of preaching. That was embarrassing to me, but I got no criticism. Some of the deacons were overjoyed at hearing short messages. Deacon Williams clapped me on the back joyfully for my brevity. Don Gagnon was a good and lively preacher but tended to repeat himself several times. People were happy to be let out early for a change.

One interesting thing to me was how well I could see *everything* while I was preaching. Every movement of the young people far in the back was highly visible: passing notes, whispering, or smiling when the sermon material wasn't calling for a smile. It made me wonder at Gagnon's tolerance toward my conduct in the back of the church just a few short years earlier.

Toward the end of the summer a few things happened to affirm my call to ministry. Old Tom Gillespie spoke to me in the john one day when we were at some sort of a camp. He said, "Arny, I have heard a lot of men speak from the pulpit, and I just want you to know that you have a way of speaking that holds my attention a lot better than most of them I have heard." It was brief but powerful, coming from the most respected, eighty-year-old deacon. I badly needed this kind of affirmation from one of the saints, rather than just hearing "good job" when I preached short sermons. The second thing to encourage me was when Don Gagnon decided I should be licensed to preach. This required my giving a brief doctrinal statement and then being questioned by anyone in the congregation who wanted to ask me theological questions. Some of the young people showed up and asked good questions. It was good to have this formal session behind me once it was over. The final affirmation came when I was asked to preach a final message on Sunday evening while Don Gagnon was present. This time, I spoke on the would-be followers of Christ, challenging the congregation to lay aside whatever it was that was hindering a full surrender to Him. At the invitation, a half-dozen or more people came forward to rededicate their lives to the Lord. Among them were my brother and my cousin, Marveline. Don Gagnon came up to me after the prayer time with them, with tears in his eyes. In his New England brogue he said, "Ahnie, the Lohd really used you tonight. He really spoke through you tonight." It was encouraging enough to keep me plodding toward full-time ministry.

The summer was over, and it was time for my next transition—to the high plains of Colorado and the Rocky Mountains. Before heading off to Denver Seminary, I made one more trip back to Los Angeles to see Wanda. I had tried to persuade her we should get married immediately after finishing Biola, but like a good daughter, she insisted on having her parents present. They were coming home from Singapore the next December, so it was to be a Christmas wedding. I would have felt more confident having her beside me in this new venture, especially had I known that the next chapter of my life would entail a great deal more than a seminary education.

Chapter 7 – Seminary and Church Planting

Do your best to present yourself to God as one approved...
who correctly handles the word of truth.
(2 Timothy 2:15)

Don Gagnon expressed disappointment that I had not managed to save some of my thirty-five-dollar-per-week wages toward a seminary education. I'd had to put piston rings in the Plymouth. I'd also promised Wanda I would make one more trip to California to see her before starting the new semester in Denver. I had squandered some funds on breakfast rolls at the local café from time to time. A love offering at the end of summer was the only thing that got me into seminary. However, I did wish I had saved a bit more cash when, on my way from Tucson to Denver, my tires started blowing out. I barely made it on a beat-up, used spare tire I purchased. I drove into Denver after dark and could not locate the seminary, so I slept in the car near some railroad tracks. The next morning the sun seemed to shine into my car windows from the wrong direction. I never got my directions straight in Denver as long as I lived there. The lower oxygen content in the air of the mile-high city made my Plymouth seem very sluggish. That was nothing compared to the way I felt. It took awhile to adjust to the altitude.

Denver Seminary was in an old residential part of town. The Bonfils Mansion housed the classrooms and chapel. It was still amazingly original, with gold tapestry still adorning the halls. The library was in the basement where the swimming pool had once been. The "French Room" still had a huge crystal chandelier hanging from the ceiling and a seemingly twenty-foot-long table under it. That is where the faculty met. The chapel was large enough to seat fifty or more people comfortably. Here the students, mostly men, thundered out the old hymns, and it felt good to be one of them.

The downtown residential area of Denver was a dramatic change from the busy downtown of Los Angeles. The gigantic elm trees that lined every street were shedding their yellow-brown leaves in abundance. The crisp wind swirled them around my feet as I walked the short distance back and forth from the seminary building to my boarding house. The biting, but not yet bitter, wind and the sound of crunching leaves underfoot seemed to wake me up. They made some kind of romantic impression on me that I cannot quite describe. It made me yearn for enjoying Denver life with my bride-to-be back in Los Angeles. My Southern Baptist roommate, Nathan, was a pleasant fellow who was eleven years older than I. He had already been a pastor and was a bit jaded from his pastoral experience, but he carried with him a wonderful sense of humor. He often begged me on Friday nights to go to the "visual aids" with him. This was his picturesque language for attending the movie theater.

Planting a Church

My Friday and Saturday nights were soon to be consumed with other things, such as sermon and Sunday school preparation for the new church I was starting. Before leaving Tucson, Don Gagnon had warned me that if I was not careful, "seminary" could turn into "cemetery." He felt that men who concentrated totally on academic issues could starve for lack of practical application of the material. Starting a new church, he thought, would be the answer to that problem. I consulted a couple of faculty members, and they thought it was unwise for a full-time seminary student to try to plant a new church. However, after interviewing for a couple of church staff positions, I found out my main tasks would be to run the youth department and head up Sunday school attendance contests. Those assignments sounded less appealing to me than starting a church from scratch.

I contacted the local Conservative Baptist pastor in charge of outreach who was a friend of Gagnon's. On a fall evening just as the sun was starting to set, Pastor Williams took me on a windshield survey twelve miles west of Denver. It was near

Morrison, a little town that was nestled at the entry point into the Rocky Mountains. As we toured the hilly area, somehow I did not notice that many of the houses were poorly kept, some just a shade this side of pitiful looking. However, there was one very positive attraction. In contrast to some of the less attractive homes, the Durwood Nichols were offering their spacious ranch-style dwelling as the meeting place. Marge and Durwood Nichols made a handsome couple in their early thirties. He was tall, good-natured, and had an infectious laugh. She was a beautiful blond who had come to Christ very recently. Not long before, she had been a blues singer and saxophone player in a traveling band. They had three delightful children. We all seemed to hit it off right away. When I reported back to my faculty advisor that I was planning to plant a new church near Morrison, he advised me it was unwise to try to start a church while one is in seminary. However, I was following the advice of Rev. Gagnon who had urged me to do so in the first place.

The next Saturday I started knocking on doors in the Mountain Valley community near Morrison. I was asking if people would be interested in attending a new Baptist church in the area. Not many people seemed interested, but a handful said they were. Several of them invited me in for a cup of coffee and a friendly chat. Some of them were not so friendly. These were independent folk who had moved out of the city to get away from congestion and did not even want a knock on their door. I naively thought that surely people who had expressed interest would show up for the first church service. They did not. Not one of them. We sat and waited awhile in the large living room. The Nichols had family in Denver, so that swelled our ranks to eight people, including me. We went ahead with the service, singing without use of a piano or hymnals. We simply had some words written on song sheets. The only encouraging thing was that the Nichols expressed great appreciation for my message. None of us knew one another's capabilities, so they were glad to hear I could preach without stuttering. I suppose it would have been common sense to admit that this community was not ripe for church planting. However, I did not know any better. I just kept knocking on doors on Saturdays and was pleased when a few people began to show up. Marge Nichols was a talented Child Evangelism worker who always had a little story before Sunday school classes were held. Durwood was a very pleasant, smiling Sunday school superintendent who functioned as the MC more than anything else. A fellow student at seminary, Cliff Schieffer, led the young people and did some calling on his own. Things were looking more encouraging by the time I was ready to go back to Los Angeles at Christmas break to marry my bride and bring her back to Denver.

"The Two Shall Become One…"

I had to sell my almost-new typewriter for seventy-five dollars to get gas and food money for the trip back to the coast. I slept in the car on the way to avoid renting a motel room. I arrived a few days before the wedding which was set for the twentieth of December. I found Wanda at the Overseas Missionary Fellowship (OMF) house with her parents, who had recently returned from Singapore. It was my first meeting with her parents. Dad Hazelton brought me a German-made camera from Singapore and tried immediately to explain to me what an "f-stop" was. Dad had been photographer for China Inland Mission for many years and was avid about his picture taking. He was never a talker, but always a gentleman. Wanda's mother was in full swing making wedding preparations.

The Hazeltons brought Chinese silk cloth for Wanda's wedding dress, and it turned out to be gorgeous, tailored perfectly by a faithful church member. Because of the generous help from so many people at Eagle Rock Baptist Church, the wedding turned out beautifully. My financial investment in this important life event was somewhere between paltry and zero! The cake was contributed by some of the faithful ladies of the church. Bridesmaids provided their own pastel-colored gowns. Since it was a December wedding, they carried white muffs decorated with holly. I did hand Dr. Roy L. Lauren a fifteen-dollar check for performing the ceremony, secretly hoping he might do it gratis. He didn't. After a four-day honeymoon in an OMF mission bungalow in Manhattan Beach, we came back for Christmas with the Hazeltons at the OMF guesthouse in Highland Park. A few days later we were headed for Denver, spending one night in an overly warm little cabin near the edge of snow-covered Grand Canyon on our way back. It was my first glimpse of this creative handiwork of God, though I'd been a resident of Arizona for seven years. It added awe to the already awesome new life I was entering.

Back in Denver, we spent our first night in the guest room on the top floor of the Bonfils Mansion, which housed the seminary. The next day we found an apartment close to St. Luke's Hospital on Seventeenth Street, paid seventy-five dollars for our first month of rent, and had exactly five dollars left to eat on until I got my thirty-five-dollar paycheck a few days later.

Together in Ministry

Wanda was a welcome addition to my budding congregation at Mountain Valley First Baptist Church. The Nichols' living room was getting too crowded, so we decided to revamp the horse stable behind the Nichols' house for a worship center. With Wanda's coming, the youth work was surrendered to her. She was a magnet for the rural teenagers. The Denver Seminary staff finally softened in their opinion as to whether I should plant a church. Their December issue of *The Seminarian* featured our church on its front cover. "It Started in a Stable" was the title, and Wanda and I were pictured in front of the stable-church. Young people were being saved and baptized. Then one Sunday a young engineer, Bill Coppfer, and his wife, Jo, came forward to accept Christ. Bill really meant business as was seen from his broken voice and his tears. Bill's parents also came forward. I was so happy I pounded the steering wheel of the Plymouth all the way home, saying, "Praise the Lord" over and over again. No human experience for me ever quite matches that of seeing people come to Christ. For months there seemed always to be someone accepting Christ, or about ready to. I could tell when they were under conviction. They would either make a decision or stop coming within a short period of time.

I had paid a price for the harvest that was coming. My nose was to the grindstone every night of the week with seminary assignments. Every Friday and Saturday night I anguished over these people who were coming to church, that they might be saved. I mention it because I have never since been as burdened, as prayerful, or as tearful for people as I was in this my "first love." The morning congregation totaled sixty-five people by the time we left. We had moved into a refurbished home up on a hill, on property donated by Bill Coppfer. Over half the people in the congregation were those we had baptized. Almost none of our growth came from people transferring membership from another church to ours. Many of them were young people who came from dysfunctional families, whom Wanda, and Bill and Jo Coppfer, had brought to the Lord.

During my senior year at seminary Wanda became pregnant with our first child. She delivered Cheryl Ann on June 24, 1959. She had huge blue eyes that captivated anyone looking at them. I finally had to ask Wanda to sit on the back row of our little church rather than have the ladies ogling her while she was being burped over her mom's shoulder. Their adoring smiles tended to distract me from what I was preaching about. Cheryl got used to moving around a lot early in life. Wanda and I lived in seven different houses during the three years we lived in Denver. These moves had to do with trying to live near where the church was being planted, but also because we always seemed to be looking for less expensive housing. I pulled night duty in giving her the first bottle-feeding of the night since Wanda was unable to nurse her. Cheryl was only a few months old when she would often remove the bottle from her mouth and sincerely converse with me at 1:00 a.m. in some kind of language only she understood. From the expression in her eyes and the sincerity of her coos and gurgles, I could tell she was trying to communicate something very important. I usually let her finish what she was saying before shoving the nipple back in her mouth and dozing a bit myself.

Called to Foreign Fields

I loved the people at Mountain Valley, but as I neared graduation I was feeling the "push and pull" that often extrudes one into the next phase of life. It was my senior year at Denver, and I was not feeling fulfilled at the thought of nourishing the flock I had brought into existence. Preaching the gospel came easy, but preparing meaty sermons was a burden to me. That was the "push." The "pull" was my remembering that Wanda and I had married on a premise that "The place of greatest need demands first consideration in your life." Certainly there were millions of lost people overseas who had never had a chance to hear the gospel.

I was convicted by a vivid concept of heaven and hell. It did not seem right that people should be allowed to enter the next life without ever hearing about Christ. Dr. Raymond Buker, professor of missions at Denver Seminary, further influenced me to consider serving overseas. The "will of God" thing came back into sharp relief in my life, so that I felt compelled to search out whether we should become missionaries. Together Wanda and I decided we should try to discover reasons why we should *not* take the gospel to the uttermost part of the earth, rather than why we should. We could find no reason why we should not.

As we explored our options, the Conservative Baptist Foreign Mission Society (CBFMS) seemed a natural fit for us. We applied to the mission and were appointed in September 1959. But, like Abraham, we did not know to which land we were going. The CBFMS board made our decision just a bit easier by adopting a brand-new field in Indonesia the same year—the Dyak tribal people of West Kalimantan, Indonesia.

There were several reasons that Kalimantan appealed to us from a human standpoint. First, it was in Southeast Asia, and Wanda's parents were serving in Laos at that very moment. Second, we felt a natural affinity for Asian people in comparison to Latin American and African. Third, it was the very province in which our friend Dr. Arthur Mouw had labored and about which he had shared his heart-capturing stories. Finally, it was a brand-new field, and there would be no senior missionaries looking over my shoulder. This was actually a negative factor, but I was too green to recognize that. I had just pioneered a church plant in America, and I liked the idea of pioneering a new foreign mission field. Some ego was definitely involved here, and I would pay for that later.

Perhaps I interpreted the call to mission wrongly in those days, but to me the missionary "call" during the fifties was a call to die to one's own desires. I knew the kernel of wheat could not flourish unless it first died (see John 12:24). There was a kind of sad satisfaction in the belief that self has to die, not be fulfilled. Possibly a bit of masochism, too! The slides we saw of "Borneo" (the old name for Kalimantan) made it look like a really good place to deal harshly with the flesh. Living conditions would be primitive, and it appeared that our field would be remote from civilization. The path of obedience and self-denial seemed to lead in that direction. The CBFMS board approved our appointment to Indonesia, and six months later they appointed Bob and Barbara Chapman as our co-laborers. Our support came in over a seven-month period. This brief support-discovery period could be attributed to the fact that "Borneo" was a brand-new field for Conservative Baptists, and many CB churches wanted to put another light on their world maps. It was also due to God's blessing on Wanda's and my teamwork in presenting the field. Wanda was a chalk artist, and "black light" was the going thing in those days. It was fairly dramatic in an era when most people still just had black and white television sets. I preached and told missionary stories while Wanda drew a picture, and then the lights went off while the black light came on, exposing brilliantly what she had embedded in the picture. People often audibly gasped at this point.

I said earlier that I felt I was going to the mission field to "die to self"; however, our preparations for departure tended to contradict that self-effacing thought. Packing "missionary barrels" has always been an art, and Wanda expertly packed several of them plus a number of wooden crates. We were taking clothing, tools, and supplies for four years. Workers from other missions, such as RBMU, had told us there was virtually nothing usable for our needs unless we were expecting to "go native." The Conservative Baptist Women's Missionary Societies of Arizona and California showered us with every conceivable clothing need, plus linens and toiletries. All of this was to be shipped to Singapore where it would be stored while we entered into Malay language study in preparation for learning Indonesian.

We were all packed and ready to leave for the field by December 1960 but decided to delay until after the holidays. When the day came, we were sent off from the Tucson airport by a contingent from our Emery Park Baptist Church, plus other friends. My friend NT Dellinger says that at some point I put my arm around his shoulders and said with tears in my eyes, "NT, if you can be anything else in the world, don't be a missionary." Mom and Dad did not go to the airport. (I have told the story of parting with my dad in an earlier chapter.) Mom always kept back her tears until after we left, holding strong in our presence. We stopped over briefly in Los Angeles to transfer from a propeller to a jet-powered plane. Another group of friends sent us off from the Los Angeles airport. Among them was petite and elderly Mrs. Hooker, Wanda's favorite teacher at Biola. A few seconds before we boarded, she looked us squarely in the eye as was her way when she was making a point. In her own deliberate fashion she simply said: "When He putteth forth His sheep, He goeth before them." (John 10:4 - Old King James Version). Quoted by this godly woman, this powerful word of encouragement to us kept ringing in our ears long afterward. The shore lights of Los Angeles were just coming on as we lifted off for this first overseas trip. We had said our good-byes to family and friends, knowing we would not see them again for four years. While it was not easy, I did sense the presence of God. I recorded in my journal: "If this is an example of the peace You give as I am leaving my relatives and homeland, it is enough."

Chapter 8 – Singapore and Travel to Kalimantan

The LORD reigns, let the earth be glad;
let the distant shores rejoice. (Psalm 97:1)

Singapore was a charming island city in the early sixties—not quite as clean as it is today but much more appealing as a place to live. Since Wanda was a child of the OMF, we tired travelers were joyfully welcomed into their guest facilities at an excellent room rate. Our fellow workers, the Chapmans, arrived a day later and took up residence in the New Leoni Guest House nearby. We bought them orchids and left a welcome note for them in their room. Our gesture somehow implied to them that we were the old-timers who had been around Singapore awhile, whereas we had only been there about twenty-four hours before them. Furthermore, our special treatment by OMF did nothing to promote an immediate sense of team relationship. We were slow to recognize this. However, both families soon leased three-bedroom flats in the Royal Air Force housing complex not far from the Singapore Swimming Club. British troops were being withdrawn, leaving behind perfect accommodations for people like us. The flats were roomy and completely equipped with kitchen appliances, pots and pans, and all kitchen utensils. With the Singapore Swimming Club just a twenty-minute bike ride away and Malay servants to clean and cook, it was not the hardship post we had envisioned. Even so, it was extremely hot and humid with lots of mosquitoes and no air conditioning or window screening. Ceiling fans were our only means of escape from the heat.

I have never worked as hard and consistently on anything in my life as I worked on learning the Malay language. Wanda and I each had our own separate language teachers coming to the flat one hour per day to drill us in grammar and vocabulary. We spent another five hours per day in memorizing for the next day's lesson. My teacher, Mr. Yakub, was just finishing tutoring a brilliant Oxford man going out under OMF. He showed open disappointment that it took me so long to memorize the vocabulary. I spent hours making up Malay sentences in my mind, saying them over and over to myself until I could repeat them without pausing. I tried going to the marketplace to practice, but the Chinese always answered us in English when we asked prices in Malay. I tried going to the Malay villages nearby, taking Cheryl with me in her little bamboo bicycle seat. The Malays pretty much ignored me. Wanda caught on faster by practicing with the Malay house helper. It was not culturally appropriate for me to do more than greet her or say a sentence once in a while. In time the language began to sink in, though. When Wanda's language teacher kindly invited us over to visit her and her husband, I was forced to sweat it out, making conversation for nearly two hours with my very limited vocabulary. The spicy curry she served, along with the equatorial heat, made me perspire even more than usual. It was an awkward and uncomfortable time, but that night I felt I had made the beginning of a language breakthrough.

A high point of our Singapore time was a two-week holiday with Wanda's parents in the beautiful and cool mountains of Cameron Highlands, Malaysia. In that high altitude Dad Hazelton gave me my first experience of playing golf. We bought nicked golf balls for just three cents each, and I sliced a large number of them into the dense surrounding jungle. Cheryl had suffered from a perpetual heat rash in Singapore, but in the mountain air her skin cleared up completely. Mom Hazelton packed us picnics, and we took walks to eat by small waterfalls. Nights were crisp and cool. It was a romantic place, and we were relaxed. It must have been, for here Kevin was conceived and then, some months later, carried in his mother's womb to Kalimantan.

We shouted for joy when the cable finally arrived saying that our visas for Indonesia had been granted. There had been ominous warnings we would never be able to enter this new field. The Protestant Minister of Religion in Pontianak, the capital of Kalimantan Barat, had said, "No more missionary organizations will be allowed to enter Indonesia." Our CBFMS Foreign Secretary, Dr. Edwin Jacques, had made an epic boat trip from

Singapore to Pontianak to survey the field and to persuade the Minister of Religion to grant us entry. It worked, but it took awhile. We still waited three months after receiving the visas so Wanda would not be traveling during her first trimester of pregnancy. Meanwhile two new CBFMS missionaries arrived to stay with us a few days just before we left the island. Nurse Trudy Davis and teacher Norma Hasse joined us in our home and got a brief orientation to Singapore life.

In early December of 1961 we went to the Singapore pier to board the "Lalang" freighter for Pontianak. With feelings of nostalgia we watched the shoreline of Singapore disappear in the distance. This stay had been a great interlude for us, giving us a chance to get reasonably fluent in Malay. There was also a bit of acculturation to Asian life and food.

I began this section by speaking of "transitions," and now it was time to face up to the greatest transition of all. It would take us four days on the "Lalang" to make the 390-mile trip from Singapore to Pontianak. We rented seamen's cabins in the lower bowels of the ship, two rooms located on either side of the diesel-powered engine. There was a good strong roar accompanied by considerable vibration day and night. No porthole graced our cabin, or anything else to move the air. The tiny fan in the ceiling of our cabin had apparently stopped turning long ago. It was the days before DDT was outlawed, and that insecticide dealt almost instant death to the abundant cockroaches under our mattresses and in the cracks. We had not planned adequately in bringing enough food on the trip. We were allowed seamen's food, but the boiled eggs, fish, and even the rice all tasted the same—like fish! Fortunately the Chapmans, who had prepared better supplies, took pity and generously shared their cheese, crackers, and raisins with us.

Time dragged on as we stopped several hours at the islands of Batam and Tanjung Pinang. Deck passengers boarded carrying everything from live chickens to a fully decorated artificial Christmas tree. The deck was nearly packed as people laid out their *tikars* (grass mats) for sitting, dozing, and smoking. They were mainly Chinese and Malays, a friendly bunch of people, and there was plenty of time to practice our language.

On the morning of December 3 we caught our first glimpse of Kalimantan. About five o'clock in the morning we entered the mouth of the great Kapuas River, which finds its source hundreds of miles inland in the very heart of the island. The pilot negotiated the sweeping curves in the river as the prow nearly touched the trees growing along the edges. Seven hours brought us to the docks of Pontianak. Dilapidated "go-downs" stood behind ancient piers made of the ironwood for which Kalimantan is famous. Since it was Sunday, no officials were around. Immigration was called, and three hours later the officials appeared to check passports. Not a breath of air stirred after the ship dropped anchor. Meanwhile a brief torrential rain first alleviated and then intensified the noonday heat as the sun returned with a vengeance after the brief cloudburst.

Finally a large flatbed barge came alongside, and our ninety deck passengers began scurrying aboard. Meanwhile we stretched our necks looking for a missionary to greet us. We assumed that our cable sent six days earlier had by now been received. When every square foot of the barge seemed to be covered, the captain finally advised that we no longer wait for a private reception but rather go ashore with the deck passengers. A mad scramble ensued as two families grappled with twenty-five pieces of hand luggage and shepherded four small children aboard the barge. Ashore, we continued our lesson in patience, waiting several hours for customs officials to arrive and process our hand baggage. We stood in long lines, sweating with the other passengers, to go through customs. We were briefly frightened when a customs official threatened to strike a Chinese merchant who tried several times to bring a large basket of goods through customs. After repeatedly telling him he had to store his goods with the customs authorities until the next day, the customs official grabbed the basket and hurled it carelessly in our direction. It came dangerously close to Cheryl when it landed. He then leaped over the low counter and raised his fist to strike the merchant who by then had fallen to his knees, begging with hands clasped in front of his face in a praying position. With fake jabs coming close to his face, the man pleaded, "Please, please, please, don't hit me." It was sickening to see a grown man beg with such humility in front of so many people.

By now it was getting dark and still no sign of the missionary on whom all our hopes were pinned. While the children were fed the remaining food supplies in a corner of the customs office, I left the dock to rent a three-wheel trishaw affair and went in search of the Chinese Protestant church of which Dr. Jacques had informed us. The Muslim trishaw driver obviously knew little of Christian churches. First he tried the large Catholic church, then to the Protestant Church of West Indonesia. Finally a policeman at a night watch post directed me to the home of an Indonesian widow whom he knew to be active in the above Protestant church. She had never before seen my face, but upon hearing of our two families with four small children waiting at the harbor without accommodations, Mrs. Hetariah insisted that we come immediately to her house for the night. Indonesian Customs Department had temporarily confiscated all of our foreign money, and there had been no opportunity to procure Indonesian currency even to pay the trishaw driver. We were literally penniless in a strange land. Mrs. Hetariah paid him and then ordered a young man named Jack to take me back to the harbor on the carrier of his bicycle. Engaging a total of five trishaws for our eight people and baggage, we made an eerie little parade as Jack led us through the dimly lit streets of Pontianak to our destination. This former judge's widow gave us our first taste of Indonesian hospitality by providing baths, food, and shelter to total strangers who could barely speak her language. Being familiar with the ways of Westerners, she even opened a priceless can of cheese and offered us fresh bread to go with it. She was the instrument God chose to use in proving to young missionaries the truth of His promise that: "When He puts forth His sheep, He goes before them." And so, on our first night on Indonesian soil, we rejoiced in the goodness of God's provision. We were grateful that a precious cultural trait of Indonesians is their generous hospitality.

PART 3 – LIFE IN KALIMANTAN

The next morning after our wonderful hospitality at the hands of "the widow of Elijah" we saw more of the city of Pontianak in the light of day. This port city, built on swamplands before 1771, lies just three miles south of the equator. A few minutes after the sun came up, it was extremely hot and humid. The ditches that ran alongside the major streets were small waterways where sampans carried their wares—mostly coconuts, it seemed. People were bathing in these little canals, brushing their teeth, or washing their clothing in the brown water. City dwellers are mostly Chinese and Malays, plus a few Dyaks and a mixture of ethnic groups from other islands of Indonesia.

Chapter 9 – Early Impressions

*For with stammering lips
and another tongue will he speak to this people.
(Isaiah 28:11)*

With the help of Rev. Philip Chung of the Chinese Protestant Church, we found the RBMU guesthouse. It smelled musty and to our eyes appeared rundown. At night, we lay in our own sweat. Any movement of air from our ceiling fans had little chance of penetrating the thick mosquito nets hung over our beds. The humidity alone made the bedding feel damp. Well-worn kapok mattresses allowed us to experience the firmness of the boards supporting them. There was no sign the place had been repainted in recent history. Water ran only in the early morning, at which time someone had to be alert to fill several drums stored in the back for bathing and cooking. Tides from the ocean came and went, backing up the great Kapuas River, which in turn raised the water level in the ditches surrounding the house. Overall, it was a depressing atmosphere.

We were not grateful enough for this place of rest because we had experienced so much better in America and Singapore. Later on, we would grow to love and appreciate this old guesthouse. It was a haven for missionaries coming out of the interior, offering a secluded space in which to relax, while purchasing supplies or doing mission business. We were immensely grateful that a sister mission would generously allow us to stay in their facility. It became a meeting place where we got to know all the other missionaries scattered across this vast jungle region. They came from well-known missions of that era such as Christian and Missionary Alliance (C&MA), Regions Beyond Missionary Union (RBMU), Go-Ye Fellowship, and Worldwide Evangelization Crusade (WEC). Our initial impressions of a house that would eventually become precious to us were undoubtedly due to some cultural shock. Perhaps we were spoiled from having just left the beautiful city of Singapore.

With the help of a Mr. K. from the C&MA, we managed to find the bank and cash some of our traveler's checks we had retrieved from customs. At the bank, we learned it was illegal to sign a check with a ballpoint pen; it had to be a bona fide fountain pen. Indonesian officials tended to retain the trivial rules such as these that they had learned from the Dutch. We got a paltry forty-four rupiah for each U.S. dollar. The black market rate was more than ten times that amount, so buying power was extremely limited, making us feel taken advantage of, and that we were squandering the Lord's money.

Wanda and I ventured out on our own to do the early morning shopping before sunup. We quickly learned the cost of taking a trishaw to the market place. We also got a general idea regarding the going price for food and how to bargain. Fortunately bargaining skills had begun in Singapore, but it still felt quite foreign to us to haggle over prices. We even had to bargain for the little trishaw called a *beca* to transport us to the central meat market located next to the Kapuas River. There we bought chunks of beef slashed from the quartered animals hanging in the open market. In the vegetable market nearby we found tomatoes, cabbage, onions, and several kinds of greens we did not recognize. We felt at a loss as to how much to buy and how to cook the Indonesian raw products from scratch. Fortunately Barb Chapman was a good cook and did a lot of the meal preparation. Adding to the physical discomforts and awkwardness of a new culture, we also faced some interpersonal issues. We had not yet learned how to live in harmony with the Chapmans, so there was added tension from that perspective. To top it off, we were baffled as to how to get our shipment out of customs.

There was one bright spot for me in the midst of the negative things I faced, and that was Wanda's buoyant spirit. She was five months pregnant and feeling the heat, but she still showed a consistently cheerful nature in all of this new life. Perhaps it was having grown up on the mission field herself, but she seemed to have instant acculturation without the usual signs of depression. She loved to happily converse with the little Malay man who was the RBMU house guard and water boiler (all water had to be thoroughly boiled before drinking). Her cheerful spirit may have been part of the reason for her being less able to live in harmony with her fellow missionaries. Her maintaining such a pleasant spirit must have seemed out of place to those who were suffering from cultural shock. It would be easy for them to wonder, *Why is this woman always smiling?*

In the first few days we were thoroughly screened by police intelligence and registered by Immigration and regular police. Even our small children had to be fingerprinted. The process appeared to be endless. It seemed terribly odd to spend so much time in dilapidated old government and police offices that had shelves and shelves of musty papers stacked up. For me, it was not easy to keep smiling during this time, but it seemed important, so I made my best effort.

Four long days passed, and then our Indonesian sponsor called on us. Mr. Haniz had come from our future mission station in search of car parts. First impressions are lasting, though not always accurate. Mr. Haniz of the PIKI (Indonesian Evangelical Christian Association) church spent more than an hour pouring out his tale of woe. There were problems of hunger, low salaries, and immorality at the mission station that was to be our home. He was visibly overwhelmed with the whole situation. In retrospect I see that he was expressing how happy he was that we were finally there to share the burden. In his own way, perhaps, he was telling us of his joy at our presence on the field. Unfortunately we, his audience, were already feeling new and inadequate in everything, including even such matters so simple as grocery shopping. We tried to show interest regarding all the problems Mr. Haniz was facing, but our hearts got heavier as he unburdened himself. We were pleased to be able to communicate reasonably well with him in our Malay brand of Indonesian and wondered what it would have been like had we arrived on the field with no knowledge of Bahasa Indonesia. One thing impressed us immediately about Mr.

Haniz: his utter pessimism regarding the work did not affect his own personal bearing. The Christian humility often encountered in Indonesian believers was markedly absent from his personality. Perhaps being left with full responsibility for Mr. Brawni's work the previous six years had given him a self-esteem beyond what was appropriate.

After Mr. Haniz's departure we went back to trying to unsnarl the red tape of importing our goods through customs. It is difficult to say how long it would have taken had not Elmer Warkentin of RBMU arrived on December 8. He had just received our cable sent from Singapore on November 28. The next morning at customs we followed an experienced hand. Elmer walked rapidly between the customs offices but slowed his pace several strides before reaching each official's door. Then he knocked gently and proceeded very slowly to enter the office, bowing slightly to communicate his respect for authority. At the same time he exuded open friendliness with a wide smile. It became a ritual, which I tried to imitate for the rest of my life when doing business with Indonesian officials. A hurry-up attitude is usually offensive to these people.

The polite ritual paid off. Our forty pieces of freight and twenty-two crates of food were released from customs within the next three days. Duty charges amounted to $45. Elmer gave the officials a small gift of some of our flashlight batteries and some powdered milk *after* we cleared customs. To offer it beforehand would have constituted a bribe. We rejoiced in the goodness of God and the obviously benevolent attitude of Indonesian officials. Throughout the 1960s and half of the 1970s, the Indonesian customs department generously allowed missionaries to bring in most of their personal goods without charging duty.

Having cleared customs, our freight was stacked high on the ironwood porch at the RBMU guesthouse, ready for shipping to Sungai Betung. This 125-mile trip was an approximate ten-hour drive in an overloaded truck. Freight prices were outrageous because of the poor dollar exchange rate. The best bid a Chinese Christian "friend" could offer was $250 per load (more than it had cost to ship from America). Still hoping to find a better bargain,

Bob Chapman and I decided to make a quick visit to Sungai Betung while shopping for a less expensive trucker.

Travel to our future station was via the local bus system. Chevrolet trucks of 1940 vintage had been revamped to make twenty-eight passenger buses. A sturdy wooden frame covered with sheet metal housed the passengers. Windows made of wood and tin were slid up and down by the passengers, making it very dark inside when driving rain required their being closed. Benches were made of wood with a bit of padding on the seats, but not on the backrest. A heavy rack on top provided freight space for huge vegetable baskets, durian (thorny fruit) and raw rubber. Original truck springs were stiff and gave the passengers many a jolt. An early report from the field tells of the five-hour trip from Pontianak to Singkawang:

> The road in places was very bad, but the driver was little aware of it. At times the stiff-springed bus would slam you hard enough from the bottom to give you a headache. The country grew more beautiful as we progressed north toward Singkawang, with mountains rising toward the inland. Along the coastal road were healthy-looking rice fields, a fairly-well-populated area with most of the people living in *atap* (thatch) and bamboo dwellings on stilts. (1/26/62 Indonesia Report No. 3:4)

At Singkawang Mr. Haniz met us in the old Chevrolet carryall left behind by Mr. Brawni. Attempts to report to Immigration were thwarted by a flood surrounding that office. Hopes for a midday departure to Sungai Betung were dashed when the PIKI car developed battery trouble. Finally by 3:00 p.m. we were on our way. The first seven miles toward Sungai Betung had at one time been paved. Now it was a sequence of potholes. Still, the beauty of the area continued to impress us. In contrast to the wretched road, we were surprised by beautiful mountains rising up just beyond the outskirts of Singkawang. The farther inland we went, the more beautiful was the terrain. We were impressed by our first glimpse of Gunung Pendaring and Gunung Bawang (*Gunung* means mountain). Mr. Haniz was a jubilant chauffeur, picking up a passenger here and there but grandly refusing all payment for fares. Honking the horn enthusiastically in each marketplace, he jabbed his thumb triumphantly toward his two new missionary recruits in the back seat. Even in our naïveté we could grasp that he was gloating over some who had doubted his promise that Americans were coming to help in his work. We continued to feel like two very incapable and unworthy messiahs!

It was just past 6:00 p.m. and getting dark when we reached our destination. A handful of people were waiting for our arrival. The former missionary had left behind a bamboo house with thatch roof. Out front was a large concrete slab also sheltered by thatch, which served as a spot for visiting. Kerosene pressure lamps were hung, and more of the local Dyak people began to gather. This was our first glimpse of the tribal people we came to reach. Most of them were smoking or chewing betel nut, which dripped crimson red down their chins and stained their teeth black. Their clothing seemed quite worn and unclean. Somehow these exterior signs had a bit too much significance to us new missionaries. We asked Mr. Haniz which of these were believers and were told that they were all Christians. Unrealistically, we had expected to meet *clean* Christians who were devoid of addictive habits! It was in pagan villages we thought we might meet what we were seeing here. A few of them were conspicuous by their cleanliness. These were mainly the employees of the mission station. We were at a loss for words after exchanging first greetings with the people. We sat on the rough benches and stared at one another, making small talk for a little over an hour while the kerosene pressure lamps hissed overhead. Finally we were excused to shower and look around the station with the aid of a pressure lamp. A couple of rooms in the clinic building would serve as the Humbles' first home. Chapmans, with their larger family, took over the former missionary house. Our report back to our boss said: "Our first impression of the field was somehow rather one of despair. Perhaps it cannot be analyzed, but we both knew in our hearts that we were completely cast upon the Lord for strength and wisdom as we stepped into this new situation."

Despair escalated to desperation when, on our way back to Singkawang the next morning, the old car broke down. With a captive audience, Mr. Haniz was able to unburden his troubled soul for three solid hours regarding the frustrations of the work. No one escaped his criticism. Stories of immorality seemed to be his favorite subject. His tale of woe became an intolerable weight until we wanted to scream at him to stop. Undoubtedly he was hoping for us to offer consolation. Our feeble attempts to give comfort from Scripture fell short, not only because of our lack of language, but also because he seemed an intolerable and intolerant egotist, determined to show us there were no easy solutions to the burden of this great work. Many of the problems he mentioned could obviously be solved by more American subsidy to the work. But these new recruits felt that indigenous church-planting methods included a decrease of foreign funds, not an increase. So we remained silent and just tried to hear him out.

When an overcrowded bus suddenly appeared, we were jubilant. Somehow room was made for two more passengers. In spite of the press inside the bus, we felt like we had just been released from prison. Mr. Haniz returned to the station for car parts. Farther down the road more people crowded on. The back of the bus was loaded with foul-smelling durian and the spoiled smell of raw rubber. A mother boarded with a young boy whose arm, leg, and ear were charred black from his having fallen into an open fire. She got the seat directly in front of me. The combined smells of the rubber, durian, and burned human flesh added to our feelings of culture shock and depression. I had a plate of fried rice when we arrived in Singkawang but could not keep it down. I had a terrible aversion to fried rice for the next year or so!

Back in Pontianak we finally contracted the hauling of our freight for what was at that time an astronomical $778. The cost was more than it had been to ship the goods from America to Singapore. However, the cost had to do more with the devalued dollar than inflated Indonesian prices. It would take three truckloads to get our stuff up to the station. On two of those trips I was perched high up on top of the truckload of freight. From this vantage I had a great view of the coast, the jungle, and the mountains. I could also hear clearly the singsong music blasted out of Chinese shops as our truck drove through the Chinese town of Singkawang. In my heart I said, *How could I ever possibly feel at home in a place like this?* I had no idea that later on this same sound would truly be music to my ears.

It was December 24 and time for the last load of goods to be transported to Sungai Betung. Wanda particularly was starved for something familiarly American as Christmas Day approached. Her goal was to reach our station and dig out some colorful decorations and presents that very day. The strangeness of our new surroundings made us feel a bit compulsive about getting a taste of home. The truck loaded with our goods left Pontianak early enough in the morning, but many people along the road needed a ride. Our driver soon had a dozen passengers perched on top of our freight. Stopping here and there, he seemed to be running a regular shuttle service. Time dragged on so that we did not reach Singkawang until 4:00 p.m. It was another four hours to our station, but Wanda begged the driver to take us on so we could be there Christmas Eve. Born in China, she used all manner of persuasive flattery and praise to encourage our Chinese driver to push on to our destination. Knowing his love for children, she even appealed to him that our little daughter must receive gifts on Christmas Day or be terribly disappointed. But the driver, wiser than the sentimental missionaries, just laughed and dropped us off at the Chinese church to spend the night. Wanda's prayer letter of January 4, 1962, tells the story of our first Christmas Eve in her own words:

Sentimental Wanda was heartbroken—and even more so when she and her husband and child were shown the room that was to be theirs for the night! My first thought was: *What worse situation could happen to us on Christmas Eve?* You see, the church was having their big Christmas program—which meant that many of the participants were staying overnight. Every available room had been taken when we arrived—except for "the manger" (a windowless tiny room) as we have now affectionately called it! We now appreciate that room, for it was given in love—and was sufficient! But oh, how the attitude counts. Our bed was made of two burlap cots; a tattered mattress was spread on top, and a grass mat over all to hide that which was underneath. Two single mosquito nets were put up over the cots—and that was home! But the Lord was to teach me something! How much the tradition of Christmas had become a part of me. A tree, gifts, candy, and cookies—just had to be. But not so the first Christmas! I, who had accused others of commercializing Christmas, had in my heart commercialized it! It was the King's birthday, and we were all together as a family—what more could I be thankful for?

And so we were proving that missionaries could be as humanly sentimental as others, especially at Christmastime. We were also proving the faithfulness of God in His just being there as our source of comfort. His "going before" did not always mean as cozy a nest as that provided by the judge's widow in Pontianak. It did mean that our world did not fall apart when sentimental hopes were dashed and schedules were not kept. "Immanuel" was our sustaining strength.

Christmas Day we were up at 4:00 a.m. and soon on our way to our future home. The night before we had dined on a few chocolate candies and some *rambutan* (hairy fruit) I bought in the marketplace. By the time we got to the little marketplace of Serukam, we were starved. It was a stopping place for truckers to eat, and so we feasted on duck eggs, rice, and curry of some sort. It seemed a very strange but tasty Christmas Day breakfast.

We felt very conscious of our richness as our many crates and barrels were being unloaded at our new home in the little clinic building at Sungai Betung. It was a feeling that would never quite leave us during our twenty-three years in the jungles of Kalimantan Barat, a certain uneasiness over being so much wealthier than those around us. Certainly we had not had that problem in America where by comparison we were never quite in the middle-class income bracket. We were impressed when we set up our kerosene stove and refrigerator. We had used kerosene stoves on the farm in Kansas. However, to observe the flaming wick at the bottom of a refrigerator creating ice in the freezing compartment up above was a new and wonderful thing! We decided to delay our Christmas celebration until New Year's Day.

The Rehoboth Church at Sungai Betung held their big program on the night of our arrival. Here we observed how Western influence was mixed with Indonesian decorations. Palm fronds were artistically formed in an arch to make a grand entryway into the churchyard. Inside, the church was decorated with colorful crepe-paper streamers, which extended from the walls to the bell hanging in the center. A Christmas tree was decorated mostly with Christmas cards. White candles were placed in bamboo holders to be lit while the congregation sang "Silent Night" in Indonesian. Several kerosene pressure lamps were hung to totally illuminate the scene. People began to gather at 6:00 p.m., and the church was jammed by 8:00 when the service started. Children, not used to attending Sunday school, were packed in solidly, seated on the floor in front of the benches. Many of them were Chinese from the local marketplace and understood no Indonesian. They all talked at once. All attempts at keeping order failed. It seemed total bedlam to us.

Noise rose and fell like waves. It was never quiet enough to hear what was being said from the pulpit. School children shouted Bible verses they had memorized, and young choirs sang their songs. Live candles on the Christmas tree were lit as we sang "Silent Night." This is always the peak of any Indonesian Christmas program, as we later learned. Bob and I gave brief testimonies with what vocabulary was available to us, and Mr. Haniz preached. We shouted some words into a microphone but could not hear ourselves talk. Then Mr. Haniz gave some gifts from American churches to any village chief present. Most of these were packages of flannel baby bibs to be distributed in each village. Finally everyone received some kinds of local special cakes and drinks. Every ironwood bench was packed. Honored guests, including a few local government officials and the two new missionary families, were seated in front on rattan chairs. Little tables before us held tasty cakes to eat and milk to drink. The whole service wound down in about three hours. Tired missionaries expressed *"Selamat Hari Natal"* (Merry Christmas) to hundreds of people. Little did we realize the fine cakes and drinks were all an ill-afforded splurge on the part of someone (probably Mr. Haniz) during the hungry part of the year. They were practicing the cultural norm in Indonesia: celebrate the occasion, even if it requires a sacrifice.

The next few days were spent in getting our house in order, but also in receiving a seemingly endless string of villagers welcoming us to the area. It was *rambutan* season and a bumper crop at that. Every foreigner we ever met loved rambutan at first taste. Inside the red, hairy skin is a white, delicious, rather grape-tasting fruit, but it is impossible to describe its sweetness. We had them piled everywhere in our kitchen, not comfortable in rejecting anyone's welcoming gift to us. Mr. Haniz warned us ominously that we should be keeping track of all these offerings since the givers would be expecting a larger gift from us in the future, a warning that did not come true in the days ahead.

Every morning began with the clanging of the church bell to call together the faithful for a 7:00 a.m. church service. Mr. Haniz always appeared in spotless white trousers and white shirt with a black tie, looking very much a contrast to the ragged people on the benches. Local villagers and some school children from the mission school filled up some of the ironwood benches. The idea was to give the people something biblical to think about before they headed off to do their day's work. Under ordinary circumstances, Dyak farmers would have been on the way to their fields at daybreak. Morning devotions became a monotonous ritual with Mr. Haniz giving a morning diatribe on whatever subject he chose, using a Scripture verse as his point of departure. Bob and I were soon asked to alternate in giving the morning message, and we did so to the best of our ability with our limited language.

Mr. Haniz had waited a long time to get help in the work and wanted us to shoulder the financial burden. We, on the other hand, wanted to just study the situation and gain a better grasp of the language. He often summoned Bob and me into the little hospital business office for discussions about the ministry, but we were not ready to talk. He became very angry and sometimes shouted so loud that our wives could hear him across the compound. Tension mounted higher in each session. He spoke negatively of virtually everyone in the area as well as of neighbor missionaries working miles to the south and east of us. He also gave us incessant warnings as to how we should carefully guard the young girls whom he recommended as our kitchen helpers. He seemed obsessed with the subject.

Once we were a bit more settled into our temporary homes, we decided to have a look at some of the thirteen villages that were within walking distance from the church. We found people living a subsistence level of existence. They never had enough rice to last out the year until the next harvest. Most homes consisted of a dirt floor, bamboo walls, and thatch roof. Some villages, such as Keranji, still had homes built up on stilts five feet tall, with multiple families under one roof, reminding one of the early longhouses of Dyak life. Pulling rubber helped supplement their income and was in fact essential to it, especially during the hungry season when the rice had run out.

Bob and I tried to visit several villages in a single day, just for survey purposes. We sat in homes where people were eager to show us their baptismal certificates and relate to us that they had already become Christians. Several of the men we met spoke quite knowledgeably of Jesus and the Bible, but seemingly had little if any change in their lives. This attitude seemed to radiate out from the mission station to the surrounding areas. In truth, there was little evidence of idol worship among them. It was more that they still clung to their addictions, which included gambling, drinking, tobacco, and betel-nut chewing. They would readily agree with all we said regarding the Bible and Jesus and in fact could quote the Indonesian Scriptures better than we could. Somehow this took away any feeling of purpose for my being there. These people needed deeper teaching but did not seem interested in hearing it, especially from a couple of men who could barely speak their language. *If I had wanted to deal with people like this, I might as well have stayed home in America,* was my thinking. As missionaries, we had come to tell people about how Jesus can change one's life. These people had heard about Jesus and, to us, remained unchanged.

I wrote a prayer letter in April 1962, which pictured the Sungai Betung situation as "Semidarkness." It goes back to the very first night we settled into the bedroom of our new home in the little hospital building. A large double bed with a tall iron frame at each end suspended a very thick mosquito net. The only ventilation in the room was a six-inch by thirty-six-inch slit above the window. It was unbelievably stifling—Wanda was very large with child—and like an oven under that heavy net. The only light to work by was a little kerosene *pelita* lamp.

There was a small kerosene lamp burning in the bedroom of our new "hospital home" in Sungai Betung as we came in to spend our first night there. The glow of that little lamp, whose light is now familiar only to our fathers or grandfathers, seemed insignificant when compared with the electric brilliance to which we Americans are accustomed. While unpacking our things, we fumbled in the semidarkness, often bringing various articles very close to the light to distinguish their identity.

Perhaps this little lamp best illustrates the situation on our field here in Kalimantan. There has been light here, the Word has been preached here, but somehow it has not been that searching, penetrating light that so characterizes the gospel. Rather, it has left the people groping in a semidarkness, aware of the Light but failing to be illuminated by it. Villages we enter speak of Christianity but still cling to worldly habits and oftentimes to heathen customs. We have a beautiful church building here...but they know nothing of a separated, regenerated church membership. We have stood beside the crude jungle grave of an infant and heard the Scriptures read in halting Indonesian but felt that those who attended had neither sensed the Source of Life in Christ nor glimpsed the reality of the Resurrection. With heavy hearts we have refused to use the name of Jesus Christ to bless a household that was…sacrificing animals—this of course in a "Christian village."…

Certainly there are those here who want to believe— that do believe—but to draw a fine line of distinction between the true and the false in semidarkness is a difficult thing. Pray with us that we may have the discernment and the wisdom to intensify the Light to some degree. Pray that the Holy Spirit will do a genuine work in the hearts of some and call them out to a clear testimony for Jesus Christ.

We desire to acquire the language in great gulps, but somehow it doesn't come that way. Progress is being made, however, and we are learning to use the Word in preaching services…. Pray that we may come to the place of being able to communicate with all clarity and fluency. As Bob and I were gone into a village for a burial service one day, Wanda read a very appropriate Scripture in Isaiah 28:11—"For with stammering lips and another tongue shall he speak to this people." This verse aptly portrays our present situation.

I wish I could say that I accepted this "semidarkness" situation without being affected by it personally. But there were days when I felt my own soul was dwelling in semidarkness. Even after we moved from the hospital building to our brand-new bamboo and thatch-roof house, I was at times attacked by feelings of depression. I spent some daylight hours under my mosquito net in my bedroom, brooding over my own inability to change the situation around me. Indeed, I seemed unable to change the feelings in my own heart. There was obviously a spiritual battle going on, and I was feeling Satan's attacks. Before leaving

America, I had expressed that "death to self" was the only way any Christian should live, missionary or not. I had said that if one is going to be dead to self, one might as well be a missionary as a carpenter or a doctor, since to be dead is to be dead! Isolated from input from a wider Christian fellowship, I now found that self does not die so easily. In reality, it should be easier to practice death to self on the mission field, far from television and the enticing temptations of American life. I later joked, "It would be a lot more satisfying to experience this kind of death to self if there was someone around to applaud me while I was dying."

In spite of the feelings of despair, I was held fast by the *golden thread*, the intense belief that only surrender to the will of God would see me through. Times of low emotion would come and go, and then I would be back at studying language and talking to the people around me. I don't think the nationals ever had any hint of my struggle with depression even though I was often miserable in the village, trying to get a handle on how on earth to help these people.

I was greatly helped by the fact that Wanda seemed never to succumb to feelings of depression. She remained her happy self. Almost immediately she began Bible studies with her first house helper, Salome, and kept up this pattern with other helpers as they came into her life. Many poor people came to our door for some kind of financial help. During the hungry season, when rice supplies gave out and were very expensive at the marketplace, she would loan them rice, to be paid back at harvest time when prices fell to rock-bottom levels. She also did a lot of trading our extra clothing for fruit and live chickens brought to her back door. Everyone went away feeling they had gotten a good bargain. It saved them face because they would rather feel that they had made a trade than to feel they had received a handout. She had a cheerful smile for every person who came her way.

Chapter 10 – The Good Things of Our New Life

Fear not, O land; rejoice, for the LORD will do great things.
(Joel 2:21)

It is tempting to remember the earliest years of our missionary life in terms of perpetual semidarkness. However, as we began to adjust to our new life in Kalimantan, there were many positive and happy moments that came into our lives as well. Some were small things, some were greater, but all of them helped us survive a depressing situation. I will deal with the smaller things first and then go on to some of the greater ones.

Small Delights of Daily Life

Life gradually took on a new rhythm, so different from that in America. Little delights of life become meaningful when there is no television to distract or malls to visit. Perhaps they are not really rituals, but when performed regularly, they lightened up our quiet days and added joy to them.

The Bathing Ritual

When we first arrived at our station, we noticed how two beautiful rivers came together just above the bridge, making a watery Y visible from the road. This part of the river was shaded by huge trees. Because the nationals often used the river for their toilet facilities besides using it for their baths and clothes washing, we felt squeamish about enjoying its coolness. For Wanda and Barbara there was also the question regarding the technique of taking a good bath in a wraparound sarong. However, when Ingrid Stippa, a missionary from RBMU, came over to visit our station, she took the ladies down to the river and showed them how to use a sarong to take a full bath in public without exposing too much of their white skin. Soon we were all going down just before it got dark and enjoying our evening bath at the river as a family. Dyaks always take a bath before eating the evening meal. It became a regular family ritual for us also to go down and soak out the heat of the day in the cool water. By evening whatever we were wearing was always soggy with sweat. Nothing was quite as refreshing as to let one's body temperature be brought down by the coolness of the water. Such a deep soaking caused a veritable change of attitude. We did not realize how much difference it would make to have that experience to look forward to each evening. It was the children's play time and often served as a brief adult social time at the end of our day. The evening meal even tasted better after the bath. We put on pajamas instead of street clothes to spend the rest of the evening.

The "Milo" Ritual

Milo is a malt-flavored, light chocolate drink powder made in England. We had learned to love its taste when we were introduced to it in Singapore. We brought several cans of it along in our shipment. A large dollop of sweetened condensed milk was added to the drink to make it taste rich, almost like a hot chocolate malt. When river baths were finished, along with cleanup after dinner, Wanda and I always had this dessert to look forward to after Cheryl was put to bed. It was our debriefing time to relax and review the events of the day. Yes, a hot drink did cause us to perspire, but an occasional gentle breeze would give us a sense of coolness. At least that was our perception at the time. There was no television to watch, and even the short-wave radio did not function well at night, so this was our evening entertainment. The Milo made us feel we got a taste of luxury as the night noises of the jungle joined in to serenade our moment of reverie. Being so close to the river, every night we heard the wonderful and mysterious sounds of life. Insects, small animals, and even a very strange-sounding river bird with a bass voice chimed in to the chorus. In fact, it took awhile to get used to the many noises so we could get to sleep. Eventually they became friendly sounds rather than threatening or strange.

The Friday-Night Ritual

I suppose this event could be called our "fun ritual." We were far from any city and social activity. Even if we went to the city, there was not a nice restaurant to eat at or hotel to sleep in. Chinese-restaurant food was usually tasty, but it was a common saying that, "The dirtier the walls, the better the food in a Chinese restaurant." If you doubt this, ask any of your old-time missionary friends to the Chinese world. Atmosphere was something not to be had under any circumstances. Any social activity would have to come from our own genius. So, on some Friday nights Wanda hung up a Mexican blanket on the kitchen wall and invited the Chapmans over for tacos. It was a great change of diet and always seemed like a special event, especially for the wives. Tacos still took a lot of time to prepare. All food preparation had to be done from scratch: grinding the beef with a hand meat grinder, rolling out flour tortillas, grating cabbage as a substitute for lettuce, etc. A few drops of Tabasco sauce from our food shipment went a long way toward transforming the little taco into an ethnic wonder food. We did not always eat together, but we did always try to play together on Friday nights, usually Rook, but sometimes we got crazy playing a game of charades. The hissing of the kerosene pressure lamp above our game table diminished from time to time as the room gradually darkened, reminding us to give the lamp a few more pumps in order to get the maximum wattage available. No matter how the week had gone, this seemed to be our best way of coming together with our fellow missionaries in a socially relaxed way. Something to look forward to was essential during those days, and the fun nights relieved us of some of the stress. We could even joke about the stress in such downtimes as this.

Larger Joy Factors That Affected Our Lives

As we gradually made adjustments to a new culture, God brought special blessings into our lives. Some of them came in the form of additions to the family, special places we would cherish forever, and even the beginnings of spiritual fruit.

A New Son

Childbirth is a momentous occasion for any family, and of course, especially for the mother. Our bedroom in the little hospital building was adjacent to the maternity ward. It seemed to us that most expectant mothers visited this room close to 3:00 a.m. The board wall separating us from women in the throes of childbirth was thin, so we heard the full expressions of birth pain. Groans started in small waves and crested in agonizing screams. Eventually the groans ended with the cry of the newborn baby. Shortly after that cry, one of the relatives would start marching back and forth across the room with the baby, making a loud "uh-uh-uh-uh-uh-uh-uh-uh" noise that seemed to be the standard lullaby for newborns. It was nearly as sleep-disturbing to us as the earlier groans of the mother. God's promise that women would "bring forth children in sorrow" was proven repeatedly in the wee hours of the morning in the delivery room next to us. Wanda often went next door and helped our nurse, Trudy Davis, when she was needed.

The time came for Wanda herself to deliver her second child. Our nurse felt it best to have a doctor present for Wanda's birthing experience. Dr. Muthalib, the local government health director, sent his Jeep and driver from Singkawang to escort her into town three weeks before the due date. Cheryl and I waited at the mission station for a phone call that would come through the one and only local phone at the Chinese marketplace. For nearly three weeks Wanda lived at the Catholic hospital in Singkawang, whiling away the hours by making trips to the post office across town. Young boys often followed her, calling out and jeering at her large stomach, a crude but common custom in some parts of Asia. The Chapmans graciously fed Cheryl and me many fine meals while Wanda was in town.

The timing was perfect. One day a runner from the marketplace came to say I had an incoming phone call. I sprinted the two hundred yards to the marketplace. Phone lines were notoriously bad. People shouting into a phone could be heard clear across the street. It took a couple of tries for me to understand the voice on the other end of the line yelling in Indonesian, "It's a boy!" I shouted for joy, startling the shoppers in the little Chinese store. The miracle was that the bus that came through just once a day was sitting right there on the road in front of the shop where I took the call. I begged the driver to wait and ran back home to gather some clothing. I was actually surprised the driver waited, since that was not the ordinary custom.

I found Wanda happy and glowing. Kevin was displayed in a little bed where everyone could see him. His midwife was a Chinese Catholic sister, trained in Holland. The nurses carried Kevin all over the hospital to show him off since he was a pound or two bigger than any of the local newborns in the nursery. Wanda later said this was her easiest delivery of all four of the children, a mercy of God, since there was not a Western doctor anywhere near us. For four days after delivery Wanda had her knees tied together. This was the custom of the Dutch-trained nurses many years earlier. When no one was looking, Wanda would slip out of the knee knots and take a short walk to keep the blood from clotting. We were both in a state of euphoria, partly because of having a new son, but also the relief that all went well in a strange land, and at the hands of those whose medical capabilities we did not know.

On the eighth day of Kevin's life we took him to the Muslim Imam to have him circumcised. Muslims usually circumcise their boys at age twelve or thirteen, following the pattern of Ishmael, so we were not exactly in line with the local custom. Local doctors refused to do the operation, saying that circumcision was always done by the Imam. This ignorance on our part could have been harmful to the health of our little son, but again, God's grace prevailed, and he healed up nicely from the surgery without getting an infection. The circumcision was performed with sharp bamboo to avoid danger of tetanus. At least, that was what the Imam told us.

When it came time for Wanda to return to the mission station, she had one of her more serious ordeals of early life in Kalimantan. The doctor's Jeep broke down on the road in the heat of the day.

Wanda sat with Kevin and Fatimah, a young Muslim midwife, in the shade of a home near the road. However, the heat and humidity were intense, and she had little to drink during the six-hour wait. Her dehydration may have been part of the cause of what followed. A few days after arriving at our station, Kevin started vomiting a pink substance that turned out to be his mother's milk mixed with her blood. It may have been that Wanda lost her ability to produce an adequate milk supply on that arduous trip. Kevin was ingesting blood from the cracked breasts, so we rushed him back into town. We thought with his weight loss he was looking terribly skinny. However, when we got to the doctor's office in Singkawang, we found a long line of mothers who held babies that looked far more emaciated than Kevin! The doctor seemed little troubled by his appearance and put him on powdered milk as first a supplement and finally a replacement for his mother's milk.

A New Home

At first we thought we would live in the hospital building for a few months before moving out to another location. Several surveys to areas near Singkawang and farther up the road beyond Bengkayang seemed promising, but we never felt the freedom to make the move. I will describe in a later chapter why God's sovereign hand was keeping us in Sungai Betung. Letters to friends in America spoke of our restlessness and lack of contentedness in general. One thing pushing us toward moving was the facilities in which we lived. Already mentioned was the delivery room right next to our bedroom. On the other side of the delivery room was our kitchen, so we had to go outdoors every time we moved between the two rooms. The little clinic building was right across from the hospital building we lived in. Patients lined up on its verandah to wait for examinations, chatting loudly, smoking, coughing, and spitting. A large percentage of them had tuberculosis. Often they stepped across the way and stared into our bedroom window to entertain themselves while waiting for a family member to be treated. We shared an outdoor toilet with these patients. The thatch on the outhouse was in bad shape, so on rainy days we had to balance an umbrella over ourselves on a squat toilet.

Given these conditions, we decided it was best to build a temporary house until our final placement was determined. Local Dyak carpenters were hired to do the job. They drove five-foot-long ironwood stakes deep into the earth and fastened to them the floor joists, which supported the floorboards. Walls and partitions were made from woven bamboo. Bamboo poles were first crushed at the joints. Then the pole was opened up and flattened out to become a "bamboo board." All boards that were used to hold the bamboo partitions in place were hand-sawed and hand-planed. These flexible "boards" were then cross-woven in checkerboard pattern in sections about ten feet long and eight feet high. When a section was completed, we had a woven bamboo piece of wall, ready to stand upright and nail to the round posts that were the studs. Doors and windows were crafted of planed wood, and the roof of thatch was put on to cover it all. We were told that the dry weevil would eat up the walls in a short period of time, so I sprayed them with an extremely strong insecticide brought from the States. I increased the recommended concentration about tenfold and sprayed it on the bamboo. (For my extreme measures I ended up with a deep chest cough that lasted several months.) A surprising number of embedded insect larvae fell out of the bamboo onto the floor. The walls were then varnished and proved to last more than fifteen years without deterioration. Moving into our new home was one of the happiest events of that first term. The bamboo walls were porous and much cooler than the board walls of the clinic we'd lived in. We knew people could peek through the tiny cracks in them because we could often see the eyes of small boys peering in. Somehow, it did not matter so much as time went on.

Discovering "Long Beach"

The coast that extends for many miles along the west side of Kalimantan is for the most part an unattractive stretch of muddy black sand, often decorated with stumps of dead palm trees. I caught glimpses of it from time to time from the bed of the truck hauling our freight up-country. Nothing about it was attractive. We were surprised to learn that there was one stretch of golden beach within easy reach of our jungle home. *Pasir Panjang,* translated from the Indonesian language, means literally "Long Sand." It is located ten miles south of Singkawang. We first discovered it when a local medical doctor generously suggested we might want to use his beach cabin.

I was not prepared for Pasir Panjang's beauty and had to admit it was love at first sight. It was a pristine strip of clean, unpopulated beach, with a little cabin, decorated in front by a huge bank of brilliant bougainvillea flowers. It was virtually the only building on the whole beach. Large tamarisk trees grew along the shore, providing good shade. In some places, farther down the beach, there were huge boulders twelve to fifteen feet high. These could be scaled in order to sit atop them and absorb the quietness, with only the lapping of the water to soothe a troubled heart or, as was often the case, give rise to worship of the Creator. The sense of peace here provided a stark contrast that was most needed at this time of our life. The beach was free of human clutter and pollution. The local people had not yet discovered the concept of beach recreation, so it was virtually devoid of all human activity, except for the occasional fishermen passing by. We soon discovered that just a half-kilometer walk down the beach local fishermen brought in a fresh catch every day, so we could get first pick of their harvest before it was taken to the market in the city.

It is impossible to imagine what life in the jungle of Kalimantan might have been like if we had not had the reprieve of the beach from time to time. When the jungle and its people problems seemed to be closing in on us, we could take an occasional trip to our Long Beach to look out over the vast expanse of the South China Sea. It never failed to be a time of respite and healing, a place where we seemed more able to worship and have family times. Because almost no one but us stayed overnight in the little house, we ultimately christened it as "our beach" and felt we owned the place, though we had no legal right to it. As the family grew up and as Dr. Muthalib's place eroded, we took tents to stay in and bathed in a freshwater stream that flowed into the sea from a nearby mountain. Our four children remember this as the most precious piece of natural real estate on earth. We read books in the heat of the day and played games together at night. Anticipation is one of the greatest pleasures of life. Our annual vacations there were anticipated months in advance.

Today there are many little hotels and stalls for people to eat at scattered along the beach. There is clutter and pollution. I still hold in my heart the beauty of it in my first impressions. It was God's special provision for us to enjoy at that time, and the memories of those times stand out as some of His most beautiful gifts to us.

New Personnel

When we first arrived in Kalimantan, we found the little medical clinic barely functioning with the help of a loaned government nurse. Few patients visited the clinic, partly because of high prices. Medicine was highly subsidized by the government, but somehow Mr. Haniz had been unable to get it from the local health department. We learned that our neighboring mission was purchasing medicines for a fraction of what Mr. Haniz was paying on the black market. Bob and I made a fifty-kilometer bicycle trip over very muddy roads to the RBMU station at Ansang, Darit, to learn more about it. There we got a great deal of advice from the Warkentins regarding life in Kalimantan. Later I called in at the provincial health department in Pontianak and introduced myself to Dr. Sudarso. He gave me the needed permission to buy subsidized medicines. In June of 1962 we received a great boost for our field and our morale in the person of Trudy Davis, R.N. Trudy was a nurse with ten years of experience behind her in the Belgian Congo. With minimal language from her brief time of study in Singapore, she plunged into the work with great dedication. Overnight the word spread that medical help was available. Regular clinic days were scheduled for the mornings, but emergencies were treated at all hours of the night. She trained a few local people to be her assistants. Her sense of humor and her love for coffee soon gave her the nickname of *Nona Kopi*, which being translated means "Miss Coffee."

No medical statistics are available for the end of the 1962 year, but it was reported at the end of 1963 that 11,172 patients had been treated in the out clinic, with an additional 572 patients hospitalized for a day or more. The latter were housed in a makeshift set of buildings that still had dirt floors and thatch roofs. The hospital was located right next to the river, behind the clinic and the newer little hospital building that was our first residence.

Because it was right on our doorstep, the success of Trudy's work seemed like our success as well. People were being healed, and the gospel was being preached on the little veranda of the clinic every morning the clinic was open. The medical work proved something was actually happening at a time when we felt we were spinning our wheels. Sale of medicines generated income to buy more and better medicine. A few Chinese from the marketplace began to show up at church on Sundays, partly because they were being attracted by Nurse Davis's ministry among them.

Another source of encouragement came in the form of a vivacious young lady named Norma Hasse. Norma had a passion for reaching children and starting Sunday schools. She arrived on the field in October 1962, and by November was already submitting goals for the growth of Christian education in the four little village churches we had inherited from the former missionary. Her upbeat spirit and healthy sense of humor added spirit to our small team. Raised in a home where she had lived with six brothers, she was courageous in facing the many challenges and hardships of a pioneer field. One of her first projects was to get fresh, new materials for Vacation Bible Schools prepared. The lively choruses that came with this program created new enthusiasm for children and adults alike.

First Fruits of the Harvest

The Dyaks have a traditional feast day called *Pesta Makan Padi Baru.* Loosely translated this means "New Rice Feast." Rice ripens gradually and a bit unevenly at first. The villagers pluck these ripe heads of grain to get a taste of what is to come. We were often invited to nearby villages to enjoy the occasion. Rice cooked in lengths of bamboo, seasoned with coconut oil and tiny bits of garlic was the special "cake" offered as the appetizer. Dry rice raised on the sides of hills and flatlands, without irrigation, is aromatic and has an almost nutty taste when freshly harvested—so very different than it is when it has been stored several months in a burlap bag. These were joyous occasions for the villagers, and they were eager to share the occasion with us. At this time there also gradually began a spiritual harvest.

Sungai Betung was a spiritually "burned over" area. The men had heard the gospel, but with few exceptions they seemed unchanged in their lives. The women and young people, however, were ripe for harvest. The harvest was under our noses while we were struggling with, "Where do we go from here to dig into ministry?" It all began with what might be seen to some as a misinterpretation of Scripture. Wanda was reading in her quiet time one day out of Isaiah 28.

Isaiah 28:7-8 tells of the priest and the prophet having gone out of the way and having erred "through wine and strong drink." The passage speaks of spiritual leaders who are swallowed up with wine and then goes on to describe an ugly scene of tables being full of vomit and filth, with no place clean. To Wanda, it pictured some of the men who had gone to Singapore to study the Bible, then returned to become drunken prophets in our area! Finally, the passage seemed to speak of a target group. Verses 9-11 say:

> Whom will he teach knowledge? And whom will he make to understand the message? Those just weaned from the milk? Those just drawn from the breasts? For precept must be upon precept, precept upon precept, line upon line, line upon line, here a

little, there a little. For with stammering lips and another tongue He will speak to this people.

As Wanda shared these verses with me, she felt God was clearly telling us that we should reach out to those who were still young. She felt the Holy Spirit was telling her that the "stammering lips and another tongue" part pertained to us, as we still struggled with language. Undoubtedly the prophet Isaiah had another context in mind when the inspired Word was originally written, but it seemed to us like a mandate from God.

Taking the passage literally, Wanda started meeting with the young people after church on Sundays, *teaching* them the gospel. They responded enthusiastically to her teaching, and many of them accepted Christ as personal Savior. Often I would return after preaching in Bengkayang to hear her say excitedly, "There are three young men who want to accept the Lord today. Would you come and pray with them?" I would do it gladly, feeling as though I should be the one drawing people to the Lord but so very glad Wanda was there, doing it so effectively while I dealt with the older generation.

Wanda also started Friday women's meetings, teaching illiterate women the gospel. Using flannelgraph, she taught the exact same lesson three weeks in a row. They had been taught that they were ignorant females, and they did not at first believe they could learn anything. It took many weeks of teaching to prove otherwise. Finally a few of them grasped the good news of the gospel and prayed to receive Christ as their Savior. Apat was one of them. She liked to tell the others that before she knew Christ she was no more than an animal, but that now she was like a lost sheep that was found. As other women came to accept Christ, Apat was there. Soon she was interrupting Wanda to tell them in their own dialect exactly what to pray and how their lives would be changed if they did. Indeed, their lives were changing. One old lady named Manta eventually memorized 104 Bible verses.

Mr. Haniz was not happy with the women's meetings. He did not like it that scores of Dyak women were coming to Christ, learning Bible verses, and singing heartily every Friday afternoon. It appeared to undermine his position of influence on the local people, and it posed a problem to him that he was not in charge of it. He liked to quote to us what he claimed the husbands of the wives were saying: "These women should be out chopping down weeds in their rice fields, not just tramping down the weeds on the path as they go to study what they can't understand." His implication was that women should be out in the fields where they belonged. Mr. Haniz seemed to have an unusual interest in the affairs of women in general.

Encouraging News Beyond Our Mission Station

Four hours to the northeast of us lay the village of Sejajah, only reachable by four-wheel-drive vehicles. One day a handsome young man from that village paid us a visit. He was uncommonly polite and educated compared to the folk we had been experiencing near the station. He came across as a very humble young man and showed respect we had not seen among the local people around us. Yohanes was a sixth-grade graduate from the Catholic school in Bengkayang and yet had maintained his Protestant roots. (There was only one other person in our area who had graduated from elementary school.) Sejajah was one of four village churches left to us by our predecessor, Mr. Brawni. Yohanes hoped that we might visit the believers in Sejajah and also wanted us to marry him to his fiancée. Bob and I agreed to pay them a visit.

In Sejajah we were welcomed into the home of Yohanes's parents. The people were warm and friendly without making special demands on the new foreigners. It was our first experience at overnighting in a Dyak village. At bedtime we strung our mosquito nets in the living room. Bob blew up his air mattress, a fascinating sight for many neighbors who had gathered, apparently to see us off to sleep. Earlier we had feasted on rice and chicken, which was so spicy we could only eat a few bites of it to push the steamed rice down. We soon learned that the village diet meant rice three times a day, except in the hungry season when they have to resort to cassava root as an undesirable substitute.

A simple chapel of bamboo, with its little steeple topped by a cross, stood in the center of the village. Benches for seating consisted of posts driven into the ground with thick, hand-sawed boards nailed to them. Dyak villages have personalities all their own, and this one was distinctly friendly and open to us. They were hungry for learning more about the Christian life. We gathered every morning for worship, probably because of the practice already established at Sungai Betung. For the first time, I began to feel what it was like to experience joy in village ministry. Everyone vied to get us to come to their homes for a special time of singing and opening the Scriptures later in the day. In each home either tea or coffee was served, and whichever it was, it was syrupy sweet. But the fellowship was sweet, too.

We left Sejajah a few days later, feeling encouraged in heart. Yohanes was particularly eager to receive new truth and asked many questions about the faith. In later months I would often return to visit this village, sometimes leaving home feeling rather discouraged myself. But when I got to Sejajah, Yohanes's quest for answers to Bible questions had me teaching him the Word for hours. After each visit, I returned to the main station refreshed and glad to have him as a friend.

Chapter 11 – Facing My Fears

Whoever watches the wind will not plant; whoever looks at the clouds will not reap. (Ecclesiastes 11:4)

We had been in Indonesia for more than a year and were beginning to speak the language quite fluently. We were also enjoying some success in the work. However, we were about to face a string of problems, any one of which could cause closure of the work in Kalimantan. These were huge, insurmountable issues in the earliest years of our ministry. From our human perspective, we could see only darkness in the days ahead. God had a lesson in store for me that apparently needed to be repeated over and over in order for me to get it. The lesson was: *Things are not as they appear to be from your human perspective. Great obstacles that block your pathway, dark clouds gathering overhead, forces beyond your control: these are only* your *perception of reality. There is another reality, which is seen from above. Your task is to keep moving ahead, straight toward the obstacle, to see what God will do if you persevere without swerving to one side or the other.* I did not know at the time that was the lesson to be learned, which could be part of the reason I had to keep learning it over and over again.

The country of Indonesia was gradually moving toward Communism, from the highest levels of government to the poorest peasant in the village. This in itself created an uncertainty, as huge changes were beginning to take place. President Sukarno often made two-hour-long, articulate speeches aired on the radio, many of them containing anti-American sentiments. Borrowing a few words from the English language, a prominent newspaper quoted from one of his speeches in its headlines: "AMERIKA BANYAK DI-GO-TO HELLKAN OLEH BUNG KARNO." Without understanding a lot of Indonesian, one gets the idea that big brother Sukarno was clearly telling America where to go. A war, actually called a "Confrontation," was brewing between Indonesia and neighboring Malaysia. (The province we lived in bordered Malaysia.) This meant thousands of soldiers began moving into our area. The normally quiet road past our house was suddenly a thoroughfare for army Jeeps and trucks. Fourteen of them at a time, loaded with troops, would thunder over the dilapidated wooden bridge in front of our station. Popular songs from our transistor radio blared out: "Crush the Malaysians, the Americans and the English, crush them, crush them..." With the dark shadow of war looming over us, it was seemingly a poor time for the first major obstacle to arise, but we were not in charge of the timing.

Our First Major *Perkara* (Case)

A half Dyak, half Chinese government leader once told me what he thought were core values of the Dyak people. He said, "Dyaks love three things: they love to be praised, they love 'progress,' and they love a good court case, or *perkara*." Mr. Haniz was gone to Manado for a visit to see his relatives when the news broke. One of our pretty, young Dyak school teachers was discovered to be pregnant out of wedlock. Premarital pregnancy happened not infrequently in Dyak culture, but usually the problem was solved by a hurry-up marriage ceremony. In this case the father was not made known, so the dilemma was difficult to solve, and the shame was great for the pregnant woman and her family. Wanda interviewed Miss M. and, out of character for Wanda, told her straight out that fornicators go to hell if they remain unrepentant. Miss M. replied, "Mother would be surprised if she knew who the father of the child in my womb is." Mother Wanda was indeed surprised to find out that the father was none other than the nonsmoking, nondrinking, nongambling Mr. Haniz. When Mr. Haniz returned from Manado, I knew I really should confront him. He was greatly feared by the Dyaks because he had education and wealth far above them. Socioeconomic advantage was made even stronger by an aggressive intimidating manner in dealing with people when he felt like it. I talked to Miss M., and she was ready to make the accusation. I did not want to have this talk with Mr. Haniz. He was the sponsor who signed all our missionary visas to keep us in country. To make him lose face would mean no more signatures for visas. Finally, I screwed up my courage one night to approach him. My courage was considerably fortified by the prodding of three missionary women on the station who were outraged at his taking advantage of a young girl.

We sat on his little porch after dark one night as I told him that Miss M. was ready to accuse. He feigned surprise. "Who? Me?" he asked, with apparent disbelief. I continued, telling him that if he repented, he could perhaps, after a time of being set aside, minister in another location, but no longer here, where his reputation was spoiled. He denied his guilt but was not as defensive as I had expected. I left it at that and went home. He showed up on my doorstep a few minutes later and said his wife had heard our conversation through the bamboo walls and that something must be done, but he was not ready to openly confess his sin before the people.

From then on we began the cat-and-mouse game as he tried in a variety of ways to worm his way out of the problem. It was difficult for me, because I did not enjoy the role of playing the "cat." First, he called together the influential men of the church to meet in an effort to bring *damai* (peace) to the situation. They were all newly chosen deacons, untested and untrained in the Word. With no preliminaries a *surat damai* (letter of peace) was read in front of us all. It stated that Miss M. had made certain false accusations, and that she was ready to withdraw them. If charges were withdrawn, she would be forgiven and the case would be closed. There was a place for both the accused and accuser to sign at the bottom of the page to show proof that the issue was permanently put to rest. It looked like they were going to go ahead with it until I spoke up. I asked, "Do you really just want *peace* or do you want *truth*?" Several voices in unison said, "We want peace." I asked, "How can you have peace in your heart if you don't have truth to build on?" I added that Mr. Haniz would one day thank us all if, after investigation, he was proven innocent of this charge. For this I got dark glares from him and silence from the deacons and others gathered. My reluctance to go along stalemated the meeting. We adjourned without a decision being made.

About this time Norma Hasse's visa became due for extension, and I took the papers to Mr. Haniz's house for his signature. He told me curtly, "There will be no more signing of missionary visas until this case is finished." It was crisis time for us. If he could maneuver his way out of this, our mission was out of Indonesia forever. I began to look for some objective evidence, and Miss M. produced some love letters from the accused. His next ploy was his attempt to intimidate Miss M. Her father was poor, morally weak, and willing to compromise for money. However, he was also angry. Mr. Haniz often came to their house at night to badger the parents to work out a peace agreement. One night a friend informed us that he was again visiting the home of the parents of Miss M. Near midnight Wanda and I walked over in the moonlight and climbed the notched pole ladder to their little bamboo shack of a home. I told them that if the handwriting in the letters proved to be his, Mr. Haniz would have to bear the responsibility of his act. He whined to Miss M. "Do you see how I am being impaled on the fishhook? Can't you feel it?" She was not in a mood to feel mercy, though he repeated it several times.

It was time to take action. We decided to visit Mr. S., the head of the Protestant Department of Religion in Pontianak, to ask his aid. However, we were so exhausted, we decided to spend a whole afternoon at our lovely beach on the way down to the big city. We basked in the sun while Mr. Haniz jumped on a bus and beat us down to Pontianak. The people of our village said, "They are going into town to have it out in the courts." That evening I paid a visit to the home of the government official who was the Protestant Religion Director of the whole province. I produced the love letters and told my story. He let me talk uninterrupted until I had finished my whole tale. Then he said, "Finally, I understand. This man came to my office today and tried to explain to me that there was a big problem in his church. But he could never quite bring himself to explain what the problem was. Every few minutes he would jump up and run to the window because he heard a car drive up, and thought it was you. He left my office, leaving me very puzzled." So, while we were relaxing on the beach, Mr. Haniz was hanging himself in the office of the Minister of Religion. The minister believed my story, and I brought him up to the mission station in the Land Rover to deal with the issue.

It is not uncommon for the Indonesian Ministry of Religion to become involved when churches (or mosques) have legal problems. Mr. S. took charge, first interviewing Miss M. for over an hour in the church. She was drenched in sweat when the interrogation was over, but Mr. S. was thoroughly satisfied that Mr. Haniz was guilty. He called a meeting of the church leaders, newly chosen deacons, Miss M.'s family, all the missionaries, and others who were involved in the "case." The meeting was called to order at 5:00 p.m. and went on and on until 10:00 p.m. At that point they said everyone was hungry and we should adjourn. Instead, Wanda and our helpers ran to cook a full chicken and rice meal for the people involved in the case.

As the meeting wore on, Mr. Haniz became more angry and aggressive. At one point he rolled up his sleeves menacingly. Mr. S. responded by coming out from behind the pulpit and rolling up his own sleeves, even venturing down the aisle of the church a bit. The tension was palpable, the hours dragged on, and nothing seemed to be happening. Mr. S. then said he was going to show positive evidence of the guilt of the accused. He asked Miss M. to tell the exact locations where the adulterous acts took place. With great shame she reluctantly mentioned three places, one of them being the bathhouse/toilet with its cement floor. A new aura settled over the crowd. There were murmurs of agreement that he was guilty. We missionaries sat there stunned, wondering how they could be so indecisive one moment and so sure the next. It was obvious to everyone there but us that he was guilty because the spot of the adulterous acts had been pointed out. Now all they had to do was formalize the action to be taken against him.

Finally, one brave deacon, Mr. Step, said, "What do we do to finish this matter?" Mr. S. said, "Pound the bench in front of you and make a declaration." At 3:00 a.m. Mr. Step pounded the ironwood bench with his fist three times, proclaiming authoritatively, "We declare this man to be guilty and demand he be severed from any relationship with this church for now and forever." It did seem very, very final. In a state of relief and euphoria, I took Mr. Step and a couple of other deacons home to get a few hours of sleep in our house. Early the next morning I drove to the little city near us to buy legal stationery from the post office. It had a government seal on it and was required for any legal document. Mr. S. typed out a statement that Mr. Haniz was fired, citing the Seventh Commandment as the reason for his dismissal. He stamped the letter with an official *tjap* (seal) he had brought from his office. Copies were sent to all government officials in the area, including the police.

The firing of Mr. Haniz began a new era for us. We did not know how much he stood between us and the local people until after he was gone. Not long after his dismissal, we held the baptisms of our first sixty converts. "Sin in the camp" had definitely been an obstacle to spiritual growth. God had used Mr. S. to remove the obstacle. My "perception" had been that our work in Indonesia would have to be aborted before it was seriously begun. God's "perception" was that He would provide a way through for us if we would just move ahead in obedience to Him. The problem of Mr. Haniz was taken care of, but the political and military situation continued to be a major issue.

The Little Major

Problems come in all sizes, and this one was in the form of a five-foot-two Indonesian military major who was an army chaplain. Our area was overrun with military personnel because of Indonesia's miniwar along their border with Malaysia. Soldiers often stopped by to drink tea and chat with me on my porch, so it was no surprise when Major Patty came by one morning with his friend Captain Alex. Being an American, I thought that military chaplains would focus exclusively on their own army personnel. It was a shock to learn that he felt his primary task was to take over the spiritual responsibility of the civilian population of the surrounding area, including all professing Christians. In fact, he saw dealing with the public, not the military, as his primary task. He had boundless energy and often went to villages for surveys and preaching. On the surface, it seemed like a wonderful asset to the work. I did invite him to preach sometimes at the main church and to be one of the speakers at our annual church conference. He began stopping by for tea and homemade cookies and to talk about the work. On the surface all seemed cordial.

Unfortunately, he did have another agenda. He planned to establish the "Hosanna" church. His ambitious goal was to baptize three thousand people in our immediate area. For fifteen hundred rupiah he would furnish every new member with a baptismal certificate, plus a set of used clothing. He jubilantly proclaimed his intentions to me in his gravelly foghorn voice, "I am going to baptize three thousand people," and then he would roar out his belly laugh. It seemed like a wonderful game to him. He had found a gold mine of unbaptized, nominal Christians, ready to be sprinkled into the kingdom. I was in agony. It was my impression that there were already far too many unrepentant but baptized people in our area. He was already visiting our village church in Madi where we were teaching the Word and praying for conversions, preaching rebirth before baptism. He wanted to baptize all of them, not just the few we had in our baptismal class.

The tension continued to build over several months. Not his tension, mine. We had many apparently cordial conversations over chicken and rice in my bamboo dining room after Sunday church. But underneath I was writhing inside during this whole time. It was a situation I could do nothing about since the little major had much more authority than even the local police chief, or any other authority figure to whom I might appeal. You just don't mess with the military in Indonesia! But the sheep were at stake here, and I felt he could spoil permanently what had already been begun. He knew my position, but I had not yet asked him openly not to come into a new area and start baptizing in his own church's name. I felt it coming to a head inside of me, a building of conviction that I had to do something, even if it was wrong. A confrontation was needed, and I hated confrontation, especially with a major.

With much trepidation I finally made the decision to confront him on his own turf. There was a military base on top of the hill in the little town of Bengkayang where Major Patty was quartered. When I got to Bengkayang early one morning, I kept driving around and around the little town square trying to work up my nerve and the seeming audacity needed to confront him. Finally the Land Rover headed up the hill to his complex, almost as if against my will. Without my going inside, he came out to greet me. As a foreigner, I am not sure I was even supposed to be up there where only the officers quartered. With little introduction, but very politely, I told him my reservations about his bringing in a new church to the area, confusing the people about methods of baptism, and baptizing the unsaved. He began to bristle in his own way. He reminded me that as a foreigner I would soon be out of Indonesia. Theoretically, he was right. The country was sliding fast toward Communism. He implied that he was a permanent fixture and I was very temporary. Suddenly, from out of nowhere, a very large military policeman came alongside him. As we debated the issue, the big man began interrupting our conversation. He spoke directly to the little major, "Who was in this area first, this missionary or you?" Chaplain Patty was one of those unique people who could say whole sentences without actually using many intelligible words, mostly just grunts. He tried a few of these on the big captain, but the captain would have none of it. With what I considered some disrespect, he kept jabbing his index finger into the little major's round stomach and asking the same question repeatedly. Finally Major Patty mumbled out, "He was here first." At that point the MP told him with great finality and some extra jabs in the abdomen, that he had no right to, nor would he, baptize anyone in the area.

The conversation was abruptly over. I thanked them both kindly and drove down to the little town, wondering, *What would have happened if I had not done the confrontation?* I had done it with trembling words and shaking knees. God had come to my rescue in a most unexpected way. What I had seen as an impossible obstacle that I had brooded over for weeks, God took care of in a moment. I had suddenly gotten to see what was on the other side of the "insurmountable" problem.

The little major did not seem to be angry at me. He later even did our church association a great favor. He went to Mr. Haniz and persuaded him to turn over the papers to the old mission vehicle, as well as the official *tjap* (stamp) used by the church to make letters official. This is an extremely important item for doing business in Indonesia, and Mr. Haniz was not inclined to surrender this last bit of power, even though he had been fired. A little persuasion from an army major was all it took. Major Patty and Captain Malik suggested we add the word "Baptist" to our denominational association. The new acronym would now be PIBI (Association of Evangelical Baptist Churches). This was to help clarify our identity to other denominational groups who might want to come in and sprinkle the infants in our villages. The new name was used in writing up a new church constitution, and was officially approved by the government

To be accurate to the record, I must add that after I left Kalimantan for home assignment, the little major did baptize a number of people into the Hosanna Church, but they were few in number. However, by the time I returned a year later, he was gone, and I do not recall ever being shown a baptismal certificate from the Hosanna Church in later years. So, the little major who said we would soon have to leave the country was gone from our area in a year, while by the grace of God, we were allowed to stay another thirty-four years in Indonesia. Honestly, from my perspective, I thought the little major was right in predicting we would not be long in Indonesia. God's perspective was different. He had again shown me that He sees things from above and that every apparent obstacle to His work must be challenged rather than my viewing the obstacle only from my own perspective.

Major Patty was not the last obstacle, or the most threatening, to be overcome in our ministry. The one that followed a couple of years later was perhaps the most intimidating of my life. While we were in America on home assignment from mid-1965 to mid-1966, the Communist coup d'état took place on August 17, 1965. It was a bloody beginning and had a bloodier ending. It started with the Communists decapitating five Indonesian generals whose bodies were then thrown down a well. Pro-Communist armed forces and civilians took over the national radio station for twenty-four hours. Thousands of anti-Communist people were slain. A couple of days later the pro-democratic forces led by General Suharto retook the capital and the radio station. A countercoup ensued in which hundreds of thousands of people were slain. The canals of Java ran red with the blood of bodies cast into the water. Estimates range from 300,000 to 500,000 people being killed. While we were on furlough, our missionary colleagues were living through this epic upheaval. They were later told that their graves had already been dug near the Chinese marketplace. Probably their potential enemies saw the political tide turning and spared their lives.

This terrible bloodshed set the new Indonesian government solidly against Communism. To be Communist was to be antireligion. The cure for Communism, according to the government, was to be serious about one's religion. Therefore, whoever had been lax about joining and practicing a religion was now obliged to take on one of the major world faiths. Books have been written about this, such as Avery Willis's *Why Two Million Came to Christ*. Willis attempts to explain why between 1965 and 1971 two million Indonesians made professions of faith in Christ. Much of it had to do with the government's demand that all former Communists and their sympathizers enter a religion. The whole political scene flip-flopped in a period of a few months. When I left Indonesia in 1965, I would have been risking my life (or at least my visa) to speak out against Communism. When I returned in mid-1966, I was closely questioned by the Singkawang police chief as to why America was so foolish as to allow even the existence of the Communist Party within our country's boundaries. "Don't your government leaders have eyes to see how dangerous this murderous Communist Party is? Haven't they seen what happened in Indonesia?" Hopefully this bit of important background helps set the stage for the next major obstacle we faced.

"I'm Taking Over This Church"

He was standing on my front porch in army fatigues, though he had never been a member of Indonesia's armed forces. The clothing was to make him look as official and intimidating as possible. I had been dreading Luab's return to Indonesia for several years. This son-in-law of Mr. Haniz had gone to the United States to study for the ministry five years earlier. Before leaving, he had asked Bob Chapman and me to give him letters of reference for overseas study. However, his having gotten Mr. Haniz's daughter pregnant before marriage and his background in the Seventh Day Adventist Church made us think he was not a good candidate for a church leader, so we refused to give him letters of reference. His bitter response to our refusal was: "Some day you will be sorry for this." After the recent firing of Mr. Haniz I had received many long and threatening letters from Luab, including boasts that he was returning to Indonesia to take over the church. This morning, standing on my front porch, he soon came to the same point: "I am here to take over the church." He was tall for an Indonesian, and he was a Batak. Bataks are known for speaking directly and sometimes rudely, when compared with the polite approach taken by many of the ethnic peoples of Indonesia. They also tended to rise to the top in government offices.

I was polite to Luab but told him he was not taking over the church. He said that indeed he was taking over and that for now he was going to sleep in the garage next to the church and was here to stay. He left my house angry and insisting he had the right to take over the work because he was an Indonesian. It was just the first of his many visits to my house over the next several months. His own life was in shambles. He had attended four theological schools in America in five years but never graduated from any of them. His wife had married his younger brother in Luab's absence from Indonesia and had even borne a child by him. This was a moral offense so shameful that even the Batak cultural law, known for its thoroughness, had no rule for handling such a case.

Luab appeared at precisely the time of our annual church conference, and he invited himself to speak the next Sunday. Bob was back on the field to be our special speaker of the morning. I told Luab he could not speak to the people. He did show up the next Sunday morning, marching down the aisle of the crowded building, looking unusually tall in his white shirt and thin black tie. He seated himself on the front row, and I wondered for a moment if he would interrupt the service. Instead, Deacon Telad sent a handwritten note to me saying, "Luab wants to speak after Rev. Chapman's message." Not knowing quite what to do with the note, I told the congregation, "Deacon Telad has an announcement he would like to make this morning." Deacon Telad shuffled to the pulpit. Instead of speaking of Luab's request, he surprised me with an announcement that this coming week everyone should bring their annual rice tithes to the church.

The service proceeded as planned, with Bob giving a fine, challenging word to the messengers from surrounding churches. After the invitation, to which many responded, I gave the benediction that ended the service. With heart pounding, I walked slowly out of the church, gesturing to several of the people I had forewarned. They all got up and followed me out. At that point Luab stood and told the congregation that he had some things to say to them and that he did not know why this missionary refused to introduce him to the congregation. Gradually most of the rest of the congregation exited while Luab harangued loudly against me and the mission. Toward the end of his angry diatribe, he was complaining to a handful of people. (One of them was Wanda who was smoldering, but wanted to hear what he had to say.) I was waiting outside for him, and he did not disappoint me. He charged up to me, thumping his fist against his chest, yelling at me for what a degrading thing I had done to him, walking out like that. The muscles around his eyes were twitching with emotion, and I thought for sure he was going to strike me. A young army private standing by tried to step in and calm him down but was immediately put in his place by Luab for his peace-making efforts. However, the soldier's presence there might be the reason he did not strike me. It was a very tense moment, but we got through it without physical violence.

Luab continued to come to my home with various demands. His demeanor became more and more threatening. Indonesian friends told me he had gone crazy because of his own life situation. More than once he said to me, "One of us is going to die before this is over. I have lost everything already, so I really have nothing more to lose." One day he was in my house saying threatening things when my friend Dr. Wendell Geary was present. (Wendell and his family had joined our Kalimantan team in 1964 to take up the medical work of the field.) Wendell interrupted him several times, and each time Luab's anger rose higher. He finally turned to Wendell and said, "Does the doctor really want to get involved in this serious business?" Wendell answered boldly, "I am already involved in this business." This confused Luab for a moment, and he demanded, "Why are you involved in it?" Wendell gestured generously toward me and said, "Because I am with him!" Wendell's calling his bluff was a moment of incredible tension and relief at the same time. Luab was visibly shaken to have to be dealing with two enemies instead of one. To have a friend intentionally siphon off some of the anger toward himself left me feeling so much lighter, and it sealed my friendship with Wendell forever.

I became a bit paranoid as Luab's threats became stronger. I have never before or since felt so threatened over a six-month period of time. I had always felt it was my duty to love my enemies and show love and patience as best I could. I was trying to practice what the Apostle John said about "Perfect love casts out fear." Instead I seemed to be experiencing the exact opposite: "Perfect fear casts out love." It was not so much that I was afraid; it was that I was quite *terrified!* I disliked myself for the cowardice I felt, and I particularly feared for my family. Love for my enemies was just not the answer to this problem, it seemed.

One day Wanda and the children were gone from the house when Luab showed up with a fellow Batak on a motorcycle. I met them at the door of the screened-in porch and stopped them there. I was surprised at how much more courage I felt with my family out of harm's way. It was just Luab and me. There would be no invitation to have tea this day. He was in an especially black and threatening mood. Without polite introductory comments, he threatened me, "If you don't get me the money to go back to America in the next two weeks, I will see you go up to the sky." For the first time I told him directly there would be no help for him today or any day. He insisted that he was being lenient in giving me two weeks to live and that I should think about it carefully. I told him, "Whatever you plan to do to me, please get on with it. I can't afford to wait around any more." As he kept threatening menacingly, I kept telling him, "Bring it on right now." Gradually I could see his anger begin to give way to something else. His face changed from wrath to uncertainty as to how he should handle this situation. He finally turned and rode off behind his friend on the motorcycle, lamely offering a few last threats, but I could tell his heart was no longer in it. He had been bluffing all along, while all the time I thought he was a half-crazed person who would do anything, including murder. It dawned on me that there are times in life when acting in *courage* trumps acting in *love*. From that moment on, I was never as afraid as I had been before. In fact, I have never been that afraid again for the rest of my life! He did have one more tactic to try before giving up. He had friends in high places in the city.

He never gave up. Not only was he badgering me, he was also spending time in the offices of Batak officials (his fellow tribesmen) in Singkawang. Both the district attorney and the local Protestant minister of religion were Bataks. They were not necessarily on Luab's side, but Batak ethnicity is strong, and he wore them down with his persistent visits to their offices, asking them for help. Finally the two of them came to my house one night requesting that, if nothing else, I just give Luab a chance at ministry. What could it hurt, they asked, to at least let him have the opportunity to serve? I have never felt my foreignness more than that night, sitting in my own living room, trying to explain to two Indonesian government officials why an American should be rejecting an Indonesian offer to minister alongside me. I only knew for sure that I would rather have an enemy outside the church than inside. As I prayed desperately in my heart, God gave me the thought to say to them it was the church's decision, not mine. Luab would have his chance to make his case before the congregation and the leaders of the church. I even offered to give him a ride up to the station in the back of my Jeep, which he accepted.

A week later the church was packed. On the two back rows sat men dressed in their green semi-military-looking garb. I did not know until later that these were men Luab had recruited as members of a Communist branch of the Farmers Party five years earlier. They were now having to do one day of forced labor per week because of that former political involvement, and they were hopping mad. The tension in the air was thick. The local government minister of religion who had accompanied Luab opened the session, asking for the church to receive Luab into ministry. He then gave Luab the chance to speak. Luab strode forward with his customary bravado. His words came across as demanding and authoritative. He inserted a few English words here and there, demanding a decision "rrrright now." When he was finished, three Dyak men advanced to the front. One by one they vehemently rejected his demands, saying they did not know him and that he had no part in their church. The murmurs of support throughout the church echoed an emotional "amen" to every strong statement that was made. Not a voice was raised in his favor. When my turn to speak came, I asked the minister of religion directly if we wanted to make the final decision "rrrright now." He suggested we delay the decision for a bit. The meeting adjourned without a trace of doubt that Luab's leadership was rejected. That evening Luab and the minister of religion still visited the Dyak homes of those who had spoken out, trying to intimidate them individually, asking why they would be so foolish as to follow a foreigner. They held their ground.

The story of Luab ended abruptly the next day with his visit to the nearby town of Bengkayang. While he was there, the military police picked him up and took him to jail. They had been watching him because of his earlier Communist Party involvement. Shortly after this he was imprisoned for nine years without a trial. I never saw him again until we met in a post office queue soon after his release. Regular meals in the prison had caused him to gain weight, and he looked remarkably healthy. There was no longer any menace in his demeanor or fire in his eyes. My casual remark to him was, "You gained weight in jail." His retort to me was, "You are turning prematurely gray." It was almost comical to be relating like this to someone who had so intimidated me in the past.

The life lesson for me in this story is: *never try to do with love what only courage* and *love can accomplish.* In fact, this is the same lesson, relearned, as the ones regarding the adulterous church leader and the little major. I will never know what God wants to do with an obstacle set before me until I walk up to it and challenge it. One of my favorite Bible characters is the prophet Elijah. He was a man of God, who through God's power called down fire and rain from the sky in a single day. He saw 450 prophets of Baal slaughtered at the Kidron Brook and then ran forty miles in the rain, in front of a chariot. But I have always been curious to know what might have happened had he stood up to Jezebel instead of fearing for his life and running. The Word of God as spoken in the story of Elijah stands sure as the inspired Word of God, not to be meddled with in any way. My question remains, what might God have done if Elijah had stood up to this pagan queen? For my part, I have never taken a step of courage and had God let me down.

As I look back, it seems that the sixties lasted more than a decade because of the many stressful issues we faced. In addition to the personal threats during those years, there was an ethnic conflict that severely tested all of our missionaries. It portrayed an ancient side of Dyak life we had not yet encountered. We were not prepared to witness the savagery that was seen in their return to the ways of their ancestors. I refer to their earlier headhunting days.

Modern-Day Headhunting

It was 1967 and the Confrontation with neighboring Malaysia was over. However, trouble was still brewing in our jungle area because of Indonesia's near takeover by the Communists in 1965. Before September 11, 1965, the Communists had a strong party in the government. When neighboring Sarawak (part of Malaysia) chased the Chinese Communist guerillas out of their own territory, they ran to the close-by jungle of Kalimantan, just across the border. In pre-September 11 times, these guerillas were welcome to run to and fro across the border, making mischief in Malaysia. That is because they were seen as the enemy of the new Malaysian government. That they were Communists was no problem. However, once the Communists had attempted their coup d'état and failed, they became the archenemy of Indonesia. The Indonesian government sent crack troops into our area with orders to wipe them out. Once again, our area was green with more than foliage. Soldiers were everywhere.

Because there were many Chinese farmers and rubber tree harvesters living in the jungles, they became the haven for the Chinese guerillas as well as the target for being wiped out by the soldiers. The guerillas could always find food and shelter among their own people group. The Indonesian military figured that if the Chinese farmers were wiped out, the guerillas would have no way of supporting themselves. However, for the most part, the soldiers did not bother to drive out the Chinese farmers. They just incited the Dyaks against them. It was not hard to do. From ancient times the Dyaks had harbored a jealousy of the Chinese because of their clever ways and their comparative wealth. The Dyaks claimed that when the Chinese first came into their land, they taught them to gamble and then won their best rice fields—and some of their prettiest women. Probably a claim that history would not totally substantiate. Nevertheless, a smoldering and ancient hatred was easily exploited by the military. The Dyaks began to burn the homes of the Chinese and chase them out of the interior. We knew that the Chinese in our nearby marketplace could be attacked any time. The Chinese cook at the hospital stored several bags of rice at our house along with her sewing machine and hardwood cabinets. We stored rice for a few others there as well.

We also had several fine Chinese nurses in our hospital who were being trained by Dr. Geary and other medical staff. I took a number of them to the town of Bengkayang one day, and on our way home they saw outside the car window eleven decapitated Chinese bodies lying beside the road. The nurses became deathly pale and quiet for the rest of the trip home. It became clear that, in spite of their value at the hospital, there was no room for Chinese people to continue living in this rural area. For their safety, Dr. Geary moved them temporarily into the larger city of Singkawang.

The attack on our Sungai Betung marketplace came in the morning hours. I looked out my window to see Chinese, mostly women and children, running toward our hospital station from the marketplace, screaming in panic. Many of them had babies slung from their shoulder sarongs. They were sobbing with fear. I jumped in the Jeep to call soldiers from Bengkayang, feeling guilty for leaving Wanda and the kids behind. (However, Americans were not threatened at the time.) Fortunately I met a truckload of soldiers coming my way. The soldiers took me along with them to the marketplace. Dyaks with heads wrapped in red cloth and wielding their machetes had come upon the local merchants and were busy rifling their belongings, taking everything from sewing machines to live ducks. They were all wearing some kind of a fetish said to ward off any attackers. A few of them were wearing necklaces of some kind of animal teeth. The soldiers did nothing forceful to stop the looting. They just gave speeches about right conduct. The Dyaks paused in their looting long enough to applaud what the soldiers were saying. They gave me the bullhorn to take my turn at talking to the Dyaks, and I also got no more than some applause. The Dyak marauders were from another area, so I had absolutely no influence on them. Dyak neighbors would be ashamed to attack the people living right next to them. It is always that way in Indonesia. The troublemakers come from a distant area, not next door.

Three hundred Chinese fled to our hospital complex and our church to be housed, fed, and preached to for the next couple of weeks. Jung Nam Fu, our Chinese evangelist friend, was visiting us right at the time of the demonstrations. It seemed a God-thing that these Chinese who barely spoke Indonesian and listened only to Peking (Beijing) radio every day would run to a church in their time of fear. Many of them had never taken Indonesian citizenship and counted themselves loyal to the Chinese Communist government, even though they did not really know what Communism was. Every evening these refugees gathered in the church to sing choruses in Chinese and hear the gospel repeatedly in their own language. Many of them came to Christ and ended up in Chinese churches in the cities around us. I also preached in open-air meetings in Bengkayang where even larger numbers of Chinese were gathered because of the ethnic cleansing taking place. Some of these people also turned to the Lord and became part of the Chinese Christian community in Singkawang and eventually migrated as far as Jakarta. It was hard to accept the "inhumanity of man to man" that we witnessed over the next few weeks. In ethnic upheavals it seems that there is always the element of one people group dehumanizing another group. Dr. Geary walked a couple of hours to see the remains of several Dyaks whose charred bodies were found in their own rice granary. They had been burned alive. This sort of thing was happening in many places. One day several Dyaks rushed up to my house demanding to be taken to the police in Bengkayang. They pulled a freshly decapitated human head from a burlap bag. They wanted to show it off to the authorities. One of them held the head up by its hair and said he was the one responsible for taking it. I was unable to eat my lunch after looking at it. I declined to take them anywhere, telling them they had cut the head off of a farmer, not a soldier.

What happened in Sungai Betung happened in every marketplace and Chinese home in our whole area. It was not so much a killing spree, but a beheading here and there with much looting and burning of property. The purpose of the military was to eliminate every Chinese from the interior. The purpose of the Dyaks was to enrich themselves a bit and to do payback for many decades of feeling themselves the inferior people group of the area. Eventually sixteen thousand Chinese were evicted from their homes. I saw a strange and eerie sight when I drove into Singkawang one day. On one side of the road I saw a long line of Chinese people walking, heads down, some of them carrying a few articles of clothing wrapped in a cloth of some kind. On the other side marched the Dyaks, going in the opposite direction, wearing their red headbands. They seemed to be robots, walking fast and determined, not appearing to be human, carrying machetes and the possessions of the people they had robbed. Four of them were carrying a huge hog that someone had just chopped in two through the center rather than cutting it down the middle. Two men were carrying each half. It was the utter quietness of both lines of people that was striking. There was not a word spoken. Both parties seemed to be in their own dream worlds. I picked up a couple of Dyak policemen on my way back. When a Dyak group flagged my car down, the police jumped out and began to beg the marauders to have mercy and told them we were all on the same side. Their fear was far too obvious. All I can say is that God protected me that day.

However, in the midst of all this upheaval, God had something special in store for our family. The Chinese were not the only ones to come to Christ in this awful drama. It started off badly. Finally it seemed that the lives of the missionaries were being threatened because we were sheltering the Chinese. We decided the women and children should move temporarily to Singkawang. Wanda at first refused to go, preferring to die beside me if there was death at stake. I finally convinced her to go, along with the other women and children on the station. Kevin was just five years old, and with death talk all around him, the fear of the Chinese seemed contagious, affecting him as well. We were all living in a kind of dread, and Kevin's fear was that he was not sure where he would go if he died. He was a very serious five-year-old, mature for his age. Rather late at night he called his mom in to ask her what would happen to him if he died. After Wanda explained exactly how to receive Jesus into his heart, he accepted Christ as his personal Savior. She told him, "We are in the hand of Jesus, and if He keeps His hand closed over us, we are safe to live on. If He opens His hand, then we go to be with Him forever in heaven." When the whole ordeal was over, Wanda had nearly forgotten what she had told him. She was reminded one day when Kevin tugged at her skirt and said, "Mom, Mom, God didn't open His hand, did He?" It sticks as a lasting and clear memory in Kevin's mind that this was the time of his coming to Christ.

A few weeks after the ethnic war had passed, we were surprised to receive a calendar from the Women's Missionary Fellowship of Canoga Park, California. After all, we were into the month of November already, so most of the year had already passed. It was a baby picture calendar so common in the sixties, portraying babies with all their cute expressions and a comment below them. Then we read the note included with the calendar. It said, "The Humbles were the missionaries of the month of October, and we offered up special prayer for you every day of this month." The name of a prayer partner was printed in the square for every day of October. We realized that the Dyak uprising had happened on the first of that month, and everything had calmed down by month's end. God had mobilized His prayer force to hold us up before His throne during that whole traumatic period. Even though we had not had time to warn anyone of the danger around us, the Lord had let His people know in advance of the threats against us.

Chapter 12 – Growing the Church

I sent you to reap...
(John 4:38)

By the late 1960s and early 1970s there was a surge in the Indonesian harvest that continued to some extent in the years to come. It was happening in many places of the country, but the area we worked in was special to us because we got to see Him at work firsthand. There were several factors that played into this ripening of the harvest. First, we had been teaching the Scriptures to lay preachers for about eight years, bringing them in for intensive times of Bible study once or twice a year. These men were going back to their villages and to neighboring villages to spread the good news. Second, there was the social upheaval caused by the attempted Communist coup d'état and the government's ensuing demand that "everyone must have a legitimate religion." Animism was not considered a legitimate religion. An additional social upset was the border warfare going on with the emerging country of Malaysia and Indonesia's resentment of that new nation. Military troops stationed in the remote villages also helped Dyaks to see there was a better way of life. Finally, and primarily, it is truly the Lord of the Harvest who prepares His people for receiving His message into their hearts. No one knows for sure why one village is accepting of the gospel and another is hardened to it.

Americans usually speak of individual hearts that are receptive toward God, but in Kalimantan it was more common to think of receptive villages. During our first years in Kalimantan, many people still lived in the Dyak longhouse, which in some cases housed the whole village. I once paced the length of a longhouse to find it to be 165 meters long. More commonly the village was broken up into several housing units which put a roof over several extended families, rather than one longhouse. Individuals live in close-knit community, and no single family or individual can make a radical decision without its profoundly affecting his family and neighbors. Of course, it is usually the life and heart of some individual that influences the village for change when change does occur. Here are some of the key people who stand out most in the early days of our missionary work.

Laborers in the Harvest

It seems almost unfair to select just a few people from among hundreds to illustrate how the church grew in Kalimantan. For the most part they were unschooled laymen, who had learned of Jesus and wanted to tell others. I describe these people because I knew them personally, not because they were the best or the only heroes of the early days of church growth.

Yohanes of Sejajah

Yohanes was mentioned earlier as the church leader from Sejajah village, a man who was hungry for the Word of God. I had a unique bonding of spirit with this young Dyak man. He was humble and teachable. He was also one who seemed never to ask for personal favors, though he was no more wealthy than others living in his village. In general, he was just easy to hang out with. We depended upon each other in village evangelism. His courage to speak the truth grew as we reached out to villages around Sejajah. One night, he preached the gospel forcefully in the village of Kandasan. On our way home he said, "I would not have the courage to speak to my peers like that if you were not with me." It was this kind of transparent talk that drew us together. With other men of his village he brought the gospel to villages such as Minso where a new little church was born. Sejajah became my launching pad to reach out to other villages. Yohanes was always with me on the back of my Honda 90, traversing the rough roads and jungle paths of the area. One day he was speaking in my ear as I dodged the deepest mud holes in the road. He said, "I used to think of you as my father, but now I think of you as my brother." It stuck in my mind as one of the most touching things ever said to me by a tribal person. To be his brother felt like a high privilege to me. Later he became the president of our National Association of Baptist

Churches, where again, he served with humility and cooperation with our mission. He was the first Dyak tribesperson with whom I established a true friendship and came to love as a brother. Unfortunately, his life was cut short by a heart attack in his early fifties. I mourned this loss, as did the whole Christian family in the area. Sejajah was on the road to another village and another person of great influence in the early history of the church.

U. T. Simatupang of Dawar

With over five hundred inhabitants, Dawar village was one of the largest villages of the Sanggau-Ledo District. It boasted nine witch doctors and shamans and was deeply steeped in animism. I had wanted to visit Dawar for a long time, mainly because we had received Christian book and Bible orders from an elementary school teacher named U. T. Simatupang residing in Dawar. In May of 1965 I got my first chance to visit Dawar. Wanda, Cheryl, Kevin and Norma Hasse, along with a team of three nationals, went as far as the village of Sejajah where they held a three-day Vacation Bible School. I had no way of knowing how God was planning His harvest in this village.

Yohanes Bujang, who lived in Sejajah, joined me for this first trip to Dawar. Lieutenant Sardono who was an assistant chaplain in the Indonesian army, and rabidly nationalistic, came along with us. His presence and prejudice against "American imperialism" during the sensitive time of the Indonesia versus Malaysia confrontation did little to encourage me on this journey. Dawar is on a high plateau and therefore cooler at night. After a couple of hours the almost-invisible jungle road was no longer accessible by four-wheel-drive vehicle. We trudged uphill in the rain for two more hours beyond where the Land Rover could take us. When we were within half a mile of the village, I began to hear what sounded at first like rolling thunder. It turned out to be the pounding of a log drum, which beat in staccato rhythm. Closer yet, I could hear the clanging of the brass gongs. It was the time of Rice Harvest Festival, which would last for three days, giving praise to Jebata, the rice god who got full credit for a rice harvest, whether it was good or bad. It was celebration time in the village. Many pigs and chickens were slaughtered, and rice was consumed in great quantities.

We found Teacher Simatupang where he had made his nest in a corner of the makeshift schoolhouse, built from bamboo and thatch. His looks were surprisingly different from the villagers around him. Well-dressed, healthy-looking, with a pencil mustache, he was a handsome young man of twenty-six. I could not help but ask this smiling, educated young man, "How on earth did an educated, handsome young man like you find his way to this remote village?" His answer, with twinkling eyes, made me laugh. He said, "I was just going to ask you the same question." We seemed to become instant friends. He welcomed us royally and wanted to show us around the village immediately. People were feasting in many of the homes. Since rice is scarce for several months of the year, this was the time for the villagers to eat their fill and more. He led us to where the *Joget* dance was being performed on a large front porch. The Dyak men and women dance opposite each other, but never touch. They mince up to each other in a shuffling step, to the music of some scratchy violins, almost touching each other, then retreat back again. It looks quite provocative in a culture that allows no public expression of male and female relationships. The *Joget* was often done in times of celebration and often was a cause of jealousy on the part of the wives who were never involved in the dance. Men paid a small price in rupiahs to dance with one of the young maidens who came from different villages. Sometimes these men paid a bigger price when they got home. One husband found his clothing heaped in the front yard when he got to his door one night, with his wife screaming, "If you like that girl so much, go live with her!"

Simatupang also escorted us to the "spirit house." This was the place from which we had first heard the thunder of the drum. The drum was a fourteen-foot-long hollowed-out log, with deer skin stretched over one end of it. It was so long it went right out through the wall of the house. In the same room, men took turns beating sixteen brass gongs with their five-note semimelodious sounds. The din of the gongs blended with the intermittent beating of the huge drum made a clamor that, in my opinion, could make only Jebata, the rice god, happy! Lieutenant Sardono jumped in and enthusiastically took a turn at the beating of the big drum. Nearby an offering was laid out to honor the spirits. Several freshly dressed raw chickens were suspended from a piece of rattan, like hanging them from a clothesline. Their blood had been shed to pacify the spirits that lived in the old and blackened human skulls that lay directly below them on a shelf. These skulls were taken down annually from the upper structure of the spirit house. This was the worship center, expressing the heart of Dyak animism. Blood had to be shed to appease Jebata.

Later we followed the shaman and his assistant from house to house as he gave a little séance for each family, beating a gong and giving thanks for the individual family's rice harvest. It was a dismal and depressing ceremony. Feeling the depression of the evil spirits, I asked a young man standing by, "Wouldn't you like to know a better way?" He agreed he would and then added that they did not know a better way. I then asked Simatupang if it might be possible for us to hold a meeting for the villagers to share some good news with them. He felt the timing was not right. After all, they were in the midst of their annual rice harvest celebration, and it might not be received well, and in fact nobody would come to a meeting. While it seemed culturally inappropriate, the Spirit of God would not allow me to let it go, and I kept gently trying to persuade him that we should have a meeting. Finally he said he would see what he could do the next day to get the men of the village together for a meeting.

By the light of kerosene pressure lamps that evening, Simatupang told me what he was teaching the village young people about Christianity. He said, "I am requiring them to memorize the Lord's Prayer, the Ten Commandments, and the Apostles' Creed. When they have it all committed to memory, can they be baptized?" I said as tactfully as possible, "No, I am sorry, but they need to repent in order to be baptized." "What does repent mean?" he asked curiously. I said, "Repent means to turn away from one's old life and be born again in Christ. It means turning our backs to our idols and earthly lusts, and accepting Jesus into our hearts, and then living for Him only." When I had explained it to him as clearly as possible, his little smile returned and he said, "Maybe I myself need to repent also." Simatupang was a Batak, far from his home in North Sumatra. He had come to Kalimantan to gain wealth by smuggling tobacco across the border into neighboring Sarawak, and then smuggling manufactured goods back into Kalimantan. Border guards had become increasingly vigilant, catching many of his fellow smugglers, imprisoning some. This action caused him to take up a less lucrative life of teaching in the village. He had a Lutheran background and knew all the stories of the Old Testament, but he had not yet experienced a personal relationship with Christ.

After we had talked long into the night, Simatupang gave me his mattress with the mosquito net hung over it as my own private little sleeping space. Everything seemed a bit yellowed with age and wear, but it smelled fine. In fact, his comment to me was, "You can have my bed. It smells good. It smells like me!" During rice harvest festival the gongs beat day and night. I slept fitfully and prayed off and on through the night as the gong noises kept waking me from my slumber, wondering what God had in store for this village.

Simatupang was as good as his word in getting people together the next day. Within a short period of time more than seventy men gathered in the schoolhouse for a meeting. It was Dyak *adat* (custom) that only men of the village participate in formal meetings of any kind. When meetings took place in the longhouse, women listened from their bedrooms, or while sitting just behind the circle of men. It was not that the meetings were secretive, just that women were not involved in the business end of village life. Here in Dawar the men were reasonably attentive as several of us took turns preaching the gospel. This was the first time that most of them had ever heard the good news. After we were introduced, we all took our turn speaking to the men. The lieutenant waxed eloquent with his main point: "I never thought I would meet brothers like you in a place like this." He was emphasizing the solidarity of the Indonesian people, he being a Javanese. Yohanes and I both gave a simple gospel message, pointing out the good news of Jesus dying on the cross to set us free from sin and bondage. The men were respectfully quiet as we spoke but not ready to make a hasty decision for Christ. Simatupang did well to ask them if they would like to hear more about this teaching in the days ahead. They unanimously said, "Yes, we want to hear more." I felt both pain and joy in leaving it at that—pain that the darkness was seemingly so thick in this place, joy in realizing that against the odds, God had opened the door for a first sowing of the good seed. Simatupang was obviously the key to future growth in this village. We had formed a friendship which I felt would continue in the days ahead.

Meanwhile, back to Sejajah, where I had left Wanda and Norma teaching Vacation Bible School. While we were at Dawar, three adult men of Sejajah decided to join their children in attending all the sessions of VBS. They even enjoyed using crayons and coloring the pictures that were handed out. They were gripped by the songs and stories of Jesus and the clear presentation of the gospel. Wanda and our children were housed in the home of Mr. Um̃ar, a blind man who said he had become a Christian years ago. However, when hearing the teaching from Wanda and Norma, he said, "You make the story of salvation so clear. I've been going to church for years now, but I've never understood that I can know Jesus in a personal way – that I must make Him my own – receive Him." (Wanda's letter of May 19, 1965.) When the call for decisions was made, three young family men, two young adult males, along with many children, prayed the prayer for receiving Christ as their Savior. Those simple truths from the Scriptures became the bedrock of their faith, helping make Sejajah the lasting witness it remains to this day. As these men shared their faith, many others in the village believed and were eventually baptized. Forty-five years later some of these men have passed away, but the remaining ones are faithful pillars of the church.

In mid-1966, after a year of home assignment, I returned to the village of Dawar. Simatupang had come to Christ in a marvelous way. After hearing the gospel from me, he read the story of Martin Luther's conversion and made his decision. From there on it was a spiritual battle all the way in the village of Dawar as Simatupang passed on to the other young men what it means to be born again. The line between light and darkness was drawn, with most of the young men on one side and the old men on the other. The tension in the whole village was palpable. I baptized the first six converts in the river that ran right beside the village. Before being baptized, each one told how he had been a lost sheep, how he had lived only in darkness, and how he had now found new life in Christ. Since Simatupang had taught them, I had him in the river beside me, helping me immerse them. When the last man had been baptized, Simatupang stepped over in front of me and said, "I, too, want to be baptized." It was a moving moment for me because Simatupang was not a person prone to humbling himself in that way, especially in front of all of his disciples.

The young people decided it was time to build a place of worship in Dawar village, but the old men violently opposed it. A three-hour village meeting was held in order to settle the decision once and for all. The old men pleaded, "Why have you turned away from our old *adat* (traditions)? Have we not shown you the good way to live by our customs?" My heart was sad, more than I believed it could be, seeing sons at such enmity with their fathers. I finally stood to tell the fathers how much better sons they would have if they trusted the true and living God. I did not feel much appreciation from them, for I spoke as an outsider. After several young men spoke, one well-built, square-jawed youth of seventeen named Tingong stood to speak for all of them. "We have followed the old way, and it has brought us only ignorance, sickness, and spiritual blindness. Now we have the truth, we have a teacher, and we have a Book. We will follow this way even if we have to die for it." His face was bright red with the passion of his testimony. The room was hushed for a moment as people were awed by his boldness. The tension was so high, I believed it might just happen that way. The old men kept insisting, "If you want to build a church, build it at least a mile and a half from this village." The meeting closed with great anger and no resolution. It is difficult to imagine how the problem would have been resolved if they had been left to themselves to slug it out. In the end, the local government officials made a trip to the village to tell the old men bluntly that religion was a good thing and animism was not. They would have to permit the younger people to build a church near the village. Begrudgingly, they allowed it.

A bamboo-and-thatched-roof church building went up, just across the little stream, very close to the river. With a building to meet in, more and more people began to attend the church and become believers. In these early days of faith, they met every night in the church to sing and share truths from the Word of God. Eventually more than half the people of the village came to Christ. After several years, a group of hard-core animists could stand it no longer, so they moved away from the Christians to found a new village. The Christians of Dawar continued to visit them with gospel teams, gently encouraging them to choose the narrow way.

My relationship with Simatupang continued over the next twenty years. He became a key evangelist in the early days, spreading the Word to villages surrounding Dawar. Taking gospel teams of young men from his village, he had them testify in Segiring, Segunde, Tuhu, and many other villages within walking distance. Most villages experienced the same trauma as Dawar had. The Sword of Truth separated those who would believe from those who would not. It is one of the ways that villagers in Kalimantan became Christians.

Simatupang was the first pastor to be officially ordained in our national church. When questioned about his theological preparation for ordination, he often said he attended "The Walking Theological Seminary." When questioned further, he added, "I walked the trails with Pak Humble for twenty years, and now I know what he knows." It was too generous a compliment, for many others had great input into his life, and furthermore he was an avid reader. In reaching out to others, Simatupang came upon another key man who was to play a significant part in the planting of the early churches. His name was Jairani.

Jairani of Tuhu

From the time of his youth, Jairani was a sickly child, suffering from asthma. His breathing was always labored, and he coughed a lot. Simatupang found him in the tiny village of Tuhu, which was located beside the great Ledo River. Tuhu was a four-hour walk from Dawar. Jairani was ripe for harvest and immediately accepted the Lord as his Savior.

When in later years I married Jairani to his bride, Adak, in the village of Madi, I listened as his father stood to give the traditional father-of-the-groom words of greeting to the guests. His words were not the predictable ones said in flowery congratulations at a village wedding. He said, "Jairani has never been strong enough to be much good for anything. I am glad he is getting married today, though, and he is lucky to find a wife who will have him. I am grateful to the family of the bride for accepting him. He has always been poor of health and can't work like other men, so he is late in getting married." I squirmed a bit in my seat at what seemed to be serious denigration of one's own son. Jairani's father, like all good Dyak tribesmen, had hoped for a strapping son who could fell trees to do the slash-and-burn agriculture or could hunt wild boar in the jungles at night like the other young men. Instead he had received a physical weakling who would be mighty in spirit and mightily used by God.

Jairani could not fulfill his father's ambitions, but he was already a successful village evangelist before the time of his marriage. I visited his little village called Tuhu at Christmas time in 1967, not long after his conversion. Just twelve families lived here, right beside the Ledo River. Several people in the village had become believers, and together they had built the sweetest little church I ever witnessed during those days. It was very small but the bamboo walls were woven with care. Fine sand from the nearby river was carried up to fill the area where the pastor stood behind a well-shaped wooden pulpit with a cross adorning it. The church steeple was constructed just as carefully, with an ironwood shingle roof and a cross on the top, while the rest of the roof was thatch from the palm tree. It was not unique in its structure, just very unique in comparison to the haphazard way many Dyak temporary churches were thrown together. It felt like a holy place in an unusual setting.

From the small village of Tuhu, Jairani started evangelizing up river to the villages of Tapen and Suti Semarang, and then on up to the mountainous area of Bentiang in 1971. Climbing the five-thousand-feet elevation to these villages, his exploding breaths sounded like a steam locomotive, but he made the trip many times, taking with him Buell Hadley, one of my fellow missionaries. Wherever Jairani went, he sat with the people on reed mats spread on the floor and "gossiped the gospel" in a most humble and attractive fashion, telling how it had changed his life. He seemed universally accepted in every village, and wherever he visited, people opened their hearts to Christ in great numbers. He paved the way for other missionaries and national preachers of the Word who would come to teach and baptize the new believers.

After his marriage he moved to the town of Bengkayang. In 1972 he became the overseer of the boys' dormitory. Wanda was teaching the young people of the Bengkayang church and offering her Bible-memory course. Jairani brought the young men from his dormitory to every Wednesday afternoon youth meeting. He threw himself into learning these verses right alongside the young people. He later said he would have felt ashamed not to try and learn the two hundred verses, since his students were memorizing them. Once he had a grasp of these verses, he became an even more powerful evangelist.

Bethesda Hospital leaders at Serukam saw his giftedness and asked this third-grade graduate to be their first full-time chaplain. It was a perfect fit for Jairani. Near the hospital he could always be treated during an asthma attack, and the attacks did come. Many times he was near death. Perhaps living on the edge of death is what drove him to be so dedicated to his task of ministering to the sick. He was a fervent evangelist who would literally get up and walk out of a structured meeting to go and make his patient rounds at the hospital. I have seen him stand to his feet before the Evangelism Committee meeting was over and with his gentle smile say, "Excuse me. It is time for me to make my rounds to my patients. I am bound by the truth in Ezekiel 33:6, which says I am like a watchman on the wall. If he fails to warn the people of the coming sword, 'Their blood I will require at the watchman's hand'." And off he would go, bringing life to many just as they were about to pass through the valley of the shadow of death. Jairani's passion for the lost set the gold standard of patient evangelism at Bethesda, and others followed. For many years the annual hospital statistics revealed a thousand or more people had come to Christ during the previous twelve months. Jairani lived to see his sons into their teenage years but died soon after. He will always be remembered as my favorite and most fruitful personal evangelist.

How Dyak Villages Came to Christ

The story of Dawar told above is rather typical of how villages come to Christ. However, every Dyak village had its own personality. Sometimes it seems it had to do with their geographical location. The villagers along the roads and the great rivers tended to have a "worldly wise" attitude that inoculated them against the simple gospel. They were also prone to take a more individualistic approach to life. However, in the interior areas the villages still had a strong sense of unity, and they made their decisions as a community. It is the Lord of the Harvest who is ultimately involved in ripening the fields. In a sense, human instrumentality seems small in comparison to the readiness with which some villages embraced the good news. Bentiang was an area God had prepared to hear the good news.

Bentiang Area

Bentiang consisted of four villages on top of a high plateau where evenings and nights were cool. It was mentioned earlier as one of the places where Jairani and Buell Hadley first went to preach the gospel. The Bentiang people's story is unique. In 1972 they were so hungry for change that one hundred men signed their names to a letter and sent it to our neighboring mission, asking them to send them preachers of the gospel. The neighboring mission did send preachers just one time, but there was never a follow-up visit from them. Kalimantan is a vast geographical area with missionaries too overtaxed to consistently minister to each needy village. Meanwhile, Jairani and Buell Hadley arrived on the scene to minister to them. To keep it clear which mission would serve this area, the villagers made a communal decision to choose our mission to serve them, even before they became Christians.

My first overnight in Bentiang was in the village of Sijanjong, the largest of the four villages on top of the mountain. Here the people had expressed interest in *masuk agama* (entering religion) but had not come to grips with giving up their old *adat* (customs/religion). Since their worship of the rice god was the centerpiece of their animism, they were concerned that failure to sacrifice a chicken in the area to be planted would mean no rice crop for the year. But they were as a people obviously being drawn by the Holy Spirit to move toward God. After the evening rice meal the men all gathered in the longhouse, with women and children sitting around the edges. Simatupang and I took turns presenting the claims of Christ to them, though it was not the first time they had heard the gospel. We could sense they were in the throes of making a great decision. Kerosene pressure lamps dimly lit the faces of those wrestling and arguing over what steps to take. We made it clear that if they were to become Christians and worship the Creator of heaven and earth, they could no longer worship other gods or make blood sacrifices, since the perfect blood sacrifice had already been made. They began to loudly debate the consequences of making a communal decision for or against the gospel. Voices were raised to the highest pitch, to be interrupted by voices even louder. They shouted with emotion, but they were not angry. They were in a great spiritual struggle, about to reverse animistic belief systems that had been practiced for centuries by their ancestors.

This negotiation took place over a couple of hours. Neither Simatupang nor I knew exactly what they were saying in this obscure Dyak dialect. What they were negotiating and weighing so seriously was this: "Do we dare plant a rice field if we do not offer chicken blood to the rice god?" We were able to assure them that the God who created rice in the first place could overrule any other "gods" who stood in His way. We also clarified for them, "Yes, of course you must pray to God before you open a new rice field." With these assurances, they decided that eleven of the forty-two heads of households would forgo the blood sacrifice this planting season. If these men had fields that produced rice, the others would enter the faith the next year. A great sense of relief settled over the gathering. They were on the road to a new life, and they knew it!

These eleven families would be the test case. The remainder of the village was not antagonistic toward them because it had been a communal decision. Not long afterward the whole village participated in building a bamboo-and-thatched-roof church where they could meet to learn more about this new faith. Even those who did offer the blood sacrifice began singing hymns and studying the Scriptures in preparation for entering into the faith. The eleven brave men who took the first step did indeed reap a harvest, and the others soon followed. In retrospect, I marvel at how they surrendered themselves to a new religion with such little information as they had about the new faith. It could only be the work of the Lord of the Harvest.

In Makdomong, another village of Bentiang, they decided to become Christians and built their own church before destroying the old "spirit house." This was a structure built on poles approximately fifteen feet off the ground. Here they stored the skulls of human heads taken years ago, as well as deer antlers that were taken when warriors went off to take heads and met an unfortunate deer on their way. They said the antlers were even more powerful than the skulls themselves because they were taken on the way to hunt heads. The skulls were stored in rattan baskets and hung up high on the walls. This spirit house was where young men age ten and older slept. These boys were considered too old to sleep in the bedrooms of their parents. Sleeping near the powerful skulls was also thought to increase their bravery and virility.

We were told that when the skulls became hungry for a blood sacrifice, they rattled themselves together to request an animal be killed to appease them. After some months of learning and growing stronger in the faith, the villagers agreed it was time to dispose of these fetishes and make a clean break with the old life. When the time came to dispose of the skulls, I climbed up the rickety old ladder of the tall structure along with several other leaders. I stood by the door of the spirit house, high above the ground, while they took down the baskets of skulls to dump them on the floor. What happened next so startled me that I could easily have fallen out the door backward. The old skulls indeed did have life in them! The rats, which were the culprits that sometimes rattled the skulls, scurried in all directions. They had found the old skulls to be perfect nesting places. It seemed amazing to me that the dark powers could use even rats to promote fear and bondage.

The Bentiang villagers were unique in their emotional response to the gospel. When the story of the crucifixion was told, they audibly gasped as they heard of the nails pounded into Jesus' hands and the spear thrust into His side. The Holy Spirit made it as real to them as if it had happened yesterday. Of the eight hundred people living on this mountaintop, 95 percent of them professed faith in Christ. Like the new believers in Dawar, they were taught a simple catechism and asked to express their faith verbally before baptism. Some of the older women did this with trembling knees and quavering voices. They were baptized in increments, depending on who was ready to leave the idolatrous part of the old *adat* (religion) completely and testify to their new life in Christ. In the Semame village of Bentiang, 147 of 150 people turned to Christ. For the first few months they held meetings in the church every night. Eventually every village built a permanent church structure. They then formed gospel teams and took the good news even farther up the trail to the more primitive area of Tengon. The story of these villages is told in the next section of the story.

While this is my record of observing God's working in the villages, I want to make it clear that I was not the moving force in seeing the Bentiang people come to Christ. Simatupang spent many days during the early years after their conversion, teaching them the deeper truths of the Scriptures. Jairani and others continued visiting them. Their churches were incorporated into our national association of churches where they enjoyed the annual training events of lay elders. Eventually the Extension Bible School established by Buell and Barbara Hadley held bimonthly sessions in Bentiang to train the church leaders. Often there would be five or more "elders" taking turns preaching on Sundays to the flock. The gospel is contagious, and the Dyak people had early on formed a practice of taking gospel teams to the villages closest to them, such as Tengon, just mentioned.

Tengon Area

By 1973 gospel teams were reaching into the Tengon area, including lay teams of evangelists from Bentiang. I myself visited them during this period, when they had not yet begun to believe. It was late afternoon as our party of evangelists reached the first village in the Tengon area. This area had been left behind by civilization more than any other I ever visited. Like all good Dyak tribespeople, they took a bath twice a day. But unlike the others, they rarely had soap and their bathing hole was quite muddy. Most of them spoke only their own dialect, and some of them dressed in the traditional clothing of their ancestors. Some of the old men still wore loincloths made of rough bark. It was the only place I visited where the unmarried women were not clothed above the waist. In all other places, only nursing mothers dropped their sarongs to their waists. A scaly skin disease called *kurap* affected many of the Tengon people, making their skin rough and nearly leprous white. They were not used to having outside visitors and must have heard stories about the diseases they brought with them. The village chief greeted us and then hurried off to put on his government-issued khakis. But he was also adorned with a necklace of bear's teeth and a red bandana around his head. We climbed the notched pole ladder into the longhouse and were ordered to sit down for a foot-washing ceremony. It was not easy to find a place to sit, since the dogs, which roved freely throughout the longhouse, had spread their excrement in so many places it was difficult to find a place to sit. When we were seated, he took a live chicken and opened one of its wings, brushing it over our feet and saying softly in a sing-song voice, "Selamat, selamat…" along with other words of an ancient incantation. He then tossed some dry rice into the air around our feet, continuing his chant. Obviously this was a spiritual cleansing of some kind to keep us from spreading disease into the village. Then the chief went out for a bath to the rather mucky spot near the village which served as their bathing area. He had charcoal on his face when he went for the bath, and wet charcoal on his face when he returned. The distended stomachs of the children showed that they were malnourished and were carrying parasites. It seemed to me that most of the people, adults and children alike, had a glazed look in their eyes.

Dyaks are always hospitable people, eager to serve what they have to any visiting guest. As we sat on the floor eating, emaciated dogs crept closer and closer, hoping for a bone. When they got within reach, a man would take up a long switch and send the dog away yelping. Then hunger would gradually overcome fear and the dog would creep up, only to be driven away again. When the meal was over, the chief asked if the children could eat the bones. My first thought was, *How can we allow them to eat these things that have already been in our mouths?* My body language must have shown that I thought this improper. But I could see in his body language that he was thinking, *How can these people be so selfish that after eating the meat, our children are not even allowed to have the bones!* Immediately we offered them the bones. They grabbed them hungrily and began cracking them with their teeth to suck the marrow out of them.

The whole scene was almost too depressing for me. As I stood up to give them the gospel that night, my thoughts ran something like this: *What is the meaning of a Man nailed to a cross two thousand years ago to these people? Don't they need something more practical? Don't they need, first of all, some transformational education in health and nutrition?* But we did preach the gospel to them, in this case using translators. They were not opposed to the gospel, but in my heart I knew they grasped little of what was said that night. They needed to be taught the gospel over a long period of time for it to really get through.

The real heroes of the faith that brought truth to them were a couple of Dyak young men who became their teachers and evangelists over the next year. Neither of them had gone to teacher training schools. One of them, Mr. Boset, was quite crippled and had to make a jerking motion with his whole body in order to throw his lame leg forward each time he took a step. It was painful just to watch him walk up the steep hills. His lameness did not hamper his zeal for teaching children and living out an example of the Christian faith before people who had no knowledge of the Savior. The other young man, Mr. M., was a strapping example of health. Together they became missionaries to an area very different than their own.

It was a year later that I again visited the Tengon area. I found that the Lord of the Harvest had been at work again. Approaching the village I saw that the former muddy bathing area had been replaced by a stream of clear water flowing from a very large section of bamboo connected to a nearby rivulet. You could actually take a refreshing shower from it, while standing. Ascending the notched pole ladder into the longhouse, it was evident that the floors had been cleaned of dog droppings. They were now cooking chickens without a few feathers mixed in with the meat. Overall, there was a sense of life and renewal about the whole village. A small schoolhouse now stood in the center of the village where the children were learning to read. The school building, which had a cross on top of it, doubled as a meeting place for the believers on Sunday. When we came together to sing and worship, I heard the Indonesian version of "Amazing Grace" sung in harmony by a group of young people. Most heartening of all, I saw the gleam of gospel life and light in the eyes of those who were beginning to believe. Nine young men were glowing with the evidence of a new life and were there to be baptized that day as the first believers in the village. And, thinking back to my first visit to this village, I knew in my heart that *a Man nailed to the cross two thousand years ago means everything to every man, woman, and child, in every country on the face of the whole earth!* Eventually every one of the villages of Tengon put up their own church building and began sending their leaders to our lay training courses.

The villagers from Bentiang later told us a story that would not be accepted by the average Westerner. They said one day as they were on the trail, going up to Tengon to teach the people there more about the gospel, they met a group of spirits coming from Tengon. The spirits were carrying their rolled-up grass mats used for sleeping, along with kitchen pots and pans. The Bentiang people asked them where they were going. The spirits told them that a powerful spirit named Jesus had moved into the Tengon area and that there was no room to live there any longer. They said they were looking for another place to live. However improbable this might sound to the Western mind, people coming out of animism have a unique sensitivity to discern the spirit world. Certainly the old spirit houses were torn down and fetishes were destroyed. The presence of the Lord of the Harvest left no room for other "gods" in the villages of Tengon.

Jagoi Area

The Jagoi people live in a chain of villages that straddles the border between the two countries of Malaysia and Indonesia on the island of Borneo. The villages on the Indonesian side of the border had only been touched by Catholics who did not require them to put aside their old pagan practices. They continued the worship of the rice god even after becoming "Christians."

Dr. Wendell Geary had different ideas regarding how one should take a vacation. In December of 1971 he took a team of young men and a thirty-five-pound backpack for a two-day walk north across the border to Sarawak. They stayed overnight in the village of Jagoi Babang, ministering to the sick and giving testimonies in the evening. Both medicines and testimonies were very well received, and he was invited to return again. Back from "vacation," Dr. Geary reported this to the evangelism committee who arranged for a team of evangelists to make a survey that would include Babang. Over a nine-month period Simatupang and I led teams through the area, preaching in each village. We returned to the area every three months. Each trip took about ten days. One or two days were spent each time in Babang. Medicines were always distributed, for which a small payment was required. Days were spent in just making friendly conversation with the people. In the evening the men gathered to sing and listen to the gospel message. Attention was good, but there was no indication of a readiness for the community to make a decision.

However, on our third trip, two young married men named Asem and Laking made known their decision to receive the gospel. Missionary Don Bryant had been sitting on the floor sharing more of the gospel with them after the evening meeting. Seeing their earnestness and sensing that something important was about to happen, I thoughtlessly interrupted their serious discussion. My first intention was to stall their decision. After all, I had seen the conflict that took place in Dawar, and I had witnessed the people movement in Bentiang. It would be most unfortunate to receive only two new converts if there was a chance we could bring them in as a group. I urged them to delay their public decision awhile, hoping to influence their fellow villagers first and then become Christians together as a larger group. They looked at us earnestly and said, "But we want to believe right now." As I prayed silently in my heart, I recalled the words of Jesus: "The one who comes to Me I will certainly not cast out" (John 6:37). I allowed the Spirit of God to override my church-growth strategy. When instructed to pray simple prayers of repentance, they asked, "Where is the prayer book?" They had obviously seen the Catholic prayer book from earlier contacts with the priest. We explained that God is our Father, and it is best to just open your heart to your Father rather than reading to Him from a book. Surrounded intimately by some of their relatives and friends, they bowed to pray with more understanding than we had expected. Since villagers usually make their first decision without visible emotion, we were surprised to see the tears in their eyes when they finished praying. We taught them some basic Bible texts to hang on to. Special attention was given to warning them not to offend others or separate themselves from their community. Leaving the village the next day, I wondered if these newborn babes in Christ would be sustained by the Holy Spirit until we saw them again. We gave them the Bible, songbooks, and Christian literature, and prayed that it would be so. We would not know the answer for another three months.

On September 30, 1972, we were again in Jagoi Babang. Asem hosted us this time instead of the village chief. He was obviously happy to be taking the role of a new leader. Flashing his gold teeth, he repeated several times that there were twenty-two men ready to become believers that very night. Even the menu that night indicated good things. In this area guests are usually served only leaves and vegetables with rice. Tonight he was cooking up a healthy portion of fat pork meat to feed us.

There was an air of excitement this time as people came together for the evening meeting. True to Asem's word, when the men gathered that night, exactly twenty-two of them made professions of faith. One by one they bowed their heads and prayed to receive Christ as their personal Savior. Most of them were strapping young married men in their early thirties. Enthusiasm ran high. They were knit together in a new community, finding special joy in just sitting together and talking far into the night after the formal evangelism meeting was over. The village poet, who had been an assistant to the witch doctor, composed verses relating to leaving the old life and entering new life in Christ. Each verse detonated a roar of laughter. One of the lines in his poetry said simply, "We don't believe in Satan and ghosts anymore. We believe in the Lord Jesus." They were still carrying on when I, worn out from the trek, had to ascend to the sleeping loft above them. I could hear them off and on until 1:00 a.m.

Of the two Jagoi men to first accept Christ as Savior, Laking became a successful merchant, who in later years has faithfully served and financially supported the Lord's work. Asem went off to Berea Bible School with his family. He later became a faithful pastor who is today building a brand-new, rather large church structure beside the main interior highway. Other Jagoi villages such as Sungai Paling and Sejaroh also came to Christ. All along the path Dr. Geary had taken, village churches sprang up. It was a wonderful time of experiencing what Jesus meant when He said, "I sent you to reap." These examples of how the villagers became Christians are representative of many other villages. I could never adequately express the faithfulness of God in building His church. To enter a village where God has already been at work preparing hearts is totally different from entering a village where the people have not been made receptive by His Spirit. The fruit rarely falls into the hand without wresting it from the Enemy's grasp. But, on the other hand, all genuine fruit is made ready by the Lord of the Harvest. All the glory belongs to Him.

Chapter 13 – Family Life in Kalimantan

Behold, children are a gift from the LORD*...*
(Psalm 127:3)

A man may think of himself as "king of his castle" or by any other flattering name, but in my missionary life it was Wanda who set the tenor of the home. I believe all four of our children would agree that they grew up in a happy family atmosphere. Wanda is responsible for that. Her smile that first won my heart in Biola days turned out to be a way of life for her. There is really nothing like having a smiling wife for one's whole life! I never once heard her say, "Why would you bring me to a place like this?" Or, "Are you sure we are called to this place?" You might wonder where she got this ability to be consistently joyful and often laughing, considering her life situation. There was a secret to it. Our daughters like to say, "One of my most vivid memories of life in the jungle was coming out of my bedroom early, on any given morning, and finding Mom having her quiet time by candlelight, tears running down her cheeks." Always an early riser, she would be up before any of the rest of us, praying, reading her Bible, and going over her well-worn pack of Navigator verses. Her joy seemed to spring from a deep well that was forever overflowing in tears of both humility and joy. Her meeting God first in the morning meant that the rest of us were going to have a really good day. This is not to say she was perfect, but she was very disciplined in having her quiet time with God.

That Wanda was joyful did not mean she was a lightweight in things pertaining to organization and discipline. Detailed duty lists were posted for every child and every Dyak helper. There was also a list of rules tacked up in the hall entitled: "Rules for The Happy Humble Household." Visitors were amused to see number one on the list, "No singing at the table." This rule was made because during mealtimes the children liked to burst into song with any new chorus they were learning. She also kept a calendar with large squares for every day of the month. She penned into every square of the calendar a long list of duties that included everything from trimming fingernails to future beach vacation dates. My own village visitation schedule was also listed on her calendar, once I told her what was planned. I credit annual family vacations to Wanda's penning them in early so I could say no to what seemed important ministry assignments in favor of keeping family commitments. The lists and calendar provided structure in a situation where we could have just floated along in a laid-back Dyak culture.

The Kitchen

Our very first kitchen was in the old hospital building. There Wanda baked her first bread on our three-burner kerosene stove with its portable oven. It was fortunate she had a good sense of humor, because the loaf could not be penetrated even when stabbed with a sharp knife. She laughed when after several days we discovered the loaf of bread that had been thrown out to the dogs. They had gnawed on it on all sides without being able to consume much of it. Not long afterward a bread recipe from a senior missionary of RBMU, Ruth Warkentin, began to produce light and wonderful homemade bread. "Bake day" was always on Monday. Wanda wanted to get the hot job of baking over with all in one day. She baked bread, cinnamon rolls, pie, cookies, and whatever else she could think up. It was a wonderful feast on Monday night and still reasonably fresh on Tuesday and Wednesday. After that I began to seriously look forward to the next Monday!

Dyaks usually built a lean-to kitchen on the back of their homes, somewhat separate from the main structure in case of fire. After moving out of the hospital building, we did something similar by building a separate kitchen behind our house. There was a short, covered walkway between the two buildings. The kitchen I remember best was the one screened on three sides, allowing the heat of cooking to escape. Several Dyak girls lived in a room behind our kitchen. They needed money for school and clothing, and Wanda needed help with kitchen and laundry duties. We gave them a bit of spending money, plus room and board, clothing, any needed medical care, and school fees. Wanda gathered them all together for Bible study and prayer several times a week. After finishing elementary school, many of them went on to Singkawang to live in our mission's dormitory for middle school and high school students. One helper, Atus, who came to us at eleven years old, became a fine nurse at the hospital. Others went on to become teachers or eventually returned to their villages and got married.

The kitchen was a favorite place for our own children and the young Dyak helpers to hang out. Without fail, we had steamed rice for lunch every day. The vegetable and meat dish that provided the topping for the rice was either greens picked from the jungle or something we purchased in the local marketplace. The girls were less than culinary experts, so apart from the hot peppers, there was not much to look forward to at lunch time. Our children did not share our tastes. Many times they would leave our supper table and go back to the kitchen to eat rice and greens with the helpers.

Christmas Celebrations

Indonesians are "event oriented," that is, they tend to look forward to whatever occasion there is in life to celebrate. Christmas is always the biggest event of the year, and they begin to prepare for it months in advance. Not surprisingly, the kitchen became the center of activity at Christmas season. First Wanda, and eventually the children, got into the spirit of the thing, and the kitchen became a production plant for Christmas creations made of candle wax. Several pounds of ordinary candles were purchased in town. The wax was then melted down and combined with half-used Crayola crayons to make rich colors, to be worked up as art projects. Pie pans, cookie cutters, and all kinds of other kitchen vessels were used to mold Christmas trees, snowmen, bells, stars, and many more creations. They learned to enhance the creation by whipping up the wax to make it look like snow, and then sprinkling it with sparkle that had been brought over in our missionary barrels. It became a major operation and a contest in creativity to see who could come up with a different kind of candle each year. Each candle had a wick implanted in its center, so it actually could be burned. However, most people who received them as gifts never lit the candle but rather stored it with other Christmas decorations at the end of the season, to bring it out again the next year. We gave them as gifts to missionary and other special friends among the nationals. Wanda's December 1975 letter to family tells of making twenty such creations, plus nineteen smaller ones for children. She also mentions how much wax had to be cleaned up off the kitchen floor. We had to take a putty knife to it to peel it off in globs, but the excitement it generated was well worth it. The kids got very enthusiastic over their work. It was a family project they grew more and more proud of each year as their expertise increased. It became a "family tradition" that provided an opportunity to give, as well as to celebrate Christmas and the Savior's birth.

In addition to the wax projects, there was the cookie and candy preparation. We bought twenty-five-pound bags of flour in town, and sugar by the kilogram. Every ounce of flour had to be sifted and then sunned to remove the black specks of larvae. I kept thinking we had bought enough supplies the first time, but then there would be an order for another bag of flour and another five kilograms (ten pounds) of sugar. Wanda cut circles out of cardboard boxes, covered them with colored paper from town, and piled nearly a dozen different kinds of colorful cookies on them. In that same letter of December 1975, Wanda says she and her crew produced forty-two trays of cookies. I was the purchasing agent and the chauffeur to deliver the goods. It was important to get them to the recipient soon after they were baked. It was always a race to see if we could get them there before the humidity made them soggy or the ants beat us to eating them. We usually won, with some minor losses to a few stray ants.

Christmas celebrations in Indonesia began around the tenth of December and ended around the seventh of January. Wanda started teaching the Dyak young people their new Christmas songs in late October. They loved singing, but it took a long time for them to get it in four-part harmony. With not much else to do in the evenings, they just loved to get together for practice anyway. Besides the carols there was always a drama that often began with the story of Adam and Eve and went all the way through the Bible to the resurrection of Jesus. They had to tell the *whole story,* it seemed. In our early years, starting in 1962, we loaded the Land Rover full of Dyak actors and took them to the marketplaces along the road as well as all the way up to Sejajah to present their programs. I doubt this created much spiritual fruit, but it made the young people's meeting a happening place to be, and this in a place where nothing else was happening apart from drinking and gambling in the village.

Since every village wanted its own Christmas celebration, I often started my preaching schedule in the villages beginning around mid-December. By December 24 I was usually back in Sungai Betung to join the main church's celebration. I went to a different village every night for a week or more. Kevin often went with me on these extended times. We spent up to ten days together in the villages. Kevin never tired of the village life. He did not always play with the Dyak children but was often present for examining the baptismal candidates and came up with his own conclusions as to whether the person being examined really knew the Lord or was just faking it to get baptized! "Look at him grin," Kevin once whispered to a Bible school graduate sitting next to him. "I'll bet he's lying in saying he has stopped gambling. Otherwise why does he keep grinning like that?" The Bible school graduate was quite amused and thought this was very insightful for a nine-year-old!

I believe God used this time in Kevin's early life to make him what he is today. As a grown man, Kevin still loves to hang out with Indonesians in the villages of Java and other islands. Humanly speaking, one could believe God has brought him full circle. Being immersed in the culture as a child prepared him uniquely for cross-cultural ministry. As an adult, he senses some of the invisible nuances of cultural ambiguity that are rarely accessible to most Westerners.

Since villagers love an occasion, everyone in the village came to the Christmas program. That gave the ones who were not Christians a chance to hear the gospel clearly. I never preached a Christmas sermon about the cradle without explaining the meaning of the cross. As mentioned above, we would get back in time to celebrate at the Sungai Betung church, and then a few days later, pack up for a week at the beach just after New Year's. We had our own little artificial Christmas tree that the children thought was absolutely beautiful once we got it all decorated. I was not a dad famous for buying expensive presents. Perhaps the poverty of the villages around me might partially excuse my conservative approach toward gift buying. Dyak children received no gifts at all for Christmas. All of their Christmas celebrations revolved around the church, not family. There was also the fact that there was virtually nothing of value to buy as Christmas presents. Local shopping options extended to blow-up plastic animals and poorly made, cheap plastic toys. Hopefully we made up for the lack of extravagant gifts by spending precious family time at our favorite beach in the world.

Flood and Fire

Kalimantan is said to have two seasons: the rainy season and the rainier season. That is not totally accurate, because there is usually a six-week period around June and July when rains decrease. This was the time to burn off the trees that had been felled to start a new rice field. In some ways we loved the rain. Most mornings the weather would work up to an intolerable, humid, equatorial heat to where one felt one could not draw a breath. Then in early afternoon we would hear the advancing rain coming across the jungle like the roar of a distant wind. At this point every hand available rushed to get the dry clothes off the clothesline. Within minutes of the beginning downpour, the water would be running over the eaves' troughs like a waterfall. Rain in Kalimantan was warm, so it was our children's playtime, especially during the biggest downpours. Running and sliding in water pooled on the grass lawn made their day. They also loved to go to sleep at night with the sound of rain falling on the thatch-roofed house we lived in.

One house we lived in at Sungai Betung was so low that the water came up over the floor of the house occasionally. I seemed often to be absent from home when this happened. Wanda thought the emergencies of life *always* happened while I was gone to the village. One such flood happened in February of 1975. Every item on the floor, plus books on the lower shelves, had to be quickly moved to tabletops to keep from being spoiled. Brown water rose almost a foot inside the house, but it was not just the water. There was a scum of diesel oil from our generator shed behind the house that was messy to clean up. Creatures also came and went with the floodwater. On two different occasions a small snake drifted in during the flood, and the back screen door had to be opened to let them float out. The children thought the floods were part of the fun of life. Sonja woke up one morning and told Yvonne, "Hey, there is water on the floor!" Yvonne did not believe her at first and put down her feet. She patted her feet in it, loving the idea of water on the bedroom floor. This was all part of the adventure of living in the jungle. She was quite disappointed when Riti, our helper, carried her piggyback to higher ground. It was during this same flood of 1975 that Kevin took his little canoe and rescued several people from the rooftops of their houses. It was a great day for him as he became the talk of the community.

The two rivers that came together behind our house in Sungai Betung were a scene of tragedy for all of us at one point. In fact, Cheryl's most memorable act of compassion as a child came one day when I heard bare feet pounding up to the back door of our house. "Pastor, Pastor, Damid is dead!" several Dyak neighbors shouted together through the screen door. I jumped up from the breakfast table to see four men carrying the lifeless body of old Damid, dripping and cold from the river. He had apparently had a heart attack while out fishing at night and had collapsed in the water. It was a gruesome sight, with rigor mortis already setting in. His hands were extended, almost in a praying position. Damid was a favorite of mine, a yard worker who never seemed to have a decent shirt. I gave him lots of shirts, but he always gave them to his sons or to the neighbors and preferred to wear his worn-out ones. I turned away, shedding tears at the sight of his inert body, surprising the Dyaks. *Tuan munse*, they marveled, meaning in their dialect, "The *tuan* is crying." They were taken aback, as they rarely showed emotion except for wailing at certain times, usually by women only. Mari, who was Damid's six-year-old daughter and Cheryl's best friend, heard the news and came running to our house. Cheryl met her friend before she could catch more than a glimpse of her father's corpse. She gently turned Mari around and put her arm around her neck, leading her off to talk and play for the rest of that whole day. They were the same age, but Cheryl was almost a head taller than Mari. Mari wrapped her arm around Cheryl's waist and away they went. The picture of the two of them walking together, Cheryl compassionately leading her friend away from the specter of death, will always be imprinted on my mind.

God uniquely used these early experiences in Cheryl's life to prepare her to be the professional and compassionate nurse she is today. I almost cried one day when many years later I found her as a grown-up nurse in the ICU of Phoenix St. Joseph's Hospital. The little missionary girl, who loved to give fake shots to her dad, was now standing among patients with tubes protruding from every orifice of their bodies. Surrounded by high-tech equipment, she seemed at home, a very long way from where she had started. God does bring His children full circle.

Though the river took Cheryl's best friend's father, it was also a place very important to the children. Cheryl and her Dyak girlfriends played so many hours in the water that her hair eventually had mildew in it! By the time Kevin was twelve, he had a small canoe, mentioned above, that he would take up and down our river for hours, learning to paddle like a professional. He also took Yvonne on river rides and thoroughly entertained her by diving under water and grabbing the feet of wild ducks as they flapped wildly before being released. Sonja and Yvonne thoroughly loved the river, too. They had a thick rope tied to a tree branch and a platform from which they could launch themselves to swing out over the deep part of the river, to let go and land with a splash.

Fire was a different issue, and is of course a hazard in every society. Without modern fire departments to do the job, Dyak tribal people had only their own creativity to rely on when it came to putting out fires. It is amazing how few fires get out of hand in the village when one considers that everything is built of such flammable materials, and open-pit wood fires are always used for cooking. I recall seeing Dyak firemen work in emergencies. Once, lightning struck a coconut tree, causing it to burst into flame in the village of Segiring where I was visiting. Flaming bits of leaves blown from the tree by the wind began to drop on the roof of the longhouse nearby. The men immediately scaled to the roof of the house without the use of a ladder and then ran from place to place on the fragile thatch roof, patting out the little fires with their hands before the flames could get a head start.

Had it not been for Dyak neighbors, our own house would likely have burned down on two occasions. The first time was when Kevin decided to helpfully burn off some dry grass that had been cut down next to our house. The fire drifted toward the house, to a banana tree with its dry leaves drooping to the ground. When the dry leaves caught on fire, they leapt to the top leaves of the tree that were touching the edge of our thatch roof. It caught on fire immediately. Humanly speaking, there was no way I could put out the fire. I immediately scrambled to the under part of the roof, and, hanging there, I tried to cut away the thatch that was stitched to the rafters with plastic string. I hacked away with all my might with my machete, utterly exhausted in a few seconds, but mostly I screamed, "Help... Fire!" at the top of my lungs. Immediately a couple of near neighbors came running. With expert accuracy they used their sharp machetes to cut the plastic string that held the thatch in place. Then they deftly sent it sliding off the roof in rows of flaming sheets, leaving the rafters bare. Other men came running and emptied our water tank, using buckets to fling the water high on the roof. The bottom of the tank was mostly muck, and some of them got plastered with the stuff being flung up by their friends, but they did not care. The whole operation was over in ten minutes or less, and we were forever grateful to them.

Another time when we were sitting at our supper table, just finishing our meal, a man rushed in our back screen door without knocking. He was yelling, "Fire, Fire!" as he came in, but we had no idea what he was talking about. He had been walking on the road in front of our house and looked up to see that a curtain in our upstairs bedroom had caught fire from a candle and was already in flames. He gave us no time to question his rude entrance. He charged up our stairs and made for the fire. He found the burning curtain, yanked it off the window, threw it on the floor and then stamped out the flames with his bare, calloused feet. That house was made of wood that was of the cheapest and most flammable sort. We were so awestruck by his swift action that we hardly knew how to thank him, but we have never forgotten his intervention that certainly saved our home. We were thankful to the neighbor, and also to our Lord, who brought him along at just the right time.

Sometimes we had a bit of intentional fire of our own making. Like most boys, Kevin loved fire and often wanted to burn the trash. One day he poured a whole tin can of kerosene on the paper trash and lit it. I heard the *whoosh* of explosion from across the street and came running to find him standing somewhat dazed in front of a smoldering pile of ashes, with nearly all of his eyebrows and eyelashes singed off. Otherwise he was unharmed. Looking back, I am amazed at how few serious injuries happened to us. None of us suffered a broken bone or debilitating disease during twenty-three years of living in the jungle. To God be the glory!

Trauma and Sickness

We never suffered chronic illnesses or broken bones, but we did have some scary moments in raising the children in the jungle. Sonja, born in Tucson, Arizona, in May of 1966 while we were on home assignment, was truly our "Calamity Jane." She had multiple encounters with what seemed to us near-death experiences. When she was nine months old she had a strange-looking bite on the ring finger of her left hand that ended up in a serious bone infection. Her arm ballooned up twice its normal size, and her pain did not cease so that she cried day and night. Dr. Geary's first operation on her finger did nothing to take away the swelling and pain. We soaked her little hand three times a day in very warm salt water. She screamed from the time her hand was immersed until it was taken out. After several days, there was still no improvement. Finally Dr. Geary had to do a second operation, this time removing the growth end of the bone, which caused the finger to be shorter than normal. After he removed a half cup of pus from the inflamed area and thoroughly scraped the bone, both she and her mother slept for a consecutive twenty hours. At first we felt a bit sad for this small blight on our daughter's ring finger. Then a visiting doctor came to our field, telling of a child in the States who had a similar problem and lost two fingers and half of her hand. Then we were reminded of God's goodness in sparing Sonja's finger and Dr. Geary's sacrificial service to our family.

Shortly after the finger incident, Sonja had another life-threatening event. We rarely had special guests come to the jungle to give us spiritual refreshment, but a very special one who came was retired India missionary Dr. Eric Frykenberg. The Dyak helper girls were supposed to be watching the children while we had a session with this visiting speaker, but they got busy playing with each other. Meanwhile, upstairs, Cheryl and Kevin started swinging on the door of a hardwood cabinet about six feet tall. As it toppled over they tried hard to get Sonja out of its path, but it was too heavy. A corner of it came down hard on Sonja's head. The Dyak helpers came over to interrupt our meeting, carrying Sonja and looking sheepish. There was a deep dent in Sonja's head, making it look like a piece of clay that was hit by a two-by-four. Even Dr. Geary seemed unusually solemn as he ran his hand over the dent, just saying, "Ummm, ummm." We prayed for her on the spot, of course. She was not crying, just moaning a bit and looking shocked. Her complexion was rather grayish in color. We feared for her being normal in the days ahead.

Wanda kept a vigil over Sonja for several days. She woke her up every three hours to be sure she was not going into a permanent coma. Eventually Wanda herself became physically and emotionally exhausted. It was at this point that she had one of the most precious spiritual experiences of her life. While leaning over Sonja's bed crying, she clearly felt another Presence. She sensed that Jesus was right there beside her and that, He, too, was weeping—that He cared for Sonja as much as she did. Feeling His great love for Sonja, she spoke to Him through her tears, "Lord, I really do not want to lose my daughter at such an early age, but I know You love her more than I do. If You want to take her home at this time, I surrender her totally to You. Let Your will be done." Wanda suddenly had a sense of peace that was beyond description. There was an immediate change for the better for Sonja as well. After vomiting once, she seemed to have no further symptoms except some lethargy for the next couple of days. The dent in her head gradually disappeared over a period of time. Again, we were grateful for God's special protection over her.

A bit later in life Sonja nearly drowned in the river but was rescued by her brother, and then again had a near-drowning experience in the ocean, and was again rescued by her brother. Later yet, when she was ten years old, a fifteen-foot fall from a guava tree left her unconscious and then in shock for several hours. Such a series of life-threatening incidents made us wonder what God had in store for Sonja in the future. Amazingly, she turned out to be a very coordinated and athletic person who loved to give everything she had when playing any sport. Mentally she suffered no loss. She made National Honor Society in high school and graduated with honors from Biola University, proving, if there was any need for proof, there was no brain damage. I believe these events in early life embedded in Sonja a sense of perseverance against all odds. Today she suffers pain in several parts of her body that is quite unexplainable apart from inflammation. It has made her a woman of prayer rather than a person who retreats from life, using discomfort as an excuse for inertia. All praise be to God! He works wonders in His children, using His own methods that are mysterious to us.

Yvonne also had her own time of crisis, just after she was born. She was delivered by Dr. Bert Ferrell at our own Bethesda Hospital in Sungai Betung on March 12, 1969. A few days after her birth she started suffering from vomiting and diarrhea. This can be fatal for a newborn child. Dehydration is one of the major causes of death for children in Kalimantan. It seemed doubtful that an intravenous tube could be inserted in her tiny veins to hydrate her, partly because she was so young and already dehydrated. After Dr. Ferrell had done all he could think of to do for her, he convened a prayer meeting in our living room. We had a visiting evangelist named Djung Nam Fu who joined us in fervent prayer for Yvonne's healing. Dr. Ferrell pulled out her medical chart and wrote: "Prayer was held for Yvonne at 9:00 a.m." From that moment on we saw a marked improvement in her condition, and we have no doubt that God intervened to bring about a healing.

Kevin had his share of incidents and accidents during growing-up years in the jungle. When he was less than two years old, he had a series of ten boils across his whole forehead, which seemed better wrapped than left in the open. For many days he looked like a little pirate in his headdress. Not much later he managed to pull down on himself a dipper of freshly boiled water that was prepared for his bath. It scalded his leg, leaving huge, bulging blisters of fluid hanging from his thigh. It took weeks for this to heal up, but with Nurse Trudy's expert care it never turned into infection. Later on, when he was eight years old, he went bike riding with another missionary family, the Ferrells. He somehow fell off a bridge, landing some fifteen feet below, barely missing sharp bamboo and rocks. Some men working nearby pulled him from the water into which he had rolled. Otherwise, he could easily have drowned.

Of Cheryl it could be said that she probably dealt with more intestinal parasites than the others because she always insisted on eating with her Dyak girlfriends. In fact, we gave worm medicine to all of our children every four to six months and almost always with results not worthy of description! Cheryl also had lice from time to time because she spent so much time with her friends. They were either sharing milk and cookies in our outdoor kitchen, playing at the river, or picking tender leaves in the jungle, to be cooked later in our kitchen.

Over our period of twenty-three years in the jungle, the children would often get a strange fever, sometimes accompanied by stomach problems, sometimes not. We hydrated them and prayed over them and waited. They usually recovered over a period of four or five days, though sometimes the malady would last up to several weeks. We often had no idea what caused the fever. In retrospect, we have only praise for God for His protective care over us as a family.

Pets, Wild and Tame

Dyak people like dogs a lot, especially for hunting game, but also in their woks. Some of our kids loved animals and some didn't. Kevin and Yvonne were especially fond of them. Our first dog was a long-haired fuzzy pup acquired from a friend in Pontianak in 1962, just after our arrival on the field. We called her Singa, which means *lion* in Indonesian. Singa was faithful and extremely fertile. She eventually produced seven puppies, four times in a row. I joked that with those numbers she should have been a gambler. Singa often followed Wanda to the villages as she went to do women's Bible studies, turning back only when the yapping and snarling of emaciated village dogs made her think the odds against her were too great. Kevin was just a toddler, and to see him tottering among seven fuzzy pups and falling down among them was quite entertaining. As he grew older, he acquired several kinds of pets including a *musang* (the dictionary calls it a civet cat) and a small mouselike creature that was quite tame when handled.

Like Kevin, Yvonne was Kalimantan-born. She was the only missionary kid (MK) from our mission who was delivered at the old Sungai Betung hospital station at the hands of Dr. Bert Ferrell. Had it not been for the animals, our Yvonne would have had virtually no playmates. The local village children had been good pals for Cheryl and Kevin, but ten years later the local culture had seemingly changed. Even the children were not the innocent, easy-going types to be easily made friends with. They would still come and sit with her long enough to eat up the milk and cookies she offered them, but quickly ran away to play with each other, leaving her behind. That left Yvonne alone to spend many long hours with the dog and cats. I often found her just sitting behind the screen door scratching our dog, Charcoal's, belly. When I came out the door she would look up and give me her sweet smile and never complain, "I'm bored," like the average child would do. Her love for animals, including some half-tamed pigeons, seemed to be enough at the time. Later, when the Longs moved to our station, she had Christy and Matt to play with, especially Matt as they shared the same interest. When she was a bit older she also had a heart for the MKs who came later to our field. She would frequently invite the Jeffreys' children, Suzanne and Chris, to go fishing with her, teaching them what she knew about the skill. She loved anything outdoors, especially swinging from the rope and landing in the river. With all her siblings gone to boarding school, she had little opportunity for social outlets. I can't help wondering if all the alone time as a child contributed to making Yvonne the deeply thoughtful person she is today. Being an avid reader gave her a thirst for even more knowledge. She has become an excellent teacher, always searching for ways to improve herself and those around her.

Family Escapes

In some ways living in the jungle is a great way to raise kids. We were far from the influences of TV, drugs, and other "worldly" temptations for young people. In spite of this seeming isolation and potential for boredom, we did at times crave privacy, as do most Americans. It was remarkable how hard it was to ever feel we could enjoy alone time as a family. Even in our own home there were the three or four Dyak girls who lived with us while attending the local school.

Children of all ages and all places seem to need something to look forward to. Promising a picnic to our kids always picked up their spirits. Wanda often made plans in advance for a picnic, especially when I was gone to the villages. She would pack sandwiches in an antproof powdered milk tin, add some fruit and cookies, and start looking for a place to be alone in the jungle surrounding our house. No matter how many times she tried it, they would no more than get settled into a shady jungle spot than they would look up to see brown eyes all around them. Peering from behind trees or tall grass, they were probably wondering why people who had a nice house would prefer to eat outside, sitting on the ground. That did not cause Wanda to give up the picnics. They still looked forward to the outings, and our children just got used to the idea of never being alone!

A more successful and almost daily escape was through reading books together at night before going to bed. Wanda started it by reading Nancy Drew books to Cheryl. Reading became a nightly tradition nearly as addicting as TV in America, but certainly more healthy. Every night we were free, Wanda read to the girls and I would read to Kevin. He especially appreciated the Lord of the Rings series. Actually, we both got into the story to the point I could no longer tell whether I was reading it to him for his pleasure or mine. It turned into a remarkable time of sharing a great story that drew clear lines between good and evil. It not only drew the lines, it graphically described glorious wars fought to the death. The Narnia series by C. S. Lewis had a similar effect on all of us, taking us into great escapes from our jungle setting to the mysterious other world that only Lewis could create.

We took all kinds of books with us on vacation to our beach haven of Pasir Panjang and enjoyed them there as well. When Kevin went off to boarding school in the Philippines, I took my turn reading to Sonja and Yvonne. They especially liked Mark Twain's writings because I would imitate Huck Finn or Tom Sawyer's accent as best I could. The rural setting of those old books took us to a faraway but somehow familiar world, at least to me, being the farm boy that I was. Sharing these book getaways with the children gave us a bonding experience with each other and with both the classic and popular literature of our own culture. It is one of our fondest collective memories, reading together at night as the rain pelted softly on the thatch roof above us.

MK Education

In the early 1960s, our mission treasurer, Fay O. Richardson, once said, "The greatest single problem I face in my job is the education of missionary children." Fay was not talking about mission finances only, but also about the concerns that always surround the values missionaries place on the education of their children. Our family was no exception. We tried a little of everything in the early days. My sense of well-being was highly influenced by how I felt my children were doing in their educational progress. Wanda was the key person who worked hardest to see that our children were educated, whether in or out of the home. Here are some of the things we tried.

The Little Co-op School

Our first MK schooling experience was when Wanda and Marge Geary got together to teach the Gearys' son, Wendell Jr., and our daughter, Cheryl, in their first and second grades respectively. As teachers, they threw themselves into the task, even taking on the alias names of "Mrs. Hill" and "Mrs. Brown" so their children could not whine to "Mom" when things got tough in class. They had to respectfully call their teacher by her formal name. Wanda and Marge created a Native American tepee in the corner of the schoolroom and did as many things as possible to make school an authentic American educational experience. I was the principal of the school if conduct issues arose that seemed beyond the ability of the teacher to manage. Cheryl was sent to the principal's office just once but was so intimidated that she needed no serious disciplining. The thing that was most interesting to me was how much the school influenced the atmosphere of home life, and how time-consuming it was for the women. Their efforts proved worthwhile as "Mrs. Brown" did teach Wendell Jr. to read, and Cheryl's math skills improved under the instruction of "Mrs. Hill."

The next year we had a MAC (Missionary Assistant Corps) teacher, Mr. Wilbert Ratledge, share the burden of teaching the children, this time with Paul Geary and Kevin joining in as kindergartners. This relieved the women of a great responsibility. Wilbert was a fun-loving man who did his best to keep them busy, even getting involved in their building a tree house in the great banyan tree in our front yard.

Bamboo River Academy

It was a great relief when Stan and Nancy Hagberg joined our team as full-time educators for our missionary children in 1968. Their first schoolhouse was our old bamboo house in Sungai Betung. The building was enlarged and improved, with tin replacing the tattered thatch roof. The first students were the children of our own missionaries, later joined by some children from the other surrounding mission agencies. School worked fine for Cheryl who was good at reading, but unbeknownst to all of us, including his teachers, Kevin had severe dyslexia. In that era no one understood why he could not learn something as simple as his ABC's. He was stuck right there for a good part of the year because if he could not say his alphabet, how could he read actual words? When he finally did get to vocabulary, he could not spell or recognize the words. We were all frustrated by his learning handicap because he seemed like a smart kid. In a desperate effort, Wanda cut out footprints and wrote the words on them. She then tacked them up like a walking word trail across our dining room walls. That way they were always visible for review. Poor kid, even at home he was surrounded by words he had difficulty reading. Toward the end of his first grade year he was able to do his math but was still far behind in reading. Wanda finally took over and made some small progress in the area of reading.

The next year we moved into the city of Singkawang and put Cheryl into the boarding school at Sungai Betung. The new school was named Bamboo River Academy. That was an extremely stressful year for our whole family. One thing I did not understand about Wanda, even after we had been married several years, was how important it was for her to keep her children at home during their growing-up years. As a teenager in Chefoo Boarding School located on cool Mount Lushan in China, she had been one of the older girls responsible for putting the younger girls to bed in their dormitories at night. The little ones often clung to her and cried for their parents, sometimes even pretending she was their mom. It made an indelible mark on her that I was slow to understand. In the years before "core beliefs" had been defined, Wanda had a core belief that it was not right for her to be separated from her children, at least not until their high school years. So, placing Cheryl in boarding school went against her deepest heartfelt convictions, and Cheryl herself was not ready for the experience.

During that school year torrential floods between us and the boarding school made the road impassable except by motorcycle, so we could not even bring Cheryl home on weekends. I would occasionally make it over the muddy roads to the boarding school on my trail bike. There Cheryl would pour out her heart about how miserable she was. I held her on my lap, and we would both cry together on some nights. Neither Wanda nor Cheryl ever totally adapted to the separation and in some ways perhaps never totally recovered from it. Wanda's mother had often told us, "The only thing missionaries really suffer from is the separation from their children." We would experience the reality of this statement throughout our whole missionary career. However, that was the only year any of our children was separated from us before they went off to high school.

Homeschooling on Our Own

Wanda made two valiant efforts at homeschooling the children. While Cheryl was in boarding school in Sungai Betung, Wanda taught Kevin at home during the year (mid- 1969 to mid-1970) we lived in the city of Singkawang. Both Wanda and Kevin gave their best in the struggle, but there seemed to be no solution to the problem of his dyslexia. Kevin was willing to learn but just could not do it. They both grew more and more frustrated. I came home one day to find both of them crying. Kevin's sobbing was uncontrollable, and he seemed unable to get his breath. In his efforts to learn to read, he had apparently gone beyond what he could endure. He seemed to be broken, and I myself nearly panicked. I took him in the bathroom and poured dippers of cold water over him and dried and hugged him. His mother wept too, feeling guilty, feeling she had pushed him too far. There was nothing to do but keep doggedly pursuing the task, and neither one of them ever gave up.

Wanda had a reprieve from teaching during our home assignment year of mid-1970 to mid-1971. It was a relief to put the kids in public school at Sunnyside Elementary where brother Marvin was principal. Wanda's second stint of homeschooling came after that furlough year, beginning in mid-1971. This was the year that Simatupang encouraged us to move to the little town of Bengkayang. There we turned the garage into a one-room schoolhouse where all four of the children were taught. Yvonne was prekindergarten but had her own little desk where she colored pictures and joined in the education of the family. I really do not know how Wanda was able to teach the children, manage the kitchen, and care for the large number of Dyak guests who daily came from the villages I had visited to drink tea and talk to me. At the same time, she started a youth group in our large living room, and many of the kids attending junior high and high school came to learn their verses and study the Bible with her. Mrs. Mui Hiong was the one who saved Wanda's sanity. Half Chinese and half Dyak, she was an excellent cook who not only served delicious meals, but also cheerfully served a cup of very sweet tea to everyone who visited us.

Back to Bamboo River Academy

In spite of Wanda's magnificent effort, it was too much stress on the family to teach all four children at home and still be in ministry. Marge Geary, Wanda's close confidant, had a unique suggestion to solve our problem. She suggested that the oldest two children commute the seven miles to the school in Sungai Betung by motorcycle. We happened to have a little blue Honda that was just the right size for an eighth grader to ride and transport her younger brother to school. Wanda continued to teach the two younger children at home. Rain or shine, the kids took off early in the morning on a poorly maintained gravel road. Every morning we waited for the words: "The travelers have arrived," to crackle over the single sideband radio provided by MAF. And in the evening someone faithfully radioed us the message: "The travelers have departed." This rather vague way of communicating was because the radios were provided only for official use, not personal. They came home with stories of huge snakes crossing the road just in front of them and trees falling just behind them. The blessing was that it was a little-traversed road. Just an occasional truck, bus, or Jeep passed our house each day.

To God be the glory for His daily protection of them in travel. For the whole school year of 1972–73 they never had a single accident or even a flat tire on the road. Two handcrafted leather saddlebags slung over the back wheel of the Honda kept their books dry in torrential rain. It was a great relief to have some of the teaching in the hands of professionals. It did not solve Kevin's dyslexia dilemma, however. He nearly drove a short-term MK teacher crazy as he was quite brilliant in logic and yet unable to read. A full chapter could be written about Kevin's struggle to learn to read and spell, but I will summarize by saying that many years later he graduated magna cum laude from Biola University, then earned a doctoral degree at Fuller Seminary.

In June of 1973 we moved back to Sungai Betung to be closer to schooling for our children. Bamboo River Academy had just moved over the mountain to a lovely plot of ground just above the hospital complex in Serukam. For the next several years our kids commuted to school, riding over the curving roads of Mount Pendaring every day. The new campus was beautiful. I referred to Bamboo River Academy, or as it was later named, Bamboo River International School as, "The Oasis." Kalimantan life is messy, but school was different. It seemed to be a little piece of orderly,

American life. It always started and ended on time, had twenty-four-hour electricity, and running water with real flush toilets. The school also presented wonderful musicals from time to time that were very moving to the parents who came to watch. Sue Michaelian was especially good at presenting these programs. Dedicated teachers such as Barb Pio, Beth Yancey, Ivan King, Sue Michaelian, Joyce Sheely, and many others joined the Hagbergs to help each of our children throughout the years. We are forever indebted to those who helped us stay on the mission field, teaching our children and giving them a sample of the orderly life they might expect to find in America in the days ahead.

Faith Academy Days

As Cheryl, our eldest, finished junior high school we had a hard decision to make. Where would she go to high school? Choices were limited. The American International School in Jakarta was prohibitively expensive on a missionary budget. The only other options were the Christian and Missionary Alliance school in Penang, Malaysia, and Faith Academy which is located in the outskirts of Manila, Philippines. The dormitory situation in Penang seemed not what we needed, so we chose Faith Academy. Manila was a very long way from our jungle setting in Kalimantan. Our children had to overnight in Kuching or Kota Kinabalu, Malaysia, on the way, making it a two-day event just to get to the school. Even now it is painful thinking back to what it meant to us to send each of them off to another country for their high school education. Only my preoccupation with the work could keep from my mind the dread of parting with, and living separately from, our children during their formative high school years. Many times, as I walked the trails to villages, my thoughts would be upon them, wishing they were not so far away. Writing this as an old man, I could almost feel it was criminal to part with them at this stage of life! It was even more difficult for Wanda, who knew what it was like to leave her parents and home at age fourteen.

Cheryl entered Faith Academy in 1973 as our first pioneer to leave the family nest; Kevin, four years later; Sonja, three years after that; and Yvonne, another three years later. Our kids studying at Faith Academy spanned a thirteen-year period by the time Yvonne graduated in 1987, and every one of them did complete their senior year at Faith. They always came home for Christmas and summer vacations, so we got to spend some time with them twice a year, time that flew by all too quickly. During the kids' vacation times with us in the jungle, they debriefed thoroughly on what was going on at school. It sometimes seemed we just lived from one vacation to the next.

We tried to make the most of their home holidays, including encouraging them in their areas of interest. They all loved sports, so they spent part of their vacation times with us just staying in shape. The hills around us in Kalimantan were ideal for training for cross-country. As Kevin puffed and perspired, jogging the mountainous terrain, he was often surprised to find Yvonne, seven years younger, puffing along not far behind him. She always had remarkable endurance, and in later years would treat most hills with contempt when it came to competing with other runners. Because of Kevin's interest in wrestling, I made crude barbells for him out of a piece of pipe with cement-filled Blue Band margarine tins on each end so he could practice at home. I even started working out with him.

By the time Kevin, Sonja, and Yvonne got to Faith, there was a new provision made by our mission for us to fly over to Manila once a year for a full week to be with them and to see them perform in some sport they were playing. This helped a great deal and gave us all something to look forward to. Each of them was active in some sport, so it was an exciting time, cheering them on in their sports and meeting their friends. Cheryl excelled in tennis, Kevin in wrestling, Sonja in softball, and Yvonne in cross-country. During her freshman year Yvonne came in first for Faith Academy in cross-country. One especially memorable event for Wanda was watching Kevin compete in the annual interschool wrestling tournament. In his final match for his weight class he pinned his man in just twenty seconds. His response was euphoric. He leaped up in the air off the wrestling mat, spotted his mother in the stands and shouted, "Mom, *we* won!" They had been through so many battles together fighting dyslexia, Kevin felt they were truly a team.

Wanda and I took turns making the annual trips to Manila to be with the kids. We made great memories. Besides watching them in sports there were a lot of picnics, eating out, movies attended, and talk time. God was good to allow us those precious times together. While it was painful for us to part with them, there were great blessings in the children being at boarding school with a large group of peers, and getting a good American school education. There would have been few social, and no sports, experiences for them had they stayed in the jungle for homeschooling.

There were some negative factors that our children faced so far from home. Some dormitory parents bordered on being abusive in their treatment of the young people entrusted to them. However, there were some mentors in the school who were powerful influences on our children. Kevin received great benefit from being mentored by Steve St. Clair. Steve was the wrestling coach and took special interest in Kevin, even taking him camping. Just the two of them would sit at the campfire talking about serious things that had to do with a life totally dedicated to God, that such a life wasn't all roses. All four of our children made lifelong friends at Faith Academy, still corresponding with them to this day.

Chapter 14 – Leaving Our First Island Home

See, I have placed before you an open door that no man can shut.
(Revelation 3:8)

Exciting events were packed into our last days in California at the end of our furlough that ended in mid-1982. Cheryl graduated from Biola University on May 30 and married Craig Morgan on May 31; we departed for Kalimantan the next day, on June 1. It was probably the most hectic three days of our lives. Just a few days later I received my diploma, *en absentia,* a master of theology degree from Fuller School of World Mission in Pasadena. I had been taking courses, a few units at a time, during home assignment years, beginning in 1971. Going back to Kalimantan seemed right, but at the same time I had feelings difficult to explain, even to myself. It is hard to recall exactly when these feelings of restlessness began, or what was the cause of them.

I believe my missiological studies strongly influenced my thinking that a church movement cannot be an enduring one if it is based solely in a jungle setting. Everything I read pointed to the fact that great cities are the power centers of society, and from these centers the villages can be reached. I had once told my friend, Bob Chapman, that I could never leave Kalimantan without feeling guilty for abandoning my call. However, for about seven years, beginning in the late 1970s, I had a certain restlessness that it was time to move on to another phase of ministry in another place. I felt that our mission should branch out to the more-populated island of Java and start city churches there. I knew also that it was time for our Dyak leaders to take full responsibility for their own church. There was also the factor that we now had personnel on the field such as Grey Jeffreys, who, with his administrative gifts, could more than adequately continue to do the field-chairman work he had already been doing. The deepest motive for my desire to move on came from my inner compulsion to take heed to the *golden thread* of knowing, *What is God's will for me at this point in my life?* There would be discontent until I knew and obeyed His perfect will for me.

Since the time of my appointment with the mission, I had been thinking about Java as the most strategic place to minister, primarily because of its enormous population. Now, with this sense of restlessness, Java seemed the most logical place to go. After all, Jakarta with its more than ten million people was the capital of the nation. I knew church planting would be difficult in Java since the Javanese context is so different, and Islam was such a resistant force compared to the animism of Kalimantan. I debated it over and over in my mind, realizing the risk involved in taking on a challenge that would cause me a lot of spiritual stretching at age fifty. I still had mixed feelings about leaving. I felt reasonably experienced in ministry among the Dyak people after working among them for more than twenty years. At one point of wavering I wondered out loud to Wanda, "Don't you think it would be easier if we would just find a new area of unreached Dyak villages and settle in there to minister to them for the rest of our career?" Wanda's answer was a terse question, "Have I ever asked for an easy place to serve the Lord?" That was a good enough answer for me.

Fortified by her resolve, we decided to do a survey trip to Java in January of 1984 to see what might be the potential of our establishing city churches on that densely populated island. At the top of our list was to check on the possibilities of working with the Evangelical Theological Seminary of Indonesia (ETSI) based in Yogyakarta (Yogya). Our most helpful contact in Yogya was Greg Grippentrog, one of the professors who was also involved in the pioneering of this work. One of the first things Greg said was, "Pak Chris has been waiting for you." Dr. Chris Marantika (Pak Chris), who had established this school in 1979, was looking for partners, especially Baptists, who held unswervingly to the inerrancy of the Scriptures. We met with Pak Chris and were immediately welcomed as potential church planters to participate in what the seminary was already doing. ETSI had been established on the premise that every student, in order to graduate, would be required to win fifteen people to Christ and see them baptized and formed into a church body. It was a bold strategy that had been uniquely successful in a 95 percent Muslim context. Pak Chris made us an irresistible offer: "You can work with the seminary students to plant village churches, and you can start your first city church in my house." It seemed to perfectly fit our goals and dreams.

We invited Pak Chris over to Kalimantan to be the keynote speaker at our annual Bethesda Hospital Spiritual Renewal Week in February that same year. Dynamic speaker that he was, he made a great impression on both nationals and missionaries. He made it clear to our missionaries that Wanda and I were invited to teach in the institution he had established. However, there were four major obstacles that still stood in our way. First, our mission had a policy that there must be at least three couples to open a new field. Second, our own missionaries had previously vetoed our request to open a new work in Java back in 1976—would they still feel the same way? Third, Mr. Simatupang, head of our national church association and my good friend, would most likely object to my leaving the Kalimantan field; and fourth, the Indonesian Religion Department did not look kindly on missionaries leaving Kalimantan to move to highly populated Java. Government permission was required for any foreigner to move his residence to another island. But we sensed that God's call was upon us, and we began to pray earnestly about all of these obstacles. The Lord dealt with each of the issues as follows:

(1) Our mission executives in America relaxed the rule, agreeing to let us go as a couple without a whole team accompanying us, to open a new field. This was partly because of our years of experience and partly because we were moving into an established seminary with lots of support personnel.

(2) Contrary to what we expected, our own missionaries appeared quite willing to let us go; in fact, some of those on our evangelism team, whom I thought would object to our move, said, "The Humbles are not nearly as effective here as they were ten years ago. They seem to have lost some of their enthusiasm for the work. They perhaps do need a change." This was not very

flattering, but their words were true. We had lost our zeal for continuing jungle ministry, even though we had many friends among the Dyaks.

(3) As for Mr. Simatupang, I knew he was not likely to accept my departure in order to open a new field if I brought it up as a point for discussion in a joint meeting between church and mission. Though we had been friends and partners in ministry for many years, he was a different person when it came to a formal setting where his authority seemed to be at stake. So I invited him to our house for supper one night where Wanda had a fine meal prepared for us with lots of chicken and vegetables. We ate leisurely and talked long and cordially about many things. Supper was over, and we were headed for the door to say good night when I stopped and turned to him. "Pak Sima," I said, "I believe God is opening the door for us, and that He would have us move on to a new ministry in Java." Without even a slight pause he answered, "Well, you have to do what you have to do." And that was that.

(4) With three potential red lights turned green, we were discouraged to hear that the Indonesian Minister of Religion in Pontianak was not willing to hear of our moving to Java. This word came via our legal representative, Mr. Jan Thin. The Muslim Department of Religion officer had a reputation for being difficult where mission affairs were concerned, though his Protestant subordinate had always helped us where possible. After hearing his decision, I decided to go to the port city of Pontianak to see the Head of the Religion Department personally and hear his opinion for myself. Mr. Simatupang was beside me when we entered his office with some trepidation. The trepidation was on my part. Simatupang never appeared intimidated by government officials and had a confident way of speaking to them. After some preliminaries, he suggested that if I moved to Java and taught in the seminary there, our local church association could send their students over to Java for higher education. In spite of all the ominous warnings, Mr. R. seemed in an exceptionally good mood that day and was impressed with the idea of further education for Dyaks. He approved it on the spot, just assigning us to do the

paperwork of getting a new sponsor in Java. As if that was not enough, he even offered the polite and traditional Indonesian parting apology: "If I have ever done anything to offend you, I ask your forgiveness." I was stunned to hear this kind formality voiced from the man I thought might keep us from making the move we felt was God's will for us. I believe it was prayer and the *golden thread* of the will of God that intervened on our behalf to make him pliable that day. If He has a purpose, none can thwart it.

We were ecstatic regarding the move. I had not been excited like this for decades! Downsizing our belongings and packing up what was left was a major task. My brother, Marvin, and his wife, Ginny, flew over from America and worked for days, building crates for a few large items such as filing cabinets, and packing drums that were then padlocked against thievery. They were expert packers and perspired a lot over our drums and crates to be shipped. We held a yard sale, marking down our belongings to a fraction of their value. Even at giveaway prices, our good friends would sidle up to us and ask if they could perhaps have the motorcycle helmet for half the price it was marked. It is just not Indonesia if you don't bargain for a purchase! I always gave in to them; sometimes I just gave it to them free of charge. In the end we had a parting celebration with our national friends and church leaders. Our August 1984 prayer letter recounts that time:

> On Sunday afternoon, June 24, a lovely service was held to commission us to Java. Over 100 special friends from church and our mission reminisced with us over some nostalgic memories of our earlier years of service in Kalimantan. The traditional "pesta" of delicious and spicy Indonesian food followed the commissioning service... Saying good-bye wasn't easy. The program concluded with slides calling up special memories.

It was wonderful to have family helping us to transport our many boxes and bags by car, plane, and train to a new area. We were escorted to Yogya by Marvin, Ginny, and Rick, their son. Travel to Jakarta was uneventful. However, the train cars from Jakarta to Yogya were jammed because it was toward the end of the Ramadan fasting time when everyone returns to their hometown. The train that usually takes eight to ten hours took fourteen because of its many stops. The heat was stifling in the passenger cars. The cars were not air-conditioned but had ceiling fans to circulate the air. At least they could have had air circulation. In actuality the other passengers were afraid of *masuk angin* (air entering their bodies). We would turn on the fans, only to wake up sweating a few minutes later with the fans turned off. It took us a few "on" and "off" times to understand the situation. As soon as we realized what was happening, we gave up and slept as best we could while perspiring. Arriving in Yogya, exhausted, in the wee hours of the morning, we took taxis to a rented house that just had mattresses on the floor and no furniture. The mattress seemed enough for that night at least. Furniture could come later.

We were looking for a change in ministry after twenty-three years in Kalimantan, and a change we got! I had just turned fifty and was excited to see how God would use us in this new world.

Mom and Dad Humble in early years

Arny and Marvin on the farm

Arny on Joker

Our favorite farm dog, "Chub"

Rose School – the whole student body

Dad buys us new suits

A high school senior in 1952

Rev. Donald Gagnon and family

Wedding Day – December 20, 1956.
Wanda's parents, Eber and Anne Hazelton on left -
Charles and Lois Humble, on right

The happiest day of my life!

My first church in Morrison, Colorado, and some of the men.
From L to R: Bill Coppfer, Pat Scheaffer, myself,
George Holland, and Jim Lemons

First term departure from Tucson 1961

Leaving Tucson for second term 1966

Sailing on the "Lalang" from Singapore to Kalimantan: Wanda,
Cheryl, Robbie, Ricky, Ruthie, and Barbara

First Kalimantan team: Arny, Wanda, Norma Hasse,
June Weiss, Trudy Davis, Barbara and Bob Chapman.
Below: Ricky, Robbie, Kevin, Ruthie, and Cheryl

Our beloved *Pasir Panjang* (Long Sand)

Inside our new bamboo house

Wanda with Cheryl and Kevin
in our first "hospital home" at Sungai Betung

Dyak women are amused
at Wanda's attempt at rice-pounding

Wanda samples the *lemang* (rice cooked in bamboo)
of her favorite vendor

Arny, sharing a
men's communal meal at Tengon

Rev. U.T. Simatupang and family

Yohanes Bujang and family,
my first good Dyak friend

Visiting a village in Bentiang Area

The local shaman at work

Modern head-hunting erupts in ethnic
upheaval against the Chinese – 1967

Baptisms at Bentiang

One on one with Pak Akom

Teaching in the villages

Dr. Wendell Geary on first survey to Babang Area

Lay-leadership training course – Jairani & Yohanes

Dyak children love to play in the water...

Cheryl, Sonja, Kevin & Yvonne,
playing in the river behind our house

Our growing young family

The family is complete now!

Dr. Chris Marantika, founder of
Evangelical Theological Seminary of Indonesia

Traditional Javanese wedding

Wanda teaching her counseling class

Wanda's Counseling Team,
L to R – Yohanes, Daniel, Meri, Nova, Katryn

Graduation Day for two students
who became missionaries, Eny & Hasan

Relief supplies for the Great Tsunami of Indonesia 2004

Approximately 228,000 people died
in this world class disaster

Our last trip to Kalimantan in 2009,
visiting Sejajah Village Church

Wanda with "her girls," Tennille, Breana, and Kristina

Eldest daughter, Cheryl and family: Christy and her husband,
Cody, Camille, Kennie, Cheryl, and Craig

Son, Kevin, with family:
Leilani, Justin, Kevin, Vincent, and Breeana

Sonja and family:
Nicole, Shenna, Joshua, Sonja and Dave

Our youngest, Yvonne, on a return trip to Indonesia

Wanda and me, in our *Afterglow Years*

50th Wedding Anniversary in Venice

PART 4 – JAVA AND OTHER ISLANDS

After having lived in Kalimantan, Java appeared to us a very crowded place. Indeed, it is crowded. More than 200 million people live on this island, which is the size of New York State. That is approximately five times as many people as live on the island of Kalimantan, which is larger than the state of Texas. Side roads and main highways are always bustling with bicycles, cars, trucks, and buses. The trucks and buses belch great clouds of exhaust, which pollute the atmosphere. Three-wheeled trishaws, called *beca,* often cause traffic jams. There are always people to be seen outdoors, on their porches, or squatting in groups beside the road to chat. Men are often seen flying kites with their children. Although the trend for urbanization is increasing, 72 percent of the people of Java still live in rural villages. These villages are often picturesquely located in the middle of wet-rice fields, with high mountains in the background, just like they are portrayed by so many Javanese artists.

The city of Yogyakarta (Yogya) has often been termed "the cultural capital of Java." That would place it at the opposite extreme of practical Dyak life in Kalimantan. Theoretically, Yogya's high culture flows from the historic Sultan's Palace, still standing as a destination for tourists. To this day the Sultan is highly honored, still active, and significantly influential in government and social affairs. Tradition holds that the closer one lives to the palace, the more *halus*, or refined, are one's classical Javanese language and gentle gestures. Javanese cultural dances and shadow-puppet theater portray the lore of Java's ancient culture. These puppet shows often focus on mythical Hindu epics, adapted to Javanese culture and values. The whole cultural scene promotes a polite facade of "preferring one another" with somewhat exaggerated gestures to show respect for others. A slight bowing and pointing with the thumb instead of "shooting" people with one's index finger would be simple examples. It is a self-consciously self-conscious aura that tends to make cultural outsiders feel a bit too self-conscious! No one can deny it is a fine art of self-restraint on the one hand, and a total ignoring of it on the other when it comes to practicing it in daily life. For instance, all politeness becomes theory when cutting into line at the post office or any other queue. Anyone who decides to leave a bit of space between himself and the person in front of him is inviting newcomers to cut into the queue. Drivers behind the wheel of a car, truck, or especially a bus, also leave behind any semblance of the polite concept of preferring others over self. They barrel down the wrong side of the road, coming straight into oncoming traffic, and the largest vehicles always win as the smaller ones give way to them. It took awhile to accept the fact that the superpolite manners concept often does not apply to daily life.

There were some cultural things undeniably beautiful and concrete to be enjoyed. We were awed by the intricate yet massive carvings in some hotels where whole walls and every door consisted of ornate artwork carved into teakwood. Carved statues of all sizes often decorate hotels, stores, and the finer homes.

Chapter 15 – Joining a Dynamic Ministry

I will build my church,
and the gates of hell will not prevail against it.
(Matthew 16:18)

We went to Java to plant churches. Seminary teaching was the platform that gave us the permission to be there. However, because of my perfectionist tendencies, seminary teaching was always the most thought and time-consuming of my tasks. Fortunately in this case the platform was itself one of the tools for church planting. Evangelical Theological Seminary of Indonesia (ETSI) was a dynamic institution. This is unique in the world of missions, because institutions are commonly anything but dynamic, especially theological schools, where the emphasis is usually on head knowledge. This school was different. It had been established in 1979 and was enthusiastically celebrating its fifth year of ministry just as we arrived. It was throbbing with life. Dr. Chris Marantika, the dynamic founder, was the only Indonesian in the country at that time to hold a doctor of theology degree from outside the country. His doctoral studies had certainly not tempered his passion for reaching lost souls. The school had started small, but now had a student body of three hundred. A tall chapel building set in the middle of the campus provided a center of worship, where daily services gave rise to enthusiastic worship. Fifty percent of the student body was from Pentecostal churches; the remainder from scores of evangelical groups. Every professor was from a strong evangelical, but not Pentecostal, school. That combination of Pentecostal passion and evangelical theology seemed the best of two worlds, as each complemented the other.

The thing that most spiritually charged the atmosphere of the school was a requirement that every student win to Christ and baptize at least fifteen converts in order to graduate. There was also a grandiose national plan called 1:1:1, which being interpreted means: "Plant 1: Church, in 1: Village, in 1: Generation." The One

Generation span would end in the year 2015, and the goal was that every village in Indonesia would have a church in it by that time. The plan sounds idealistic, but Indonesian Christians love a wild and outlandish plan. Introducing the practical church planting requirement caused the primary topic of conversation on campus to revolve around whether or not one was becoming a soul winner, not how well one did on one's latest Greek examination. Students left campus on Friday afternoon to spend their weekends witnessing and teaching in the hundreds of villages that surround the city of Yogya. They usually returned on Sunday night to do their laundry and prepare for classes on Monday. Classes were held from Tuesday through Friday. Student dormitories were rented houses within walking distance of the school, providing the opportunity for students to be salt and light to the surrounding neighborhoods, rather than being cloistered together in one large building.

Of the thirty professors, ten were expatriates from various evangelical denominations. It was wonderful fellowship for Wanda and me, relating to the professors from other missions without having to deal with finances and mission business. That was one of the pleasures of the new life in Yogyakarta for us. As foreigners, we were told not to go out evangelizing in the villages but that we could preach and teach in the villages once there were baptized Christians to be taught. Our task was to provide students with material so practical in the classroom that it could be "taken directly to the village" and repeated there. Obviously, this could not always be done, but it did cause me a lot of perspiration in lesson preparation, trying to bring Bible exposition down to the level where new believers could understand it.

It was important to have good language skills when it came to teaching. Fortunately I had always worked hard at speaking the Indonesian language well. However, a rich vocabulary was not something I had developed in Kalimantan, so it was a challenge to pick up new words for teaching. I was humbled a bit one day by some students. In my pride, during Kalimantan days, I had been tempted to think I was one of the best at speaking the Indonesian language. Now, at age fifty in Java, I was the new kid on the block, working among missionaries who had had their formal language training on Java. One day some of the seminary students were joking about the language accents of the various foreign professors at the seminary. They could imitate them perfectly and were having a good laugh over it. They had not mentioned me yet, so I was eager to hear that maybe I was the only expatriate who didn't have a strong foreign accent. I asked them what my accent sounded like. They grinned and said, "Pak Humble, you have a Kalimantan accent." I did not know whether to feel complimented or humbled! The Indonesian language had been my one true hobby all my life. I was always looking for just the right word, always listening to the pronunciation of nationals. Even after being there for thirty-five years, I kept finding that I was not enunciating some words exactly like the nationals were, and I worked at perfecting them. I kept a dictionary beside me and used it every day for the sixteen years I lived in Java. I was still using it the week before I left the field. I felt that I was never done when it came to perfecting language. This obsession with language perfection probably accounts for my too critical attitude toward some of my fellow missionaries during my days in Kalimantan.

Preparation for seventy-five-minute lecture classes became my full-time job, even though I was teaching only a couple of courses. I woke up at 4:30 on the mornings I was to teach, bounding out of bed (a mattress on the floor), with heart pounding, feeling the need to totally master the material. I almost never felt quite ready to teach, and I never got used to the idea of thinking of myself as a *professor*. I was a field worker who had taken graduate studies to become a better missionary, not a teacher in a theological institution.

My first class consisted of more than a hundred students, meeting in the big chapel building. There was a sound system, but there was a lot of echo. When it came time for questions, the students' voices seemed to bounce off the walls, and the tendency of the Javanese was to speak softly or to slur their words. It was embarrassing to keep asking them to repeat the question.

Occasionally wind whistled through the chapel, a relief from the humidity but adding to the difficulty of hearing. It was stronger than usual one day. Strong enough to move some of the furniture. I could not interpret the horrified look in the eyes of the students until the huge whiteboard, balanced on the stage behind me, toppled by the wind and struck me in the back, pinning me to the teaching podium. They immediately ran to the front to lift it off of me. I was able to make a joke about it, to their relief.

The chapel was still under construction. Carpenters did not politely muffle their hammers out of respect for my teaching. The clanging and banging that went on during class time was unbelievably loud and often drowned out parts of what I was saying. It was not the sort of thing you complained about to the administration office! I often went to class feeling I might not have enough material to fill the time, but never once do I recall having to stall at the end of the session, or ad-lib to fill the time. God was always faithful to me, even though I went to every class, offering myself as a burnt offering. To this day I cannot explain it. I only know that class preparation consumed my time, so that I would spend hours on end in my office at home, preparing for a few classes.

It was especially challenging when I was suddenly assigned to teach the book of Revelation. I had avoided teaching it for twenty-five years, thinking other books of the Bible were more helpful to the tribal people I had ministered to in Kalimantan. Now I had to face it. I felt deeply the responsibility of getting things right in teaching this book. The hardest work I ever did was just trying to find out: "What does this passage really mean?" Some teachers and authors had spent decades digging into these mysteries. I was given three weeks to make hundreds of decisions regarding the meaning and structure of the book, and come up with an outline to be filled in by the students. I spent hours and hours just preparing for teaching each chapter. I was such a hermit in my study that I was avoiding my wife completely. One day Wanda came into where I was concentrating and she was not wearing her usual smile; in fact it was a frown. She proclaimed, "I am sick of Java, and I am especially sick of you spending *all* your time in your study, and I want out of here, out of Java." I had never seen her like this. It was the only time in our married life that I could remember her having such a volatile reaction. It felt like I was going through the tribulation for a few moments there! My answer was, "Why don't we take the day off and go up to Kaliurang?" Kaliurang was the cool mountain resort less than fifteen miles just up the road from our house. There we sought the Lord together, humbled ourselves before Him and each other, and renewed our commitment to spend some quality time together. For the remainder of our time in Java, Kaliurang became our retreat when things got too hot in the valley. We would take a devotional book and the Bible and spend two to four hours reading and then praying about every single thing we could think of until we felt "prayed up."

I survived the Revelation class, partially by getting the students involved. I divided up the whole book of Revelation and assigned five students a passage on which to write their term paper. I figured if I had to find the answers to all the content in the book of Revelation, they would have to figure out at least some of them. I seated them on the front row of the big chapel where I was teaching. They were now "experts" on one passage and were in effect my teaching assistants, though I only called on them at the end of the class. The catch was that some of them would occasionally disagree with my answers, thus making it even more challenging than it would have been otherwise.

I discovered that preparation and teaching was not my only responsibility at the Bible College. Professors were required to mentor twelve to fifteen students, attend long faculty meetings, mentor four or five seniors in the writing of their final theses, and preach in chapel a couple of times each semester. Institutions are always time-consuming. There were additional social response-bilities. During our first Christmas season in Yogya, Wanda was asked to train the children of the faculty to put on the Christmas play. Then there was the annual faculty Christmas dinner at our home, meaning fifty or more visitors packed our house. I say all of this to explain why just teaching a couple of classes felt to me like a full-time job.

Usually the big Christmas and Easter preaching occasions fell to the president of the seminary, Pak Chris. My first year at ETSI Pak Chris was ministering in a distant city, and he asked me to preach for him at the special Easter service. This was an honor, given perhaps because I was older than most of the other professors, or maybe because I was new to campus. Just before dawn, students marched from their dormitories to the campus, carrying lighted bamboo torches and singing as they came. It was a very moving procession. The big chapel pulpit was moved outside, and students lined up in their school uniforms to worship under the morning sky. Black clouds gathered ominously overhead. I had five pages of sermon notes before me since I was a bit concerned to be preaching on this special occasion with all the faculty present. Thankfully, it was getting light enough to see my notes when the time came to preach. However, halfway through my sermon it began to sprinkle. Not hard enough to drive the students under cover, just enough to stick all five pages of my notes together. At first I was ready to panic, but God helped and I was able to complete the preaching without the notes. God always came through for me when I was most apprehensive about an assignment. On this day I sighed a deep sigh and thought, *Well, that's over, and I did survive it. Now I can take a break.* Ten minutes later students began their full day of prayer. I was spontaneously assigned to lead a two-hour group-prayer time for thirty students in the chapel. I stood before them bringing up prayer requests and asking them for the same. There was one embarrassing moment when they told me, "We now want to pray for the area of DIY." Hesitatingly, I asked, "Where is DIY?" They had difficulty explaining to me without too much laughter, that DIY was, in English, the Special District of Yogyakarta, the very area in which we all lived, and where I was standing at the moment!

Just before our move to Java, I had lunch with then-president of the Southern Baptist Mission in Indonesia, Ed Sanders. He related how he had recently preached at an all-night prayer meeting. "All night?" I asked, my voice rising. "Yeah," he said, with his southern drawl. "Makes you feel pretty skinny, doesn't it?" Skinny indeed! I found out it was the usual practice in most of the Pentecostal churches of Java to hold at least one all-night prayer meeting per week. At ETSI it was common to have at least one all-day and one all-night prayer meeting each semester, sometimes more often when the need was felt. All-day or all-night prayer meetings did not mean constant prayer, but rather prayer interspersed with praise choruses and preaching. The night sessions usually began at 5:00 p.m. and closed at 5:00 a.m. All benches were removed from the chapel, and plastic mats called *tikar* were laid on the floor so students could sit on them. For me it was a considerably unique assignment to preach at 3:00 a.m. For an introduction I told the students of my all-night driving experience with family when I'd first obtained a driver's license at sixteen years of age. I was so eager to drive that I would ask my dad and brother every half hour if I could drive. As the night wore on, they kept turning me down until it was 3:00 a.m. At that hour they gave me the wheel, and everyone promptly went sound asleep. I was wide-eyed until the sun came up, because I was getting to drive. I warned the students not to go to sleep on me like the family had done! They didn't. In fact, this is one of the blessings of having so many Pentecostals in the student body. They were eager to keep on praying right up through the closing moment of a prayer vigil without looking at their watches. I learned a great deal from them and learned to love to pray with them, getting a second wind every hour or so.

Who Wants to Start from Zero?

From the beginning I realized how dependent our church-planting success was on the Indonesian nationals. I needed a team of good men and women to work with. While Indonesia (unlike neighboring Malaysia) has a generous policy of allowing its Muslim citizens to change religions, proselytizing is against the law. Yogyakarta and the surrounding area was 95 percent nominally Islamic. For white missionaries to be openly evangelizing could mean losing their visas, as well as bringing a negative focus on the seminary. So we were to work at second-level influence, partnering with nationals to reach the lost and plant churches among them.

I was surprised at how many denominations were already at work in Java. Besides mainline churches, and evangelical groups, there were many different varieties of Pentecostals and three varieties of Baptists. Besides all the Protestant groups, the Roman Catholics had some strong institutions and one large church in the city. While it felt good to be making a fresh start, it was daunting to realize that we needed to establish our own identity among so many different kinds of evangelicals. What, after all, is the distinctive character of Conservative Baptists? It took awhile for it to sink in on me that Wanda and I were the pioneers of a new denomination, and we were its only representatives. In acquiring good national partners I got some help from my neighbor, Greg Grippentrog, mentioned earlier. He had considerable influence on students in the seminary and suggested to one promising senior classman that he might consider working with us. Noor Anggraito turned out to be our first viable church planter. Seven other students joined the team under the challenge of: "Who wants to start from zero?"

It would be my task to pioneer the city church, but these seminary students would be village church planters. While I was not an expert on Javanese culture, I had enough village experience to make it comfortable to work with rural types, encouraging them, teaching at their preaching points, baptizing their converts, and seeing the embryo of a national church come into being. Working with a national team provided the greatest joy and continuity of work for the next sixteen years. Most of the student church planters that worked with us moved on to other ministries after graduation or returned to their respective roots. Noor stayed with us, and through his influence, other good men joined us, such as Imanuel Sukardi, and eventually Sumbut Yermianto. During our second year on Java, I invited Andreas Suparman to join the team. He was a Chinese worker I had known in Kalimantan Barat who came to ETSI to do his master's degree. He was good in language and preaching, and scrupulously honest. It is common knowledge that a trusted treasurer in Indonesia is hard to find. It is difficult to describe the comfort of having an honest man in the treasurer's position that he held. He also loved to pray. The best prayer meetings in my life were held at his home at 6:15 a.m. every Monday morning, with just the four of us, including his wife, Hetty, and Wanda. Andreas would later pioneer the PIBI work in the great city of Jakarta.

"Imanuel"–The City Church in Yogyakarta

This is the story most people would probably not want to tell in their memoirs. Or, they might at least put a spin on it to make it sound positive. I include it in my story because it took so much time, energy, and finances. It would not be authentic to leave it out. There are good and generous people involved in the story, but in my thinking a good story ends well. Therefore, in that sense, this is not yet a good story. It starts out well enough, though. Pak Chris was as good as his word. He and his wife, Sara, opened up their large home for us to start the first city church in Java. They invited their neighbors, and I preached the message on Sunday afternoons at four o'clock. Meetings began in August of 1984 after our arrival in June of that year. Seventeen people attended the first meeting. It was extremely hot and humid in their living room, with doors closed and no fan to move the air. We foreigners were the only ones who noticed that, I believe. Pak Chris himself led the meeting, and I preached briefly, simply describing that humans are fallen creatures with a sinful nature, and that God's mercy is available to redeem them.

The Gedong Kuning area where the church was being planted had many retired and active military people in the community, which in those days meant people who were tolerant of all religions. Petrus Maryono, a seminary professor who lived across the street from Pak Chris, alternated with me in preaching some Sundays. Over a short period of time the congregation grew to fifty people. Wanda and Mrs. Dina Maryono started a women's Bible study. Guntar, a senior at ETSI, came alongside to help me, and together we held a men's Wednesday-night Bible study and prayer meeting. A group of people began to believe and evidence new life. One lady, Ibu Joko, stands out above all others. She had been a Catholic, but when she came to faith, she came with all her heart. She had a new radiance and became the most active person in the church, often inviting others to the meeting. Finally fourteen people were ready for baptism. Several of them were in high school, or of that age group. Guntar started a youth meeting that numbered twenty-five young people. Wanda frequently spoke to these groups. We borrowed the building and baptismal tank at the local Baptist church. Pak Chris gave the instructions as to precisely how those to be baptized should conduct themselves. Ritual was important in Yogya, and he wanted it to be done with dignity. It seemed we were off to a good start.

Even moderate Muslims in Indonesia prefer that Indonesian Christians stay low profile. There was a constant feeling that we were stepping on toes even by holding a Christian gathering in their midst. Theoretically there are five equally valid religions in the eyes of the government: Islam, Christianity, Catholicism, Hinduism, and Buddhism. However, when people begin to convert from the majority religion, there is almost always a reaction. At our first Christmas celebration we invited the local government official called the *lurah*. This Muslim official gave words of greeting, making general comments about the value of religion, urging tolerance to all faiths, and wishing us a "Merry Christmas." Most fledgling Christian groups try to get a government official to their first public meeting in order to establish the right to meet in the community. The road in front of Pak Chris's house was blocked off so chairs could be put out into the street. A hundred or so people attended. Loudspeakers were set up so all in the surrounding area could hear. This is a very common thing in Java, because celebrations of any kind are highly valued. Loudspeakers and chairs in the street are normal for every wedding celebration that occurs. However, it was the beginning of the reaction by strict

Muslims in our area. The sound system made it public for the first time that a new Christian congregation was emerging. The little mosque down the street had not yet put up their own sound system. Immediately thereafter they installed four loudspeakers, one of them pointing directly toward our meeting place. From that time on, it blasted the Muslim evening call to prayer into our meeting each Sunday evening, so loudly it was impossible to hear what was being said from the pulpit. They even slightly changed the time of the call of the minaret, presumably so they could get their message to us twice during our meeting time. This was just the beginning.

A military colonel, whose house adjoined Pak Chris's, complained of the loud Christian singing on Sunday evening. A community meeting was held to deal with his complaint. Chris faced the man at the regular community meeting time. He was a wonderful champion of the Christian cause. In a quiet way he asked those in attendance, "As a Christian, am I a stepchild in this land of religious liberty? I hear the loudspeaker from the minaret five times a day, seven days a week, and I do not complain. Can I not enjoy worship in my own house for one hour a week on a Sunday?" His logic was sound and unassailable but tension still ran high, and it seemed our young church might be squashed at this point. However a retired lieutenant living next door to Chris and an attendee at the church spoke up, "I live closer to this group than anyone else here, and I really like the sound of that music." That comment seemed to turn the tide of opinion, and our meetings were allowed to continue. Pak Chris decided not to extend his lease after our first year of holding services in his house, and our meetings had to move across the street to the home of Petrus and Dina. They were wonderful hosts, but the meeting place did not have the spacious and well-lit atmosphere of our former meeting room. Numbers began to dwindle, and honestly I did not know what to do about it. Going door- to-door to reach out to people was not permitted. Getting our own meeting place seemed the most important option, but perhaps it was not. At any rate that is what we attempted.

Wanda and I worked hard to raise special-project monies from our mission and were qualified for a city pact church. After a great deal of searching, we were able to finally purchase land not far from the original meeting place. In order to build a church building in Java, one must get the permission of every single neighbor whose land adjoins the church property. Usually all the neighbors are Muslims. The Christians began to ask permission of the neighbors and clear the land. The neighbors seemed to be in agreement, but it is often the Javanese way not to openly oppose anyone. Before we could begin building, a sign went up on the property that adjoined ours that a mosque would be erected next door. The church received a letter of objection, signed and sealed by nine Muslim groups, including heads of other mosques far outside of our area, warning us not to try to build there. The local government officials, wanting to avoid any religious strife, said it was not wise to build two houses of worship so close together, so building was out of the question. After working so hard to find land in the first place, the church members were devastated but not about to give up. After much searching and prayer, a second piece of land was found. This time, through a fluke in the governmental system, we were granted permission to build a church by the Yogya City Planning Commission. However, the highest official in the county, the *bupati*, who was a strict Muslim, was bypassed in the matter of gaining his permission. We had the strange situation of having legal permission to build a church but no permission to meet in it after it was built. But we were already meeting regularly in it because of our permission to build. Months of conflict and misunderstanding dragged on. After meeting with the *bupati* personally, he said we could meet there but could not put a cross on the building or any sign out front to indicate it was a church. This did not satisfy the local fanatics. They regularly stoned the building and threw firecrackers and "Molotov cocktails" in the form of plastic bags of paint or ink to mar the walls. A bullet hole from a small-caliber rifle decorated one front windowpane.

There were Muslim demonstrations against the church. One Sunday night, when Wanda and I had just left the service, a group of a hundred men descended on the church in a riotous mood, shouting and screaming, "Allahu Akbar!" Our fellow missionaries, Carl and Cindy Reed, were still in the building as Carl had preached there that night. Whether for good or bad, a large group of college-age students from Irian Jaya (now Papua) were in attendance that night. Reportedly they walked into the middle of the crowd of demonstrators and told them, "We eat people like you where we come from." Some of these Irianese men would rather fight than eat. This actually seemed to cool the ardor of the threatening crowd rather than stir them up. They were not used to resistance of any kind from Christians. What was obvious was that God brought along a military colonel who was also in attendance at church that night. He went out and stood before the crowd to chide them for disorderly conduct. The crowd dispersed, because God put His man there at the right time. However, demonstrations and vandalism continued. According to the young pastor, who lived in the building along with his family, it was stoned at least fifty times. On numerous occasions he would call me in the middle of the night to say they were under attack. We prayed with them and offered to pay a hotel bill for them until the rage subsided.

This sort of tension went on for years. Finally, the police and military grew weary of our calls for help and would no longer come when called to put down demonstrations against the presence of the church. Courageous Christians continued to meet in the building anyway, but many potential members were intimidated by this constant threat, so the church did not grow significantly. In the end the government stepped in and said we could no longer meet in the building because: "It was not in the interest of national security." Meetings had to be moved, first to a local hotel, and then a large restaurant. With church members having to leave their own building, morale of the Christians decreased further. The church body did not cease to exist but eventually split into two factions. The reason for the final split was sadder than any outside persecution.

Going back toward the beginning of this story, I should mention that during the church's second year of existence, a young student and his wife returned to the seminary for further studies. Pak Chris recommended Mr. S. to me for the pastor of the church, since I as a foreigner could not continue to be the permanent pastor in this context. Wanda and I met regularly for prayer with Mr. S. and his wife, sharing the burden of planting the church. They became very close to us, and I felt we shared a mutual respect. However, Mr. S. was of a different ethnic group than the local Javanese. His concept of a church was that members should be a mixed lot from all different ethnic groups, not just the local Javanese who composed 99 percent of the population. Eventually, he had a falling out with one of the Javanese men in whose name the church property had been purchased. It was my error to leave the land certificate in the hands of Mr. S. He took the certificate to the bank and somehow bribed an official to remove Mr. G.'s name, and then he put his own name on the church property. When the church members found out about it, a number of them, already unhappy with his leadership, objected. As tension grew, they split off to form their own group. They have taken Pastor S. to court and twice won rulings against him in his claim of title to the land. Just because you win a court case in Indonesia does not mean that anyone takes steps to restore the rights of the party who wins. Mr. S. claims he will take the case to the Supreme Court before he will give up his rights. Both groups still meet in separate quarters, and the property remains in the name of Mr. S.

I have abbreviated a very long story that took place over a fifteen-year period of time. In fact, the story still goes on even today since no one has given in. I learned a hard lesson the hard way, especially as it pertains to keeping people morally accountable on an ongoing basis. I discovered that if I think something is not going well, or that a person is dishonest, I'm probably right and should do what I can to remedy it as early as possible. I had seen little dishonesties in the life of Mr. S. and failed to confront him about them. I grieve over my own failures in this our first city church plant. It is not all negative, however. Many sincere people have been saved and baptized in this group during its existence. Some of the seminary students who ministered alongside Mr. S. and me have gone on to be fine evangelists in other islands of Indonesia. God is the final judge of results of ministry. I exhort myself to say with the Apostle Paul, "I do not even judge myself" (1 Cor. 4:3). It will all be sorted out on Judgment Day, and I must take Paul's position, trusting the Lord to make all things right.

Village Churches in Java

I had come to Java to plant *city* churches. However, the emphasis at ETSI was on church planting in the villages. Since every student at ETSI had to plant a church, village churches were springing up all around the Yogyakarta district. We had the privilege of getting to know and teach some of these new believers. Noor Anggraito had started a work in the village of Sikuwung. While we did not get to be involved in actually leading the people to Christ, we were invited to baptize the first converts and preach to the people after baptism. Sikuwung was approximately an hour from Yogya and close to the city of Magelang. God had led Pak Noor to this area that was ripe for harvest. God's selection of people is amazing. Noor had a friend living in the area who was open to hearing the gospel. After Noor led him to the Lord, they began Bible study classes in his home that soon brought other people to the faith. Finally it seemed time to show the *Jesus Film*, which brought even more people to trust in Christ. The believers of Sikuwung had been nominally Muslims, but the good news of Christ had appealed to them and they received the Word gladly. They were like an oasis in the jungle. All around them were villages of Muslims, but no mosque had yet been built in their village.

The first couple of times I spoke to the believers, they were gathered in a very large room in the home of Pak Bambang. They sang mostly in Javanese, and my message had to be translated into Javanese. With sixty million people speaking Javanese, there seemed little need for using Indonesian in daily life, even if it was the official language of the land. We felt comfortable among them and found it easy to make conversation, since we were used to village life in Kalimantan. They fed us generously, and always sent us home with several pounds of palm sugar harvested from their trees.

Someone has said, "A village is a village is a village." Meaning that though there were significant language and cultural differences between Dyaks and Javanese, village life still held many similarities. In less than a year, thirty-two people took the step of baptism. To those who live in a Muslim culture, this is considered a huge break with the old life and is considered the final step toward "apostasy" from the Islamic faith.

There was a spirit of excitement when I arrived at Sikuwung to perform the first baptisms. We had to go a little ways from the village to find water deep enough, but they knew exactly where there was a small pool with crystal clear water. The floor of the pool was covered with large rocks. It looked as though it was made just for this occasion, with palm trees growing around it, and green rice fields surrounding the periphery. A very small shelter was set up so the women could change their clothes in private. Before baptisms began, I gave a short message on the meaning of baptism and we sang a hymn. Then, one by one, they came into the water to be immersed while a prayer chorus was sung between baptisms, giving time for people to ascend from and descend into the pool. As always, I took the leader, Pak Noor, into the water to help with the baptizing, honoring the one who had led them to Christ. I could sense the joy surging in them as they followed the Christian ritual with solemnity and yet with great spiritual energy. The climax seemed to come with the baptism of Mr. Tumat who was all of five feet tall. When we lifted him up out of the water, he spontaneously began to sing and dance, if you can imagine dancing in the water. His face radiated joy and laughter as his hands patted the surface of the water. He bounced up and down jubilantly while praising the Lord. It was a sublime moment of worship for all of us gathered in a peaceful setting. Everyone in the group gathered round the pool laughed with him. I have baptized hundreds of Indonesians in the pools of Java and the rivers of Kalimantan, but to me Mr. Tumat expressed the epitome of what baptism should be about.

When baptisms were finished, there was another song and prayer. I was soaking wet and had no place to change. It seemed a bit awkward, but in Kalimantan style, I wrapped a large towel around my waist and pulled trousers and underwear from beneath it. Then in similar fashion, I put on clean shorts and trousers, pulling them up under the towel for modesty, before removing it. I was standing in the midst of a group of Javanese men and women to make this change. To me it was an ordinary event, but to Noor, a Javanese national, it was astounding. I did not know how he felt at the time, but several years later Noor said publicly, "I did not know who Pak Humble really was until he did those first baptisms in Sikuwung. When I saw him change all of his clothing while standing in the midst of a bunch of Javanese men and women, I knew he was the right person to minister in the villages of Java."

Sikuwung seemed like the perfect model of how a village church plant should go. However, there was still competition. When Muslims saw that Christian activity was taking place, they hurried to put up a mosque. As stated earlier, sometimes a place of worship is forbidden if another religion gets its building in place first. It was a bit of a race to complete our structure. One member donated a piece of land right beside the road for a building. Village men and women helped in its construction. Wanda and I helped by raising a thousand dollars to complete the construction. A small room was put on the side of the building for a parsonage that would be used by a full-time pastor and his family some years later. The people of Sikuwung became our lasting friends, and we always looked forward to return visits, where we were welcomed with open arms.

Some of our village church planters were successful in winning souls to Christ in a given village. Some struggled along, having to move to other areas when Muslim reaction was so strong it upset the community. The harvest in Javanese villages is ripe, but there are lions waiting to pounce upon people eager to receive Christ as Lord and Savior. We met with our student church planters every month at our own home, serving them a meal with plenty of meat since that was rare in their diet. They gave reports and we prayed together after I had given them words of encouragement. A denomination was being formed. I often ministered in their little preaching points and had opportunity to build relationships with the villagers. When it was time for baptisms, we usually went to a public swimming pool in a small town or rural area. Standing beside the pool, we would sing gospel songs and proclaim the purpose of baptism, which amounted to preaching the gospel to people standing nearby and witnessing the event. Sometimes it was impossible to get a quiet end of the pool for a half-hour service, because children and youth continued noisy splashing and talking. Usually we could get permission from those who managed the pool so we could have a few moments of peace.

Even if it was noisy, it was still a time to witness before others regarding their faith in Christ, in a place where people are ignorant of or antagonistic to the gospel. Other public baptisms took place in rivers and on beaches. Once while performing a baptism in an ocean bay, I was nearly swept into an underground river. There was an undertow that propelled me and the woman I was baptizing toward the underground river mouth. As we "danced" toward this hazard, I kept telling her not to be afraid, trying to remind myself of the same thing. The young pastor on the shore was just removing his trousers to come and help us when we somehow broke free of the pull. They later told me that the undertow pulled people through the tunnel and out to sea as the tide recedes.

We often marveled at the liberty we had for gospel proclamation. At every public baptism I gave a clear presentation of its meaning, including how Jesus died on the cross for the sins of the whole world. We were never once accosted for openly proclaiming God's truth in a public place. I venture that there is not another Muslim-majority country in the world where there is this much religious freedom.

We also had the privilege of proclaiming the gospel at funerals. When one of our church members died, we came as soon as we heard about the death. It was a neighbor of the Marantikas. Mrs. Saria Marantika was already there when we arrived in the morning, holding the widow's hand and speaking tenderly to her.

We learned a great deal about the importance of the burial rite in Java. For one thing, *everyone* in the village shows up and spends several hours together immediately at the time of death. It is a major cultural blunder to miss a funeral. Mortuaries are unnecessary in rural Java. The people themselves take care of the body. The closest family members participate, taking turns in bathing the body for burial. Chairs are lined up inside and outside the house with literally hundreds of people present. People just sit, smoke, and chat for hours while the body is being prepared and condolences are being offered. When it comes time for the official service, the family sits inside, with all of the visitors seated outside the house. I was involved in several of these occasions and was able to clearly present the hope of the resurrection to hundreds of Muslims who were present—this with the use of a loudspeaker. They were respectful, listening without much conversation going on while I spoke. Since there is no embalming done, the body has to be buried in less than twenty-four hours, and even sooner if possible. Often they have to wait for a son or daughter coming from a city several hours away. Unlike America, most people in the community patiently wait until the family member arrives. I must admit that this stretched my comfort zone considerably. Waiting, for me as an American, was one of the hardest things I had to learn in Java. But the privilege of giving comfort to the bereaved, and the opportunity to present the gospel to those who had never heard it made it altogether worthwhile.

Backlash

Opening new preaching points and planting churches is not something well received by the enemies of the cross. There was obviously going to be a reaction on the part of the dark forces to our venturing into their territory. The Muslims of Central Java were generally known for being less fanatical than many other Muslim people groups in Indonesia. Indeed, there were times when they were surprisingly receptive of our presence. In a small village not far from the city of Solo, a Muslim government employee threw a small feast in honor of his teenage son and daughter being baptized. He invited all seventeen people of the little church to attend the occasion. He even intimated that he would become a Christian when he was safely retired from his government job. In the meantime, he feared he might lose the job by changing religions. This openness was the exception to the rule. It seemed to us that Satan attacked in various ways. One of these was a series of incidents that was too obvious to be accidental.

First, there was a series of strange deaths in our Yogyakarta city church mentioned above. In a period of six months we lost three church members through death. Only one of these people was advanced in years. The greatest blow was the death of beautiful Mrs. Joko, who was our most enthusiastic witness in the church. She contracted cancer and was taken within a few months, in spite of putting up a valiant fight. Second, there was the robbery of our home. We had been missing money from our desk drawer for several weeks, so we thought our helpers were perhaps pilfering it. To guard against this, we bought a small safe and placed it in the study. Wanda got up early one morning and called out, "Arny, the safe is gone." Sure enough, they had carried the 125-pound safe away quietly. At the same time, the place where we stored our stateside belongings in Tucson, Arizona, was broken into and several heirlooms were taken. Third, we lost our permission to stay in Indonesia. We were warned that our visas would not be extended, and sure enough we were told we had to leave the country when those visas expired. The work in Java had barely begun, and it seemed we would have to leave a fledgling church in its infancy. Fourth, it seemed that this was the time our children in America most needed our presence with them. Some of our college-age children who had been separated from us since age fourteen felt the vacuum of parental attention and made this plea: "Mom and Dad, if I ever needed you, I need you now." All of this was demoralizing and a ripping of our hearts. How does the missionary decide which is priority in kingdom of God work: planting the church, or attending to the needs of his own lambs? These were agonizing times as we tried to discern clearly, "What is the *golden thread* of God's will for us at this point in life?" The heart pull of the children, along with the above series of incidents, more than once brought us to our knees in a desperate plea for the clear leading of God. Should we pack it up and go back to the States? After talking more with our children, we felt it was God's will to continue the work and persevere through the trials on the field.

Almost every one of our preaching points also endured a backlash of some kind from the surrounding forces. At one time, when we had just eleven preaching points, I recall nine of them being under some kind of pressure to close. In most cases it was a handful of militant Muslims, sometimes neighbors, more often those from a distance away, who demanded that they stop meeting in these house churches. At the least, a neighbor's blaring radio often made it difficult to concentrate in worship. In some locations our meeting places were boarded up and a sign placed on the door that no more meetings would be allowed. This would usually be signed by a Muslim Youth organization, not the local authorities. Sometimes, though, there were ominous threats delivered by the local authorities that a riot would occur if they continued to meet. In one instance, when militants heard that believers were going to leave the village for a baptism event on Sunday morning, they blocked the road and would not let them pass. Javanese villagers were in many cases ready for a change and longing for the freedom Christ offers from fear of the spirits. However, there were always the restraining forces of a dominant religion so mingled with Javanese culture that it was hard to differentiate between the two. We experienced what Indonesian Christians had learned long ago, that the roaring lion will always be nearby, always threatening, always bluffing, always protecting his prey if possible. But the gates of hell did not prevail against the church. New preaching points were established on a regular basis. Starting lots of new churches insured that when some of them failed, others would be thriving. House churches did occasionally have to close, but it was usually because of internal relations among church members themselves, or sin within the group. One advantage of the persecution was that it kept people from becoming Christians in name only.

Spreading to Other Regions

One of the ambitious goals of the seminary in reaching the 1:1:1 goal was to plant fifty-seven satellite seminaries in various centers throughout the island world of Indonesia. From these centers the students would fan out, winning souls and planting churches, following the Yogyakarta model. The graduates of Yogyakarta were instrumental in establishing these new miniseminaries, as they were called. Early in our Java ministry I had baptized two recent graduates who became pioneer professors and administrators in establishing new Bible schools. They were part of our team before being commissioned to pioneer the schools. Imanuel Sukardi began the work in Purwokerto, five hours west of Yogyakarta. There he recruited several students who became PIBI church planters in surrounding villages. He himself began the planting of an urban church in the city limits. Sismardi moved to the southern part of the island of Sumatra where he taught in a new school there. There was some success in village ministry, but unfortunately he was never able to plant a city church. Much later, through the influence of Noor and others, Sumbut Yermianto of Bali was brought into our ministry team. Sumbut eventually established a fine Bible college and seminary in Bali that has proven fruitful in both city and rural areas. We had two students who opened an Unevangelized People Group ministry in Mataram, Lombok. Idrawus and Nasah, who had become close to us during their Yogyakarta seminary years, were sent to Lombok to bring the gospel to a tribe of unreached people.

This spreading to other islands gave us a sense of accomplishing what we had left Kalimantan to do: reach new areas of the scattered island world of Indonesia. One of the ways we could minister to our "professors" scattered abroad was to teach intensive courses in the places they were teaching. This meant five to six hours of teaching per day for the full week. If I had found it challenging to teach seventy-five-minute classes in the beginning, this was seemingly a superhuman task for me! One of the first places we taught intensive courses was in Bali. We had lived in Indonesia for more than twenty-five years and never set foot on the beautiful beaches of Bali. So consumed was I with my teaching task that at the end of the week, I had still not set foot on the beaches of Bali. All my time was spent in cramming for the next day of classes and correcting papers. We made trips to Lombok, Lampung, and Sulawesi to teach there as well, preaching in their churches on the weekends after teaching during the week.

"Building Families, Building Churches"

Before our move to Java, Wanda worried that I had important tasks that would keep me busy but that she would have nothing to do. As it turned out, nothing could have been further from the truth. Pak Chris asked Wanda to work with the women students, but we did not yet know what that meant. What it meant was her spending time with them one-on-one to encourage them. The women students gravitated naturally to Wanda and were soon telling her of their secret pains and struggles. "Mother, I have never told anyone else this story in my whole life," was the way a confidential story often began. And then she would relate a heart-wrenching story of abuse, whether physical, mental or sexual. We had always thought that American family life was more violent than Indonesian, but it was not true. Incredible experiences of freedom began to happen in their lives once the burden of the secret was shared with another and the problem was thoroughly aired. Indonesian students are good at many things, but keeping secrets is not one of them. That is the primary reason they had kept their stories bottled up for years. As word spread that Ibu Wanda knew how to keep a confidence, the students flooded to her office. I often found a line of students outside her door, waiting to make an appointment with her. There were times it seemed necessary for me to get in line if I wanted to talk to my own wife! Wanda's counseling, coupled with her teaching of child psychology, began to open up doors into the surrounding churches. The students liked her teaching with personal illustrations, and they wanted the people of the churches they ministered in to get this practical information as well.

As a result, many surrounding churches, as well as our own PIBI church groups, began inviting her to hold women's conferences. The women got enthused but soon realized that their husbands had to be on the same page if the home was to be blessed. Husbands had to be invited to the conferences, and this required a male facilitator as well as a female to gain their respect. The answer was that we began to team-teach as husband and wife at family conferences. Some of them were held as far away as Jakarta. It was both intimidating and exhilarating to work together in this way. Indonesian parents wanted an older couple who had already raised their children to be their teachers. Many of them did not know what a healthy marriage was. This task seemed to fit into our natural gifting. Probably the strongest thing Wanda and I ever had going for us in life was our own husband-and-wife relationship. The seminary students observed it as Wanda came to seminary with me every day and we sat together in chapel. In the seminary and in the churches we tried to model the "Building Families – Building Churches" theme. Students openly and often told us, "We want a marriage just like yours." Perhaps the highest compliment we ever received in Indonesia came from a fellow Chinese professor, Pak Liu, who told us one day that we had changed the culture of the seminary by the way we treated each other. Undoubtedly it was an exaggeration, for culture is not that easily changed. However, we were most grateful that God would choose to use us in this way.

There were other unexpected and unplanned ways we found that our relationship helped build churches and families. One of Wanda's main tasks was premarital counseling. The seminary was a great place to find a life mate, and many couples were headed for the altar immediately after graduation. As Wanda got close to these couples and won their hearts, they wanted to stay in touch with her. I taught missiology courses and challenged the students to do the primary task of reaching some of the 137 Unreached People Groups of Indonesia. Some of those who approached me and said,

"I want to work with you and your mission," were already being influenced by Wanda in her counseling. Between the two of us, we found that we were attracting quality couples who wanted to be a part of the greatest task in the world: planting churches where there were no churches, and modeling a Christian family while doing it. One such student was Mr. E. H. He had come from a mainline church that practiced infant baptism. Now he asked to be immersed in order to become a member and a worker in the PIBI church. At the end of the school year we celebrated a three-day marathon special event with him. On Saturday we baptized him in a village pool where he had brought forty people to Christ and seen them baptized. On Sunday we married him off to his sweet bride. On Monday he graduated from ETSI. It was tiring but exhilarating, and it formed strong bonds that exist to the present time. Today he heads up a seminary in Central Java, with a focus on reaching an Unreached People Group for Christ.

Ultimately Wanda felt the need for further education in counseling. On our home assignment in 1987 she began a master's degree in marriage and family ministries at Talbot Theological Seminary. It was a tough year for all of us as I was still working on a doctorate in missiology at Fuller Seminary. Wanda's hunger for advanced schooling had been sharpened by being on hold for decades, and she voraciously attacked her courses. Her enjoyment of schooling was a bit daunting to the rest of us, especially Yvonne who was not as enthused about her studies during this freshman year of college as her mother was. Wanda completed the course and graduated from Talbot Seminary in 1991, while it took me another two years to finish the doctoral program at Fuller Seminary. These advanced degrees helped keep us in the country. Indonesia was enforcing immigration laws that limited the number of foreign personnel working in the country during these years. If an expatriate professor held an advanced teaching degree in an area of study that was not held by nationals, that person stood a better chance of getting a visa renewal. Twice the Immigration Department told us we could not renew our visas again. In the first instance they still renewed it when we reapplied. In the second instance they put a bright red stamp of finality on our resident visa, saying when this renewal time is completed there is absolutely no chance for further extension. We knew they meant it this time. Almost all missionaries were suffering a similar fate, and there was a great exodus of missionaries. Most of the Southern Baptists and many others lost their visas during this time. It was sad to see them leave. Some of them had been in the country for more than thirty years.

Humanly speaking, our time was finished in Indonesia. However, we did not feel that the *golden thread* of God's will was prevailing in this matter, so we appealed for earnest prayer from praying people in our home churches. They had been praying for visa extensions for the Humbles for over twenty years, so they were quite practiced in this matter. Instead of accepting the inevitable and returning to America, we went to Singapore and applied for temporary visas to return to Indonesia. We came back on tourist visas and kept a low profile. The seminary went to bat in the Immigration offices of Jakarta, reapplying for a new semipermanent visa for us. Miraculously, our visas came through in a period of six months, and from then on we kept getting one-year visa extensions for the next seven years. This was one of the "little miracles" we felt God did for us year after year, to allow us to complete what He had in mind for us in this beloved nation of Indonesia. It reminded us again that every obstacle must be challenged to find out whether it is the bluff of the Enemy or the reality of God's will.

Chapter 16 – Family Reinforcements

His children will be mighty in the land.
(Psalm 112:2)

"We are coming to visit you in Indonesia." This welcome news came from Kevin and Leilani, our son and daughter-in-law. It was 1991, and we were overjoyed that we would have this three-week opportunity to show them around our island world. Justin, who was just nine months old, would accompany them. We had no idea how God would lead from there. Leilani was a music major who loved ethnic art and music, and God seemed to orchestrate her initial visit to appeal to her gifting. We enjoyed together the cultural dances of the Balinese as we attended a performance put on by a Balinese dance school. A sweet and smiling little Balinese girl came down from the stage to place a flower behind Leilani's ear on that occasion. With her half-Asian look, it seemed a kind of minianointing that fit her future role perfectly. We tasted all the local food, which they both loved. We often drank the iced, fresh coconut milk from straws penetrating the large green nut. Justin and I got our straws in the same nut, and we have a memorable photo of us savoring it together. Everything about their "vacation" with us seemed to go perfectly, especially our sense of compatibility in enjoying the sights and each other.

As we bid them good-bye, we began to have rising hopes that they would actually return to share in the work with us, but it seemed too good to be true. Their final stop as they left Indonesia was in Biak, Papua, where a group of tribal dancers performed a very traditional dance to the beat of primitive drums, right there in the airport. They had uncanny power in their legs and seemed to have built-in coil springs that levered them into the air without effort, as they danced and leaped to the beat of drums. Later Kevin and Leilani told us how both of them unexplainably began to weep as they watched the dancers. There seemed to be a magnet drawing them to this land. Leilani testifies that she felt called, then and there, to this island world. Not long after their return to the States, they let us know that they felt God was leading them to come back and join us in the work. We were ecstatic! They had been successfully pastoring a church in South Hollywood that was revived during the seven years they ministered there. South Hollywood has its share of drug addicts and inner-city problems. Dealing with problem-ridden people was the perfect training for any work that followed. It would be difficult for them ever to say in the future, "I've never seen that before," because they had seen everything! We felt fortunate not only to get to work with our own children, but also to have them come as seasoned workers. They arrived on the field to do language study in Bandung in March of 1994, this time with three children, as Vincent and Breeana had been added to the family by then.

By the time the younger Humbles arrived, the work in Java was needing a fresh infusion of vision and energy. We were planting some new village churches, but it was a matter of adding churches, not multiplying them. If we were willing to hire new church planters, or depend totally on student leadership, we could open new preaching points. However, the churches being planted were not giving birth to new churches. The principle of multiplication was missing. Indonesia is a very fruitful field compared to other Muslim countries, and we were still seeing conversions and baptisms. However, looking down the road, I could not envision paying more church planters to start new churches that could not reproduce themselves.

There was the added problem that while we had come to Java to plant city churches, we had reverted to village church planting as our primary focus. There were some city church-planting efforts, however. Andreas Suparman was commissioned to go to Jakarta to plant churches in the capital city. He recruited several other workers to begin ministries in different parts of this great city of twelve million people. One of these men he recruited was a former student of ours, with whom Wanda had done premarital counseling. The fast pace of life and the intense competition of Jakarta were serious challenges to any advance, but over a period of time five house churches began to emerge. Wanda and I visited the workers every quarter or so to give them encouragement. They all struggled with the same issue: "O Lord, give us a place to meet where we can have peace." All it took was one radical neighbor to report that they did not like the Christians meeting in their neighborhood, and there would be some kind of reaction that resulted in threats and intimidation.

Not satisfied with the lack of multiplication of our young churches, I finally made the difficult decision not to add more paid workers until the present churches began to show signs they could support their own pastors and reach out to new areas. It is hard to predict what might have happened from there on if Kevin and Leilani had not become part of our team. They completed their year of language study in Bandung and joined us in teaching at ETSI in Yogyakarta. Usually there are many problems in orientating new missionaries to the work. However, Kevin and Leilani were both missionary kids, so they were used to life in Asia. Added to this, they both truly loved the church, the Body of Christ, and the Indonesian church in particular. It seemed almost without effort that they became full partners in ministry, and Indonesians loved the idea of father and son working together. One of our fellow professors said, "Just to see you sitting with your son in seminary chapel is, right there, an indescribable blessing to me."

Beyond the blessing of our own personal and family interaction with our children, there was the relationship with the Indonesian national team that Wanda and I had recruited over the past ten years. They were nearly exactly the same age as Kevin and Leilani, and they treated them differently than they treated us. Our children gave them appropriate respect but at the same time adapted to them as peers. They had more fun together than any kingdom team of hard workers should be allowed to have! Team meetings were held to plan and strategize, but there was a great deal of laughter at the meetings as well. Kevin, having grown up with Indonesians, was able to relate better to their humor than I ever could, and they felt more free to joke with him than with me. Wanda and I were the benefactors, getting to enjoy watching and listening to our natural children learn to laugh and labor with those the Lord had called to work in our PIBI church. Our only other fellow workers in Java were Carl and Cindy Reed, missionaries we had worked with in Kalimantan. Carl and Cindy were both mature and dedicated workers who were also extremely compatible. This was probably the most harmonious team I have ever been privileged to work with. Carl was an Old Testament scholar, and Cindy was taking courses in counseling. They loved the fields in which they worked but loved the PIBI church as well.

Few missionaries have the privilege of experiencing their grandchildren grow up in the same city with them. Over the years we had accepted the fact that sacrificing nearness to family just came as part of the missionary package. Now we had the chance to live and work together. We had five good years of sharing the joys and burdens of the ministry with our children before retiring. Leilani calls these the "golden years" in which our hearts were bonded with the work and with our three grandchildren. Breeana was just six weeks old when she was brought to Java by her parents. We were able to share holidays together like normal people, especially Christmas with all of its celebrations. When the monetary crisis hit Indonesia in 1997, the rupiah suffered an all-time record loss in its exchange rate against the dollar. For a couple of years we were quite wealthy people. We gave away much of our income to needy nationals anonymously. We did not want them to know their benefactors so they would not feel indebted to us personally. For the first time in my life I got a sensation of what it would be like to be a rich man and shower gifts on the poor. It was very fulfilling! I confess also that the increase in resources allowed us some special vacations with our kids. We were able to enjoy fine meals and resorts in Bali with them. I can still picture the scene of us soaking in a beautiful swimming pool overlooking the ocean, sharing stories of my growing-up days in Kansas with the three grandchildren as well as some stories that had had great spiritual impact on me as a younger person, such as, *He Took My Whipping*. They were always ardent listeners and kept asking for more! Even at the time, we grasped the reality of, "My cup runneth over..."

As we grew in relationships with the grandchildren, so also Wanda and Leilani built their own mother-in-law, daughter-in-law relationship. Leilani asked Wanda if she would mentor her. Even after years of mentoring other women, Wanda felt some reticence when it came to mentoring her own daughter-in-law. At the same time, she embraced the opportunity. Every Monday morning, an hour before sunrise, Leilani drove over to our house at 5:15 a.m. to do a sharing and prayer time with Wanda. Both of the women had always been early risers, so this early hour fit them perfectly. If I happened to walk through the living room where they were meeting, I often would find one or both of them with tears in their eyes as they shared deeply. Later they both looked back on this as a most precious era of their lives.

We also enjoyed some unique ministry together as a foursome. Wanda and I had been doing family workshops, as mentioned earlier, but now we had partners in ministry who were the same age as our church planters. We did several workshops together, but one in particular stands out. In our mountain resort of Kaliurang, Wanda and I facilitated a workshop on husband-and-wife relationships. Unlike the ordinary workshops of that era, we separated men and women into groups for discussion time. Kevin and Leilani joined the young people for their discussion times, getting them to open up on issues that ordinarily would have been taboo for most of them. Their way of handling family issues was to clam up for a long period of time, and finally explode in anger when the pressure was unbearable. Physical intimacy in marriage was usually off the list for discussion, unless whispered between wives. For perhaps the first time in their lives they were allowed to be transparent about issues that other mentors had never discussed with them. On the way down the mountain from this conference, the nationals expressed their thanks to us for having the chance to talk about "things we never talked about before."

While we were enjoying immensely the new relationship of working with our own children, there was the struggle of dealing with the illness of our last remaining parent, my mother who was in America.

A Tug of War in My Heart

My mother had always been my most loyal supporter and prayer warrior. She had prayed me into foreign missionary service and showed her pride in my efforts to serve God. Now her health was failing fast as she endured surgery for pancreatic cancer. I was able to spend five weeks with her in December of 1994, just sitting with her, watching television, or talking when she wanted to. Marvin and Ginny graciously took her into their house for the last few months of her life and hosted Wanda and me as well when we were in the States. She said to me, "Arny, I know I am going to heaven, but I am not in a hurry to get there. I *love* life. I love my children and my grandchildren, and I am not eager to die." The statement was typical of both her faith and her honesty. After that Christmas time with her, she often spoke to me on the phone saying, "Oh, I know where I'm going, I know where I'm going."

But she had also reached the stage where she longed to be cared for. Never before had she urged me to come home, but this time, as she neared the end of her life, she did. She said, "I feel like a little child who needs to be taken care of. You have been over there long enough. I need you now. I want to die with one son holding one hand and one the other." For the first time in my life, I felt a bit ensnared by the *golden thread* of God's will and the one who had taught me most about following it. What was the true path of obedience? Should I obey God literally in His command to, "Let the dead bury the dead…" (Luke 14:26), or should I "Honor and obey my parents…" (Exodus 20:12)? I chose to try to do both. I was trying desperately to finish up a semester of teaching so I could go home to be beside my dying mother. Wanda also was deeply engrossed in teaching and counseling. Marvin phoned me faithfully every night regarding Mom's condition, warning me that she was failing fast. Often I would talk to her and hear her weak voice on the phone, growing weaker day by day. I reasoned that if I went home just three weeks before the close of the semester, scores of graduating seniors would not have their grades in for graduation day. At the time this seemed like a very serious matter. When I finally was able to complete my course work, Wanda still had a week of work left to do on hers. I did not want to go a week ahead of her and force her to make the long flight home by herself. So I delayed yet another week. I kept hoping Mom would hang on just a bit longer.

When we finally left Indonesia, Mom was still alive, but too weak to talk. The seven-hour flight from Jakarta to Tokyo, and the longer twelve-hour flight from Tokyo to Los Angeles, seemed an eternity. I feared the worst and hoped for the best. When I got to Los Angeles, I phoned Mom, telling her that I loved her and I was coming to see her the next day. She could not speak, but Marvin said she was nodding her head in agreement. There were no through flights from Los Angeles to Tucson that night. We were up for the earliest flight out of LAX the next morning. Marvin met us at the Tucson airport, silent and red-eyed. I knew before he told me the bad news. He helped me put the luggage in the trunk of the car, then turned and hugged me hard, saying, "Arny, she's gone. She couldn't wait." Then he told me how she had spit out all her sleeping medicine the night before, fearing that if she took the medicine, she would never again wake up. She had to surrender to God's calling her to heaven just three hours before I arrived. Life and death are in His hands.

I was not angry at God but was very disappointed in myself. Why would I not sacrifice a few weeks of teaching for the one who had taught me so clearly about the *golden thread*? I cannot begin to discern why God chose to do it this way. Some things I will have to learn about in eternity. Neither Wanda nor I were present for the deaths of any of our parents. There is a sense of loss at not being able to grieve with the family at these passages. I long to meet Mom in heaven and learn together what this whole scenario looks like from an eternal perspective. How will each of us perceive my being absent at this most critical time? Whether these earthly disappointments will even be worthy of consideration with Jesus Himself present, I do not know. I do know that at the seminary where I taught, many students were not financially able to go back to their native islands to visit a dying parent. I tried to empathize but was never able to put myself in their place. After my own experience, my heart was moved for them in a totally different way than before.

God enabled me to preach Mom's funeral message, calling attention to the three C's that she loved the most: her Children, her Church, and her Christ. These were her passions, and she pursued them faithfully to the end. Today I still grieve not being with her those last moments of her earthly life. However, I do not grieve as the world grieves their lost ones. I know I will meet her again.

Relinquishing Field Leadership

With our new family recruits, we began a renewed focus on the great cities of Java. The "10C–2000" Program was instigated, planting ten churches in the great cities of Java by the turn of the century. This required recruiting more capable personnel, paying them higher wages, and providing storefront meeting, or other rented facilities for them. It took considerable flexibility for me to embrace the very idea I had so recently objected to: expending more funds on establishing new groups before we saw reproduction among the earlier groups. However, I reasoned that Kevin and Leilani had come to spend their lives in this land, just as we had. I was not about to dampen their spirits by holding to a principle that did not seem to be taking us down a road to church growth. So I dived into this new program with Kevin. He was the key person to do the "resourcing" (a new word to me at the time) of our city church planters. I often accompanied him as we met with clusters of city church planters to facilitate discussions designed to meet their needs and encourage them in the work. With the exception of one man, I sensed they were accepting Kevin's role as the mission leader. I also sensed that he was as ready to take over the leadership of the mission as I was to let it go. It would not be long before I could surrender the leadership of the mission in Java to him. However, there was one very serious issue that would precede that event.

In 1997 Kevin began to experience extreme fatigue accompanied by fever, cough, headaches, and generalized aches and pains. It became progressively worse until he finally developed "foot drop" which means he could not keep one foot from slapping down each time he took a step, as though there was some kind of paralysis involved. After trying all the local labs and doctors in Yogyakarta, we finally went to the Baptist Hospital in Kediri to consult the American doctor there. The doctor was sure it was a spinal problem with the issue focusing between the fourth and fifth vertebrae. He issued Kevin a medical emergency letter in order to acquire a quick exit-reentry permit from Indonesian Immigration. The seminary staff threw a spontaneous farewell party in his honor, but he had no energy to enjoy it. I will never forget taking him to the airport in a wheelchair, looking emaciated, drawn, and old beyond his thirty-five years. He had determined to finish his seminary classes, and we had foolishly allowed him to do this, thus exacerbating the symptoms that were by now very serious.

It did not take long for the Singapore doctors to diagnose him as being in the advanced stages of typhoid fever. This happened just one month before their scheduled furlough was due, so Leilani and the children soon joined him in the States. Their beloved Calvary Baptist Church of Huntington Beach, California, nurtured him back to health and blessed the family for a year of home assignment. Unfortunately the typhoid would take its toll on Kevin's health in the years ahead, affecting blood pressure, respiration, and kidney function, to mention some of the symptoms. These maladies have seemingly not slowed him down in ministry, just become a continuing force for him to push against, requiring great perseverance over the years.

Just before Kevin and Leilani returned to the field in 1998, David and Sonja (our daughter) Daum, along with two-year-old Joshua, entered Indonesia as missionaries, partnering with Overseas Crusades (Now *One Challenge*). It seemed to us as a dream come true. We felt that God was blessing us far beyond what we ever hoped or prayed for, to have two of our children and their families living on the same island. Although Dave and Sonja lived far away from us geographically in that it was a nine-hour train ride between Bandung and Yogya, it was wonderful to feel they were still our neighbors on the same island. We were able to get together with them on holidays and family vacations. There is a bonding that takes place when grandparents spend time with grandchildren at an early age, and this was a rare pleasure for us. When we finally retired, we would already have a head start on knowing each other from the kids' earliest days. One unplanned vacation came together when there was a threat that Muslim radicals were going to deal severely with any foreigners in the country. We were given a choice of whether to take a brief excursion to Bali (where very few Muslims live) or else leave the country. We opted for Bali and spent a couple of weeks with our kids on the beach, to debrief and enjoy family time until the storm blew over. Such are the mercies of the Lord when things seem to be getting most tense.

When Kevin and Leilani returned to the field in 1998, it seemed the right time to pass the torch of field leadership to them. Because of visa restrictions, they had been the first new missionaries to join our Indonesian team for fifteen years. They loved the whole PIBI church even as I had loved it. Kevin had already taken on so much of the leadership that it seemed natural for him to assume the title of Field Chairman. And so it happened that I was relieved of a field leadership responsibility that I had carried, off and on, for the last thirty-eight years.

Before telling more of the story of our departure from Indonesia, I must mention a life-impacting ministry that began for Wanda and me toward the end of our missionary career.

A Life-Changing Workshop

Someone has asked the penetrating question, "Does anyone ever say anything new to themselves and others after the age of fifty?" The expected answer is "no," but I experienced otherwise. In 1996 Wanda and I were selected to attend a Training the Trainers workshop sponsored by our mission, called *Sharpening Your Interpersonal Skills*. Credit must be given to Ken Williams, former Wycliffe missionary who held a Ph.D. in psychology, for creating the material for this course. Ken also had a history in the Navigators program, so biblical truths were the foundation of the material, not psychology. We were among the first eight people trained to facilitate this workshop. Among the eighteen interpersonal skills taught and practiced were: loving listening, confronting, dealing with conflict, trust, managing grief, drawing people out, problem solving, moral purity, managing stress, debriefing, and several other practical subjects. Our mission meant business in training us for the workshop. The plan was that every one of our more than five hundred career missionaries would take the course. While Wanda and I were two of the first facilitators, many more were trained in the years that followed.

We facilitated our first workshop in Singapore. Missionaries traveled from Pakistan, Jordan, Turkey, and Taiwan to attend. Wanda and I flew to Singapore a couple of days early to master our workshop material in a YWCA room. We divided up the material and spent hours "cramming" in preparation for it. Part of the satisfaction of it was team teaching with my wife. The classes ran six hours per day for four and a half days. After many decades of ministry, it felt like I was for the first time experiencing what "adult education" meant. The material was solidly based on the Scriptures, and the truths came to life as participants wrestled with their own core beliefs. At the peak of the most intense discussion times, it was comparable to the high I used to get when reaching the climax of a sermon I was preaching. It was truth being discovered in community. It was also quite tiring and strenuous work. Those who attended were deeply impacted by the Word of God, worked through in community. I could safely say we received more affirmation from the participants than we ever expected. Some lives were changed on the spot in many of our workshops. In Hong Kong a pastor of a thousand-member church blurted out on the first day, "I hate my daughter." He was truly a man of God who was disappointed in the fact that his daughter was not honoring him. On the last day of the workshop he said, "Last night I stood on a hill overlooking the city of Hong Kong, and I forgave my daughter for the way she had hurt me." Such stories as these encouraged us to continue the workshop in the days ahead.

Over a period of six years we facilitated the workshop in Singapore, Taiwan, the Philippines, Pakistan, Indonesia, Hong Kong, Thailand, and Turkey. During that same time we also translated the materials into Indonesian and held several workshops with our own national church people, as well as for other groups. It was nice to "see the world" while at the same time doing kingdom work, but that was far from the greatest personal benefit I experienced. No other study in later life ever impacted me as much as this one. Much of my previous life experience was examined in the light of the core beliefs of this workshop. For instance, a clearer understanding of "Core Beliefs" helped me see why Wanda was emotionally unable to place her children in boarding school before they reached the ninth grade. For me it had seemed a missionary duty. For her it was going against every part of her fiber as a mother, primarily because of her own personal experiences as a missionary kid. To understand it as her core belief helped me to belatedly empathize with her position. It was not her opinion alone that she was dealing with; it was a belief she held to be true in her deepest core.

I also realized how, as a mission leader, I had not in the past always been faithful to my fellow missionaries in the matter of "speaking the truth in love..." (Eph. 4:15). My tendency was to speak in love, but not be straightforward enough about the truth. It helped me understand why I was once told by a fellow worker, "Yeah, Humble, I know you are a politician." He was half joking, but the words hurt. I thought at the time my brother was seeing me in caricature, that I was actually only being diplomatic, not political! However, after the workshop I understood that there was some substance to the charge. Because I lacked the knowledge of how to confront with the necessary love, courage, and skill required, I was prone to put love over truth. In an effort to save a relationship, I was not helping my brothers and sisters to grow. Perhaps the deeper reason was a fear I might embarrass myself by confronting in anger. Practicing the skills took away much of the fear of not being able to handle most interpersonal issues. Embracing the new core beliefs in the workshop, I gained new confidence in confronting with both truth and love. When an issue arose that required a confrontation, I would say to Wanda, "Let me do this, I need the practice." I should hastily add that I am still practicing and still do not say it is *easy* to confront others. It is just that I am now practicing with a confidence I wish I had had in the earliest days of ministry.

The End of an Era

Having this workshop as a new task made the transition out of the position of Indonesian team leadership easier. Kevin took over as team leader, and I assumed the role of his adviser or consultant when he needed my opinion. Wanda and I began the process of severing our long-term relationships with fellow workers and nationals. Our own missionaries gave us a beautiful filigree silver boat as a parting remembrance. Indonesians love to have a reason to celebrate, even if it is a farewell party. Their kind words of affirmation were as meaningful to us as the expensive boat from the expatriates. Our April 1999 newsletter titled, "Parting Partying" describes the atmosphere and some of the events that took place:

We are nearly through the denial stage. Reality slowly burns through the fog. After thirty-eight years of ministry in our beloved (and often frustrating) Indonesia we are being sent off with gifts, banquets, and altogether too many kind words. The sage words of Dr. Vernon Grounds from our seminary days long ago come back to me: "Compliments are like perfume, to be enjoyed, but not taken." Instead of tearful good-byes we have enjoyed "celebrations" with national church leaders in Jakarta, Yogyakarta, and Bali, giving thanks for almost four decades in this land. In addition, our counseling team took us to the beach for a day just to bask in each other's fellowship. Missionaries from other missions have also gathered to celebrate our history here. Last week the

Seminary devoted a full evening to recalling memories with us, then fervently commissioned us to our new role in CBI, lessening the pain of parting by thrusting us forth into a new work for God...

THE LORD IS GOOD AND HAS BEEN SO VERY GOOD TO US. There is every indication that our nationals and missionaries believe we have "finished well" this phase of our lives. From our own perspective we view the embroidery from underneath and it looks pretty imperfect. We wish we could have won more souls, healed more relationships, and planted more viable churches, but God is our judge, and with the Apostle Paul we refuse to judge even ourselves. Of the too many good things said, one church planter summarized how we would like to have been remembered: "They attempted to salvage every broken relationship in the whole denomination." It is not true, but he stated precisely the desire of our hearts. "Blessed are the peacemakers."

In the end we experienced nine different parting celebrations with our dear friends. Leilani managed to have a wonderful book of photos and letters put together for us to keep as a tangible memory. We felt truly spoiled, and somehow the more adulation we received, the smaller we felt. We had been discipling Indonesian leaders and establishing a new church association on Java for sixteen years. Some of the leaders felt keenly the sense of loss at our leaving. They often gave contradictory comments during their prayers of blessing for us. One young pastor prayed, "Lord, now we are no longer children. We are finally mature, and we are prepared to face the future without our mentors." Another prayed, "Lord, we are still children, and feel we still need guidance from our leaders." Such prayers often brought tears to our eyes. All of them blessed us as we moved into another phase of ministry. This was a satisfaction beyond description. At the same time, we assured them that this was not good-bye forever. We had already made plans to return to Indonesia for ministry just five months into the future.

By the time we left Java we had forty-one churches in our denomination, many of them city congregations due to the renewed emphasis on urban church planting. There were many larger denominations around us with far larger churches, but we felt privileged to have experienced the hand of God in gaining a beachhead for this national church. Still there seemed so much ground to be covered, so many souls yet to be reached. But we had this one blessing, that the church and the mission would go on without us. There is a well-known adage that states: "Success with no successor is no success." I had always found it difficult to think of myself as being truly "successful." But if the opposite of the adage is also true, I was finishing in Java with success. About the same time Kevin took his new position as field team leader, Dr. Chris Marantika was elected as the president of the PIBI national church association. He actually wanted the position, and told us so. He and Kevin had always gotten along famously, so I was leaving the work of the church in the hands of two capable and compatible leaders. I felt doubly blessed that God would honor me with a son to take my place, and an internationally known leader to assume responsibility for the national church we had pioneered. All praise be to God, I certainly did not feel I deserved this honor from His hand. His grace abounds.

I Saw China!

We had a wonderful event planned to ease the pain of leaving our lifetime of service in Indonesia in May of 1999. We were excited about a planned trip through China. Several times in the past we had made elaborate plans to visit China, only to be disappointed because of some unforeseen circumstance. Once Wanda had a whole China itinerary planned out, only to learn that we could not procure our exit-reentry permit from Indonesian Immigration in time to go. Another time she had it all planned was in 1989, exactly when the Tiananmen Square massacre occurred and no Americans were allowed to enter the country. After two major disappointments Wanda abandoned all hope of ever seeing her birthplace. I refused to give up her dream, so I planned this trip, hoping all would go well. However, in 1999, as we neared our departure date, we learned that the United States had accidentally bombed the Chinese consulate building in Belgrade, and the political tension between America and China was very high. Americans were currently not viewed positively because of this error. We were solemnly warned by our State Department it was not a good time to go into China. We could not resist going, in spite of the warning. Anticipating the rigors of travel, Wanda and I worked out at a fitness center and lost several pounds each as we tried to get into condition for this eighteen-day trip. This time, not only did we get to make the trip, we also got to do it accompanied by Kevin, Leilani, Justin, Vincent, and Breeana. They met us in a Beijing hotel, very excited and eager to see the sights. That very first night they arrived in Beijing, we saw a spectacular presentation of a Chinese opera that included all the drama and acrobatics for which they are famous.

After hearing stories about China from Wanda for more than forty years, I finally got to see some parts of it for myself, together with my children and grandchildren: the Chinese opera, the Great Wall, the panda bears, the Terracotta Warriors, the Bund in Shanghai, a five-star cruise down the Yangtze River—all the famous tourist attractions. But for me, and the rest of the family, our greatest enjoyment came from having Wanda show us around Kuling on Mount Lushan, where she attended boarding school during her high school years. We saw the boarding school and the dormitory room where she had slept. The old stone buildings were still remarkably strong, and it was in the process of being turned into a hotel. We visited the "Three Graces Waterfall," one of her favorite places during high school days. We were there on her birthday, and the family managed to find a birthday cake. I wrote her a birthday poem in honor of the occasion. The grandchildren came marching into our hotel room early in the morning, bearing her cake with lighted candles and Justin tooting on a toy trumpet, to start the day off right. Even the noise of numerous and extremely boisterous Chinese tourists could not dampen our spirits. The China trip was a fitting exodus to our nearly forty years of missionary service. We have since referred to this China venture as "The trip of a lifetime." It was the perfect transition for us, somehow easing us out of a career of church planting into the next phase of our lives.

PART 5 – TO "FINISH WELL"

When the firewood has been consumed, there remains a brief time while the coals are still hot, their redness providing the dim light of an afterglow. Though we had spent the best years of our lives in Indonesia, we still had a burning desire to "finish well." Agewise, it was time to retire. We had our formal retirement ceremony from CB International in June of 2000 in Denver. "Retire" seemed like a dark word to us. We shied away from it, substituting instead the word "retread." We borrowed this word from an old World War II ditty. Raw rubber was a precious item in those days, and new tires were nearly impossible to buy. Americans were being urged to retread their tires rather than replacing them. The song ended with the drawn-out refrain, "Don't re-tire, just re-tread."

Chapter 17 – Member Care

That they may be encouraged in heart and united in love.
(Colossians 2:2)

We felt most fortunate that we did not have to leave the world of foreign missions at retirement age. We had an offer to continue ministry with CB International (soon to become WorldVenture International), our mission board, in the Member Care Department. We did have to change our base of operations back to America. We were eager to see how God would direct our lives in the future.

We settled in beautiful Denver, Colorado, to continue our postfield ministry. In a sense it was coming full circle for us, since this is where we had spent our first three happy years of marriage. The view of the snowcapped Rocky Mountains was a daily lifting of our spirits. WorldVenture was in the process of building a new facility in Littleton, Colorado. We bought a townhouse near WorldVenture's new building site in order to stay in close contact with our mission team. Real estate in Denver was at an all- time high. We settled for the townhouse after searching for only one day. We had looked at nine pieces of real estate that day, and by the end of the day the place we liked best had been snapped up by another buyer. It was clear that there would be no chance to deliberate on a property before buying it. The place we settled on had no view, no lawn, and no appeal to the eye. It was a center apartment with an asphalt backyard and our neighbor's front door facing our front door less than fifteen feet away. Its only attractions were being almost new, clean, available, and very nice inside. It was at Wanda's urging that we bought the place. She was so eager to get settled and get on with ministry that its resale value was not a factor to her, and it was my desire to make her happy. The core beliefs of the Sharpening Your Interpersonal Skills Workshop were working in my life more and more each day. The opportunity to share this material with others was an exciting venture. Our major job assignment was to facilitate this workshop in various countries of the world. But we also had a dual commitment to keep returning to Indonesia for continuing ministry.

We were back in Indonesia for a three-month visit, five months after our May 1999 departure. Kevin and Leilani had created a cozy, one-room apartment adjoining their house in Yogyakarta. We were able to pick up where we left off in many ways, but without the stress of preparing seminary lectures and dealing with field administrative issues. We had plenty of one-on-one time with Wanda's former counseling team members who were maturing in their faith and skill. An added joy was the opportunity to stay in touch with our three grandchildren, Justin, Vincent, and Breeana.

During our earlier years in Yogyakarta our lives had been overwhelmingly filled with teaching classes during the week and preaching in the churches on the weekends. Now we returned to Indonesia with a less intensive schedule. Our ministry included visiting our Unreached People Group workers on Sumatra, Bali, and Lombok. Our national missionaries loved to have us come just to see and hear about their struggles in ministry. We also facilitated the SYIS workshop in Indonesian in a couple of different places.

Schooling for our grandchildren became a problem in Yogyakarta. Tuition was high, Christian students were few, and a New Age aura seemed to surround the Yogya International school. A large international school in Salatiga, an hour and a half away from the seminary in Yogyakarta seemed the answer. It had been founded by Christians and was run by Christians. Kevin and Leilani decided to move the family near the school and commute back to Yogya to teach their seminary classes. A plus in this move was the much cooler climate in this high-altitude city of Salatiga. The rhythmic clatter of horse hooves on the paved streets of Salatiga caught their attention immediately. Horse carts loaded to overflowing carried passengers and market supplies to shop owners. Kevin's family began to develop an interest in horses and horseback riding. My having had a pony in my youth and my love of horses led them to believe I knew something about them. In 2003 I got to help Breeana pick out her first horse. It was my privilege to try out several horses for her. One was a high-strung young paint pony that wanted to do nothing but run. She pulled at the bit and pranced every step. Not wanting to disappoint her, I finally turned her loose on the far end of a paved backstreet of the city. I flew by the owner and his friends as jaws dropped to see this gray-haired old man pounding down the street full speed on a spirited pony. Without a saddle to hang onto and just a handful of mane, I was wondering if I could get her stopped before we reached the main street. Fortunately I did, but they did not buy that one. We finally settled on another, gentler little mare for Breeana. Trying out so many horses and getting the kids started in riding was such an event in family life that 2003 was dubbed as "Year of the Horse!" We had no idea what was in store for the little Javanese Muslim man who boarded the horses for them. He was destined to play a key role in bringing scores of people to Christ. He later became a true disciple of *Isa* (Jesus) and passionately testified to others, influencing them too to come to Christ.

Our trips back to Indonesia were interspersed with travel to China and other nations with limited access to the gospel. The purpose was to visit and bring encouragement to workers who were living in isolated or discouraging places. This included the nations of Mongolia and Kazakhstan. Our mission spun off a sister and nonprofit organization which was the sponsor of our travel in these limited access nations. Our stated goal was to: "Hang out with those who are working in some of the most discouraging places of the world." Our theme verse was: "That they may be encouraged in heart and united in love." (Col. 2:2). Wanda's roots in China and our long-term experience as missionaries gave us a certain amount of credibility in the world's most populous nation. Ours was a "listening ministry" more than any other single thing. We had learned that it was not very helpful to come to field missionaries with pat answers. They needed someone who would hear their hearts, and who are not poised to pounce on them with the perfect solution to the issues they are facing. On one occasion we spent seven hours in just one day listening to a missionary, helping him resolve a deep personal issue. This worker has remained a most effective evangelist as well as becoming a very close personal friend. Even to this day I still consult with him from time to time. Another was a single lady who sincerely wanted to be married. We had always had the highest respect for single women on our field, and it was our privilege to spend hours with her, listening to her heart.

Not all of our time was spent in traveling. One of the reasons we settled back in the United States was to spend time with our family in America. We were able to visit with Yvonne in her beautiful and tiny Long Beach, California, apartment. It felt good to experience getting to know our homeside kids better. We had a tendency to feel almost guilty, as though we had been neglecting them by living overseas all these years. We made many nine-hundred-mile trips from Denver to the Phoenix area to visit the family of our eldest daughter, Cheryl. They in turn came to Colorado for a memorable vacation with us near the Rocky Mountains. It was wonderful to have this Arizona family—Craig, Cheryl and their three children, Chrystie, Kennie, and Camille—with us for a Colorado vacation time. To us it seemed we were finally investing some "member care" time in our own children and grandchildren, rather than giving it all to people on other continents.

When Dave and Sonja came home from Indonesia with their three children, they spent three weeks with us while they were looking for a house to buy in Colorado Springs. When they did purchase a home it was on the north side of the city, so we were only an hour's drive from them. This gave us many opportunities to get together, even getting a chance to watch the grandchildren in some of their sports activities. On one occasion Joshua and I hiked to the top of the little mountain called "Castle Rock," between Littleton and Colorado Springs. It is a short but very sheer climb, so we had to scramble our way up, gripping tree roots as we climbed up the rock face. The view from the top was spectacular. He was a precocious five-year-old, still unable to pronounce his "r's." But he threw out his little chest and marched around the top of the great rock, observing the view, and repeating proudly, "It was definitely woth the effoht." Living so close to them allowed an intimate bonding that holds fast to this day, even though they have redeployed to the Island of Cyprus at this writing.

An annual family event that everyone looked forward to was Christmas at Huachuca Oaks Baptist Camp, near Sierra Vista, Arizona. Two Christmases we had all four of our children there with all nine grandchildren. The "motel rooms" were rustic enough, but the large dining hall was all ours and there was plenty of room for being active, both outside and inside. The whole family loves challenging physical activity, so outdoor games like "Ultimate Frisbee" and touch football were popular, as well as hikes to a nearby cave. Creative juices flowed as the grandchildren put on impromptu Christmas dramas, acting out the birth of Christ. Then there were the very serious and intimate "debriefing sessions" which some of them looked forward to more than others. Each of us took our turn sitting at one end of a long table and opening our heart about our deepest struggles over the past year. There was plenty of laughter, but sometimes tears were mixed in, and empathy overflowed as we shared each other's pain. Today everyone remembers the Huachuca Oaks Camp experiences as times we will never be able to repeat again, but precious because God gave them to us as a family.

The most memorable Christmas at the camp was "The Year of the Bobcat." We had a particularly large family group at the camp in 2001 since Marvin's whole extended family joined us, including his oldest son, Jimmy, with his wife, Cindy, and their three daughters, Caley, Kaitlyn, and Kelsey. It was toward sunset and getting cold when I heard Yvonne shriek. I ran over to the motel front porch where she was comforting the dog, Montana, after she had been attacked by a bobcat. The cat had locked its jaws just over Montana's eyes when Yvonne jumped into the fray and bravely kicked it loose with the toe of her motorcycle boot. Under a bench on the porch, the critter was visible, a curled-up ball of grey and black fur. When I saw it I stepped back several paces, but obviously not far enough. I had just warned Yvonne, "Get back," when the bunch of fur decided to move. The cat came hopping out with strange, uneven movements. I thought it would pass me by, but instead it headed straight for me. When it was making its leap to attack, I kicked out with my right foot to ward it off. The cat dodged the kick and then used my foot to lever himself up and lock his teeth on the upper part of my left thigh, uncomfortably near the groin. There he hung, chewing ever deeper through my jeans and raking my lower leg with his claws. It felt both painful and surreal. I looked down at this rather small cat, maybe twenty-two pounds in weight, thinking, *What does one do with a bobcat hanging on his leg?* Without a weapon of any kind, I opted to throw my full weight on top of him. I slammed myself to the ground with him under me. He must have felt smothered as this did discourage him. He let go temporarily, only to come around and try to jump on my back. At that point Yvonne came screaming at him and aiming kicks at his head. Seeing the unfair odds of two against one, he disappeared around the corner of the motel. Later I told Yvonne that I almost ran around the corner myself when I heard her Comanche yell!

Later that same evening the cat attacked my nephew, Jim, who is a well-built man of one hundred and eighty pounds. Jim got his ire up and decided to strangle the creature. He got the cat down on his back twice with thumbs pressed firmly into his throat, but the cat wriggled free without effort and attacked Jim from behind. The cat finally left him, unhurriedly, looking back and yowling a few times. Later, Jim's daughters counted sixty-six claw and twelve teeth marks on their dad. The bobcat was not finished with his vicious ways. Later that night he attacked a nearby rancher's dog, and the rancher shot him.

Three government service agencies showed up to inquire about the bobcat attack. One of them asked if we had done something to irritate the cat, since it is not their usual nature to be aggressive toward humans. The dead cat's body was taken to a laboratory in Tucson where it was found to be extremely rabid, and we were warned to get rabies shots immediately. So, on Christmas Eve, four of us were at the little Sierra Vista hospital getting our first of five shots. Kevin was included in the company because he had carefully examined the teeth of the dead cat. Earlier we had been told by a very relaxed doctor that there had not been a case of rabies in these parts for over thirty years and there was probably nothing to worry about. "However," he said, "if you do get rabies it is a hundred percent sure you will die!" We knew it was the Lord's intervention that allowed the cat to be shot and inspected so we could know the truth. The next day we had our names on the first page of section B of the Arizona Daily Star, with a headline that read: "Rabid Bobcat Bites Two Men." I thought it ironic that I had crossed the ocean several times, lived through ethnic uprisings, been in the proximity of one war, and never had my name in the local paper. It took getting bitten by a small cat for that notoriety to happen.

These family times in America were interspersed with trips back to Indonesia and other countries where we ministered, making life quite full. We were back in Indonesia every year except one, from the time we retired in 2000 until 2009.

Part of the joy of being "retreaded" was having time to spend searching the Bible. Since age seventeen I have been obsessed with knowing and following the will of God, no matter what I myself desire personally. It was the *golden thread* originating with my mother and was what started me into a life of missionary service. I believe it has cost me severely in some family matters, but I have known no other way to live. This passion to know and follow God's perfect will did not subside when I left the mission field. One day during my quiet time I rediscovered John 14:21: "He who has my commandments and obeys them, it is he who loves Me. And he who loves Me will be loved by My Father, and I will love him *and manifest Myself to him*" (Italics mine). Over the years my heart had always resonated with the Apostle Paul's passionate statement: "That I may know Him, and the power of His resurrection, and the fellowship of His sufferings..." (Phil. 3:10). Paul obviously knew Christ well, but was hungry to know Him better. I determined to go on a search to discover the words of Christ in this matter. I spent several weeks reading through the New Testament, copying by hand every single commandment given by Jesus. I am not sure quite what I was expecting, but the desire to have Him manifested to me was and is still very strong. It would be wonderful if I could say that through this study I found the key to seeing the face of God in some wonderful and spiritual manifestation. Such is not the case. It only renewed my original passion in my old age. My desire is still "to know Him" in deeper ways than ever before. This is an ongoing spiritual journey for me, hopefully to the end of life. I would need His presence in a special way in the near future. I was soon to be alone in a different way than I could have ever anticipated.

Chapter 18 – Losing My Life Partner

I have fought the good fight. I have finished the course.
I have kept the faith.
(2 Timothy 4:7)

Actually, I did not lose my Wanda all at once. I lost her gradually. I believe it began on the early morning train ride from a London hotel to Heathrow Airport. It was in the spring of 2003. Wanda and I had just completed a one-day workshop for missionaries in this great city, and she was very fatigued. As we rode along she was suddenly overcome with nausea so severe that she said she would just like to die right then and there. When we arrived at the airport she emptied out her stomach, then sat there dazed, resting her head in her hands until time to board. During the long flight home she was exhausted to the point of despair, saying nothing. Back in Colorado the tiredness continued, and she appeared disoriented beyond the effect of ordinary jet lag. We were due to depart immediately for the Conservative Baptist Annual Meetings in Spokane, Washington, but Wanda was so tired that she was unable to pack. This was new to me. For the first time in her life, I packed for the ultimate packer.

When we prayed that night, before the departure next morning, she closed her prayer with, "And Lord, help Arny to stamp out his notebook." When I asked her the meaning of these words she said, "Oh, I think they just came out of my dream world." I was concerned, but did not think too much about it. For two days while driving to Spokane she said almost nothing, and what she did say often came out of that dream world, not quite making sense. In retrospect, I am astonished that after decades of transparent communication between us I could not bring myself to say, "Honey, what is wrong? What is going on with you?" I had a horrible sense of foreboding and was honestly afraid to ask. Finally, out of desperation, I called our health insurance company. I was ordered, "Go to ER immediately." In Coeur d'Alene, Idaho,

Wanda had her first MRI. A solemn doctor of neurology took me aside to give me the results: "Your wife has suffered a small, severe infarct in the right internal capsule of her brain. The effect of it is similar to being hit in the head with a two-by-four. What she has lost will never be able to be regained." I tried to comprehend the gravity of his words. He then instructed me not to start taking over everything from her, but to let her do what she could in the future as far as her regular tasks were concerned. I was devastated.

It was the beginning of incalculable loss in my life. Since finding Wanda was the best thing that ever happened to me (apart from my salvation), then losing part of her seemed to be the worst thing that ever happened to me. Over the years I had frequently boasted, at least to myself, that I had the best partner in the world. Now I felt that the good life was over. Anyone who had not known Wanda previously, before her stroke, said she was a very sweet and smiling person. In fact she still was. What she lost, however, was so profound that in many ways she was no longer the same person. Curiously, the stroke left no visible physical effect apart from some loss of balance and a heavier gait in walking. It was all higher cognitive loss, which seriously affected her judgment. Depth of feeling was also greatly reduced. When she would occasionally say, "I love you," I sensed that those words had lost most of their weight. Gone was the woman who got up very early in the morning, bouncing with energy to take on the world. Instead, from that time on she was perpetually tired, needing a couple of naps in the daytime, besides eleven hours in bed at night. Gone also was her gravitational pull toward the hurting people of the world, and the magnet that attracted them to her. Gone was the ministry passion to serve the Lord through her love and spiritual gifts.

A week after the ministroke, most of our children were present with her to celebrate her seventieth birthday in Huntington Beach, California. They were determined to make it a grand occasion. Leilani had written a catchy song for the daughters to sing. The song epitomized Wanda's formerly dynamic lifestyle. It ended with the refrain: "You're Livin' It, You're Givin' It All You've Got." A few weeks earlier that line would have been perfect. Now it seemed to the ones singing that it was a mockery. There was other poetry and fun presentations in her honor that night, but she was unable to focus or to engage emotionally in the festivities. Ordinarily she would have been laughing and crying alternately as her children poured out their love to her. Now she focused her attention on two-year-old Shenna, while everyone around her was trying hard to celebrate her life. It was a traumatic experience for the whole family to see her like this. This was the mom who was always Supermom, never daunted by any challenge, always rising to every opportunity to celebrate *anything*, always the optimist. Now she seemed to be living partly in another world. Several weeks later I asked her if she felt no emotion. She simply said she did not dare let go of her emotions, fearing it would be too much for her.

At first my life seemed totally shattered. There are not many men in the world whose life and ministry are as tied up with their wives' as mine was with Wanda. So rich was her personhood, I felt that from the beginning of our life together that I had overmatched myself. Early in our marriage I had often prayed, "Lord, don't let me hold this gifted woman back in any way." Now, she was stricken, and I felt I was left with a different partner. This was bereavement just short of death for me.

After the first of the shock wore off, I began to stop feeling sorry for myself. I gradually realized how very fortunate I was. First, I had received immeasurable help and support from a giving and godly woman for forty-seven years of marriage. It dawned on me that if I spent the rest of my life giving her my best care, I would never live long enough to repay the debt of gratitude I owed her. Second, it dawned on me that in every loving relationship, usually one partner fails in health before the other does. We hoped it would be different for us, and often spoke of how wonderful it would be for us to go to heaven together instead of dying separately. We even joked about the serious, suggesting that a timely plane crash, for instance, might allow us to go together. But in the end there are usually only two roles to be played: that of the patient, and that of the caretaker. I began to see how privileged I was to be the one to take care of her. I pictured what my life would be like if I was on the receiving end of terminal care, not the giving. Jesus clearly had it right when He said, "It is more blessed to give than to receive." She was not in pain, just tired and wanting to be totally retired. She was also totally functional when it came to caring for herself, and rarely said strange or embarrassing things in public. It would be my pleasure to serve her for the rest of her days.

At first it was hard for her to see me start working in her kitchen. "You are just taking over my kitchen," she said more than once, with considerable irritation. I tried to give it back to her, but when she attempted to do the cooking, the sequential aspect of a recipe was too much effort for her. It took a couple of years, but eventually, she was happy to be the helper and let me be the chef. I loved to cook for her and even managed to find that I had some sort of a latent gift for being a reasonably good cook. She was always pleased with what I created, perhaps because her taste buds had never fully recovered from eating boarding school food in China. Also, while she excelled in all other areas, gourmet cooking had never been one of them. Even my own daughters commented on this previously undiscovered culinary gift of mine. Every morning I got up early and cooked her breakfast, then got her up in time to eat at 7:30. After breakfast she always went back to bed for an hour or two of rest. It was a complete reversal of our early days of marriage when I could hardly drag out of bed in the morning and she would have a hot breakfast ready for me when I got up. The physical part of the relationship was not a burden to me, but the emotional pain came in trying to keep up a continuing partnership of equality in marriage.

When a man and wife have been happily married for almost fifty years, there develops a mutual respect and honor born out of *agape* love. This respect extends to allowing one's partner to help make life decisions. Even more, it pertains to engaging in deep conversations where they wrestle with life issues that have to do with everything from the mundane to the intimate. I tried to continue treating her with the same respect as I had given her when she was whole. Because I adored her, I had always tried to give her what she wanted. What she mainly wanted now was to watch lots of television, travel, and eat out a lot. It was a stretch for me to work hard at any of those things. It was also hard to keep in mind that she had lost most of her short-term memory. If she asked often to eat out, it was because she had forgotten we had eaten out just yesterday! Every day I prayed for perfect patience, and at the end of every day I realized I had failed in some way. Another heartache was her frequently saying very sadly, "Surely God has something else for me to do on this earth. What do you think it could be?" She had a deep longing for significance through service, and that could no longer be. I searched in vain for some special task for her to make her feel useful again.

Some things about Wanda stayed with her. She kept her smile, even though the bright sparkle was no longer in her eyes. It was, however, a warm and never-failing smile. She loved her family, especially her grandchildren. They also loved her, and loved her new, uninhibited ways. She was more able to connect with the younger ones than I was, playing and joking with them. She still wanted to read her Bible. Sometimes, for several days, she would forget to read it, then I would remind her and she would get back to it again. Once she got into it she would read for an hour or more. She also loved books on Asia in general, and China in particular. She would sit quietly and devour a whole book on China in a couple of days. Finally, she loved to travel and see new things. Perhaps it was because of this passion for travel that we did not give up our travels to Indonesia after the ministroke. This may seem contradictory to what I have said about Wanda's limitations, and some of our relatives thought we were crazy to continue. Our prayer letter from October of 2003 was entitled: "On The Road Again." In it we state:

> For a while there we wondered if we would ever be back "on the road again" due to concerns over Wanda's health. We are profoundly grateful for her post-

ministroke recovery [a slight exaggeration here!] and her doctor's go-ahead to travel overseas. Headed for six weeks of ministry in the Chinese world and Indonesia, we sense the familiar feelings of trepidation and excitement. The sensation never changes. Adrenalin flows through old veins as well as young ones. This is where it's at. This is where the action is. We will do our best to encourage workers in the Chinese world.

After we visit the Chinese world, we travel to Indonesia...The day after we arrive, we are scheduled to speak to pastors and wives gathered from Central and East Java, plus Lombok Island...One more goal is to spend one-on-one time with village church planters in Central Java...O Lord, Help!

When we landed in Indonesia, Wanda was so tired that we wondered if she would be able to function at all. She did want to be there, however, in spite of her fatigue, and did her best to take some part in our encouragement ministry to others. It was amazing to discover that Wanda communicated more logically and emotionally in Indonesian than in English when she gave a devotional. We made another trip to Java in 2004. Again Wanda was feeling her loss of memory. One of her favorite former students sensed this feeling of loss. He came to the Jakarta airport to see us off. His prayer for her was eloquent:

Father in heaven, if Mother Wanda fears that she has forgotten some things of the past, help her to realize those things are not really lost. Help her to know that her teachings and her life example are deeply engraved in our hearts, and will become a part of the lives of our children and grandchildren. So, comfort her with the thought that the things in her mind are really not lost at all, rather they have come to be our possession and will be with us to be taught to our children and our children's children.

On these trips we did some ministry together in the form of the Interpersonal Skills Workshop. We had done it so many times, it was somehow engraved in her mind in such a way she could still go back to it without too much effort.

Back to Tucson

We had been living in Littleton, Colorado, for five years when the cold winters began to seriously affect Wanda. To put it in her own words, "I don't want any more cold weather the rest of my life." For me, it was a struggle to move away from WorldVenture headquarters, since our lives had been so tied up in missions. It was also difficult to move away from three young grandchildren living close by in Colorado Springs. However it seemed that the Lord was moving us in that direction. Living in a three-level townhouse was a deciding factor as well. We were needing a single-level dwelling because of Wanda's knee problems. In April of 2004 we found what seemed an ideal place just being constructed in Tucson, a four-bedroom home with a living room view of the Rincon Mountains. When moving day came, men from our Legacy Class at Mission Hills Church helped us load the U-Haul truck. Son-in-law Craig, accompanied by granddaughter Chrystie, drove the truck to Tucson for us. For me, it was like coming home, since I had graduated from Tucson High School so many years earlier, and my brother and his wife still lived in the city. We felt infinitely grateful that our frugal parents had left us some funds, and along with our own savings we could purchase the house for cash. God was generous beyond what we had ever hoped for. However we seemed to be getting further and further from our world of missions. I figured I was saying good-bye to any further overseas service as we said our farewells in Colorado in October of 2004. I had no idea God had one more big mission for my involvement.

The Great Tsunami

On December 26, 2004, the largest disaster in recent human history occurred in Southeast Asia. A great earthquake at sea caused tsunami waves of up to a hundred feet high to strike the coast of Aceh, North Sumatra, wiping the earth clean where there had once stood thousands of buildings. Uniquely, this was the only region of Indonesia that had embraced the Muslim Shariah Law. A few days later I received a call from our Asia Director, Marty Shaw, asking if I might be able to assist for a couple of weeks, surveying the damage and setting up for mercy teams from our churches to minister to the remaining, stricken population of Aceh. This was a difficult decision for both of us. Wanda wanted to travel wherever I went. She was not comfortable being left alone for any significant period of time. She was only at peace when she was with me. Given her condition and her deep feelings, she was the real hero in this venture. It was a superhuman effort on her part to let me go. A day or so before my departure, she still begged to go with me. The Lord finally strengthened her resolve, and she was able to release me.

I was on the ground in Aceh with Kevin just eight days after the disaster. The media could not convey through television the awful wreckage we witnessed there, nor can my words describe it here. The sheer power of water had washed large sea vessels a mile or more onto land. Row upon row of urban homes were transformed into piles of rubbish. Shattered pieces of boards, chunks of cement, clothing, plasterboard, toys and other debris were mingled in heaps ten feet high. School homework with the scrawl of children's handwriting was found not far from a lone little tricycle. Crushed vehicles appeared to have been turned into giant accordions. Bodies were littered over the debris in many places, grotesque and bloating spectacles. The stench was something the news media could never communicate, and it was by far the most penetrating of impressions we received. One large fishing vessel was perched on top of a small house as though a giant had plucked it from the sea and placed it there. A large ocean barge was washed several hundred yards up on the shore. We surveyed the carnage and pondered what kind of a message God might be conveying to these people. Estimates of loss of lives varied. The United States government estimated there were more than 167,000. The Indonesian government estimated that 700,000 people were displaced.

In the brief time we were there we were able to network with Samaritan's Purse and other organizations, enabling us to assure teams coming from America that they would have housing upon arrival. Makeshift tents were set up in large communities for immediate refuge. We stopped at one of these centers to interview some of the refugees who had been settled there after losing everything they owned. They gathered around us, eager to talk. It was fascinating how much their worldview had been transformed by the disaster. Before the tsunami, the Aceh people often termed America as "the great Satan," and proudly spoke of their own little region as being the *serambi* (front porch) to Mecca. Even other Indonesians were not welcomed to this strict region, and were considered outsiders. After the tsunami, one woman in the resettlement center stared me straight in the eye and said, "If it had not been for *your people,* we would have certainly starved or died of thirst." In this case *your people* was referring to American military personnel who had responded immediately by racing an aircraft carrier to the area which could produce thousands of gallons of fresh drinking water per hour. Food and water were then distributed by helicopter from the carrier. Thousands of lives were saved by these measures. Their whole perspective on America and its people was transformed by our country's immediate response to this disaster. I was appointed as Tsunami Team Coordinator for WorldVenture.

Needing men on the ground to manage and organize the teams, I contacted three former co-laborers from Indonesia: Stan Hagberg, Bob Long, and Dave Henderson. All of them were former fellow workers in Kalimantan Barat. All of them agreed to go for a short-term ministry in Aceh. It was hot and humid work, but they took on the task with great energy, winning the hearts of the Aceh people and the teams from America sent to work with them. Gregarious Stan worked his way into their hearts to the point where he was told, "Bring your wife, and come and live among us when this is all over!"

Long-term results in Aceh were most encouraging. Our best church planter in Java, Mr. S. felt called to move to the area. Working with the church teams that came, Mr. S. established a beachhead for reaching out with the gospel. Over the next few years he and his team won scores of people to The Way. God did not merely open the door to Aceh, which had previously been closed tight, not only to foreigners, but to other Indonesians. He broke down the door, so that thousands now have heard the gospel from the many workers with nongovernment organizations who entered to help the hurting.

Wanda and I ultimately had three "last trips" to Indonesia. That is, we kept returning to our Indonesian friends, telling them, "This is probably our last trip to see you!" One of these was in the year of 2004 mentioned above. It was returning from this trip that I lost another piece of Wanda. On this particular trip we had participated in the thirtieth anniversary of the Bethesda Hospital where we held a workshop for the local church planters. At the close of that workshop Evangelist Mikah asked:

> Is there any way you could communicate to those missionaries who first brought the gospel to us how deeply grateful we are to all of you? Were it not for you missionaries, we and all our people would be headed for hell instead of heaven today. How can we ever say thank you as we should?

Mikah mentioned the names of the Bryants, Hadleys, Bowens and Hagbergs, besides ourselves. Mikah had been ministering faithfully as an evangelist and church planter for more than thirty years. I baptized him as one of the first six converts at Dawar in 1966. This is part of the "afterglow" of life, that we are allowed to experience, by the grace of God, hearing the gratitude of the Dyak people.

All in all, it was a very satisfying trip, but on our way home Wanda had another stroke. Even in this case the grace of God abounded to us. A quote from our May 2004 prayer letter says:

> Having disembarked from airplanes so many times over the past forty-some years, we pretty much have our

system worked out. I forge ahead with a heavy carry-on, and Wanda is right behind me carrying a lighter one. But upon deplaning in Incheon, Korea, on our way back from Indonesia I turned around to find she was not there. When she finally appeared she was "listing heavily" to the left in her gait, her balance gone. I grabbed all the bags and stabilized her. Her eyes were also failing to focus properly and I feared she was having another stroke. She was also using "word salad," or putting a bunch of words together that are disconnected from reality. After three hours of rest in a hotel she showed no improvement. An ambulance whisked us away from the hotel for a fifty-minute drive to the emergency room of INHA University hospital, siren screaming as the driver skillfully maneuvered us through the traffic lights. ER in Incheon, Korea, is not like ER in Littleton, Colorado. No curtains separated us from the emergency cases surrounding us. A man with many fresh face wounds was gurgling up blood through his tube just a few inches from Wanda's bed.

Angel of Mercy: But the care was excellent and the Korean medical personnel were professional. We were told at first that she needed an MRI but we would have to wait until tomorrow. But then the bright, young neurologist discovered that we were missionaries – and she was a Christian. Not more than four feet and eleven inches tall, she was more than adequate to the task. From then on she seemed on a "mission" to take care of us. She discovered that we *could* have the MRI in an hour or so. She made me promise that if there was an acute problem we would stay in Korea a week. If there was not, we could leave the hospital that night. It took awhile, but she eventually returned with the news that we were free to "go home." But we had left the hotel so quickly I did not even know the name of it. Fortunately I did have a number for the airline office. The airline official asked us if we had Korean currency to take a taxi back to the hotel. The answer was "no." Was there an ATM or other source of Korean money nearby? Again the answer was "no." The Korean doctor, listening in to all of this, politely took the phone away from me and chatted with the airline agent. She then took us outside in the cold Korean winter wind, her white doctor's robe flapping in the breeze. She found a brand-new taxi, dialed the number of our hotel on her cell phone, and asked the hotel clerk to give the taxi driver exact directions on how to get there. She then handed what seemed to be a fistful of Korean money to the driver and told us to get in. I begged to pay her in U.S. dollars but she adamantly refused any payment. We asked for her name, which she also refused to give until we told her we needed it to pray for her. Unlike the angel who wrestled with Jacob, this angel was willing to give her name when it was for prayer purposes. Her name was Dr. Haewon Kong. We rode perhaps a half block before I began to weep for the relief of it. The smell of new leather in a comfortable taxi was part of the pleasure. God had brought along His angel at the perfect time for us.

With experiences like this happening to us, some thought we were slightly out of our minds to continue intercontinental travel at our age and state of health. Perhaps we should have stopped all overseas travel at this point, but it seemed that the pressure built up in us over a period of time, the longing to be with the Indonesian people, and to speak the language that was as familiar to us as was our native tongue. Our final trip to Indonesia was mid-December 2009 to mid-January 2010. We had had more than our share of afterglow moments by then.

Wanda's Last Ministry

God heard Wanda's prayers for an opportunity to serve Him in her final years. It came in a surprising way. In Tucson we had joined El Camino Baptist Church in 2005 and immediately started attending prayer meeting, along with the regular church services. By 2007 I was serving as an elder and teaching a seniors' Bible study class on Sunday mornings. Besides looking out for my wife, I was quite busy with church activities. Wanda often mourned the fact that seemingly God did not have a place for her to minister. El Camino has always had a strong foreign missions program. They had supported us in Indonesia for more than thirty years. In preparation for the 2008 annual missions conference, a bright and beautiful young air force wife was given the task of writing a missionary drama to portray how better to pray for missionaries. Tennille contacted us to get some missionary background and make the drama as realistic as possible. She was so intrigued with our story she suggested we might get together as couples. This suited us perfectly. Our ministry over the past forty years in Indonesia had been among young couples and we were eager to meet with her and her husband. Thus began the most surprising and beautiful friendship of our later years. Tennille was not quite thirty years old, and her tall, handsome, air force major husband was her senior by only a couple of years. They were beautiful people, inside and out. We started meeting together as couples twice a month and found it refreshing for both of us. It seemed counterintuitive to others perhaps because of our vast age discrepancy, but each of us acknowledged the other couple as "our best friends in town."

Tennille saw something latent in Wanda that many had failed to see. She asked her to share her life experience in marriage and family with herself and two other young women of the church, Breana and Kristina. The three of them began meeting at noon at our house once a week. Although the stroke had erased much of Wanda's short-term memory, she could still draw from her deep and rich experience of teaching marriage and family courses in Indonesia. She also had more than fifty years of married life experience to draw from. Wanda and these young women adored each other in spite of the age and life experience discrepancies. I had found a workbook online called, "After You Say I Do," by

°

Norman Wright for them to use as a study guide. They all worked on it faithfully. From my study I could not distinguish the words they were saying, but I could hear their joy. Every few moments they would erupt into gales of laughter, letting me know that studying about how to grow in one's relationship with one's husband can be much more fun than most husbands could imagine. Frankly, I was flabbergasted that Wanda could still pull up from her memory the life experiences and advice that was relevant to these young women. Her ministry in their lives was probably as fulfilling to me as it was for her. I had agonized with her over her lack of opportunity for service. Now she was again feeling fulfilled. She loved serving her Lord Jesus more than anything on earth.

This ministry to young wives went on for a year. It would be difficult for me to evaluate the lasting value of the time these women shared with Wanda if Tennille did not tell me. She recently said, "Not a week goes by but what I remember something Wanda shared with us about how to live with and honor our husbands." It is a precious and lasting memory, realizing that a merciful God gave her one final opportunity to bless His people through her. Hard times were just ahead, though neither Wanda nor I had the slightest idea of how soon the end would come.

The Valley of the Shadow of Death

Over the next seven years after Wanda's stroke, I gradually became responsible for every decision to be made, every item to be remembered. Regarding things like deciding meal menus, or being sure we got where we were going on time, Wanda did not care to express an opinion. As long as I was with her, she was content. If anything went wrong in any aspect of our lives, it was my fault. I mean, really my fault, because it could no longer be hers. Looking back now, I realize I was a bit like the proverbial "frog in the kettle." Wanda's health was gradually getting worse, but it was difficult for me to see it on a day- to-day basis. If she was tired before, she was even more tired now. When she complained that she had absolutely nothing to do, I began making her a daily schedule, like she used to do for herself. It was routine things like: "Play the piano, have a quiet time, vacuum two rooms, do the Bible study assigned for deaconesses…" But she was pleased to have it because it gave her the needed direction.

I was not the only frog in the kettle. Even Wanda's medical doctor did not see it coming. To be fair, there was no way he could have seen it coming. On December 8, 2010, she had her annual physical and the standard lab tests done. Dr. Rogers typed in all caps, and highlighted with a yellow marker above the lab results, the words: "GOOD NEWS! LAB RESULTS ARE ALL NORMAL OR UNREMARKABLE." No one could have imagined such a reversal of her health less than two months later.

Before mid-January Wanda began having severe pain in her hands. We tried various pain relief medicines. We even bought a paraffin basin so she could dip her hands in the warm, liquid wax until it resembled a wax glove, which was then peeled off. It offered some relief, but the easing of pain was only temporary. On the seventeenth of January I took her to Dr. Rogers' office where she had a complete blood test. Her white blood count was an alarming 42,000. That suddenly got the attention of the medical world. When two days later her second white blood count was over 50,000 the attending physician suggested I bring her in again next week. Instead I took her straight from the doctor's office to the emergency room at St. Joseph's Hospital. She was immediately admitted. Cheryl was working an upper floor, but came down to ER to be with us. We heard Dr. Bravo say, almost reverently, that Wanda probably had Acute Mylogeneous Leukemia (AML). He was very solemn. I had no idea he was stating her death sentence. AML is an extremely aggressive form of leukemia. Consulting further with oncologist Dr. Boxer, we learned just how aggressive. He estimated that without taking chemotherapy Wanda would have only weeks to live. We were given a choice. Take the chemo and perhaps live a few months, or go without it and come to an even swifter death. It was not really even that optimistic. Chemotherapy treatments might, but would not necessarily, prolong her life. Wanda's age worked against the probability of any long-term recovery. She had many other health factors that could keep her from responding well to the chemo, including a very slushy-sounding (the doctor called it "thundering") mitro-valve in the heart. A recent CAT scan showed she also had severe narrowing of major arteries at the top of her brain. I knew the only rational decision was to choose the road that would give her some quality of life for a short time, and reject the chemo treatment. I hoped she would see it that way, too. I went home from the hospital, knelt by my bed, and wept like I had not wept for decades.

"Hope" is a word Wanda never wanted to let go of. I could see in her eyes that she would like to believe that the chemo would extend her life on earth. She was not able to visualize the trauma the chemo would cause her body and her family. The doctors made it clear that only one in four people have a remission from this type of cancer, and those people are usually without other health complications. In making the final decision, Wanda looked into my eyes and said, "I want whatever Arny wants." I can't describe the conflict in my heart at that moment. The decision for keeping her on earth a bit longer, and in great discomfort, or allowing her to go to heaven earlier, was all mine. It was the easiest and the hardest decision I have ever made. Easy, because I knew beyond the shadow of a doubt what was right. Hard, because it seemed to say I was willing to limit her days with me on earth.

It was a time when the *golden thread* of God's will again made its impact on me. Emotions had to give way to the clear values we had lived by for our whole lives. I wrote a letter to all our friends and family stating our confident belief. "It is hard to visualize how it would be consistent with the faith we profess, to prolong briefly, a life that would be lived in pain and discomfort on earth, if one sincerely believes that glory awaits us just on the other side." That was the logic of faith. The feelings to back it up remained a continuing struggle. All four of the children courageously came to support the idea of rejecting chemo treatment. Yvonne, her mother's baby, gave unexpected help when it came to encouraging her mother to turn down the chemotherapy. We talked over the decision with Yvonne by the computer Skype program, sitting on the side of a hospital bed, after just having had a tearful conversation about Wanda's soon departure. Here is what Yvonne remembers of that difficult conversation, in Yvonne's own words:

Mom looked at me and said, "Vons, what should I do? "

I said, "Mom, what do you want to do? "

She said, "Well, I want to be brave like Ginny. She has been such a special friend to me. She is so kind and brave. And she beat chemo. And, I want to be like her."

And I said, "Mom, you want to do the chemo because you think it is the tough thing to do? "

And she said, "Yes, I want to be tough."

I said, "Mom, everyone in this family knows that you are tough. This is not about being brave or not being brave. You are going to die. That is the bravest thing anyone ever has to do. If you don't do the chemo, we know you will die faster. You will have to leave that wonderful man who's sitting next to you a little sooner. And, you will get to see your mom and dad sooner while you wait for your husband. The chemo might give you more time here with us, but it might not."

Yvonne's brave words were delivered in a matter-of-fact tone of voice that did not divulge her breaking heart. Sonja, still in Cyprus, and Kevin, still in Indonesia, supported the idea as well. Cheryl, the eldest and most vulnerable to her own compassion, found it very difficult, but also agreed it was the right path to take. We had a final family meeting with the oncologist who still encouraged us to try the chemo treatment, but everyone stood firm, not wanting their mother to go through the agony. There was a sense of unity, as every child plunged into this glorious mission, "escorting Mom to the gates of heaven." This idea seemed to all of us so very lofty, compared to the usual description of dying: "Fighting, and finally losing her last battle with cancer." And so, all four of the children began the process of coming home to complete this final mission. Their mother had brought them into this world. Now they would see her out of it, with great love and compassion, and yes, with considerable grieving. The oncologist gave us a good piece of advice, though. We had planned and paid for a trip to Disney World in Florida. It included also a prepaid, nonrefundable three-day cruise to the Caribbean Islands. Wanda had always loved the world of Disney and was still quite determined to go, no matter what. The cruise was the only thing left on our lifetime "bucket list." The doctor somberly warned us that we might have to call a helicopter to get Wanda off the ship if we insisted on this one last fling at life. Reluctantly we canceled, but it was not an easy decision.

Yvonne came on a Thursday, to spend a long weekend in early February. What a relief to have her in the house. Sonja made the long flight from Cyprus, arriving just two days after Yvonne. She brought with her Nicole (12) and Shenna (9). Ignoring jet lag they plunged into care for their mother and grandmother. Both granddaughters were eager to help with every odd chore. Each of my daughters had her own special way of ministering to her mother. It almost felt like a competition of love! Cheryl was the expert in medical care, including an intuitive sense of what her mom needed most. Sonja had a way of keeping things in order, helping her girls be useful, getting me out of the house for a bike ride, and managing food. Yvonne always had a way of making her mother laugh and of cleverly dealing with her when she was not quite making sense. For instance, one night Wanda, rather delirious, found her old briefcase and declared, "I have to go to a meeting. I am going to be late." Yvonne said, "Oh, that's great, Mom, but wouldn't you like a cup of tea before you go?" Wanda accepted the invitation to tea and promptly forgot all about the meeting. All of the girls have a gift for joking and laughing under the most serious of circumstances and in the heat of a crisis. There was a lot of laughter in the house during those hard days, as the girls got silly and got their mom laughing along with them, even when she was in great pain. In every way they made life for me as easy as possible. They competed to be the one at Wanda's bedside at night, and I only occasionally took a turn with them. They wanted me to get my rest, and indeed I was weary to the bone, even with getting enough hours of sleep, because underneath the sorrow was so great.

Wanda might have been indecisive on many things in her last days, but one thing she made very clear: "I do not want to go back to the hospital." With that clarification from her, she was put on hospice soon after her fatal diagnosis. A hospital bed was set up in our large living room. It was sunny and bright, and she could look up anytime to catch a view of the Rincon Mountains. It was also noisy, but that did not bother her, because she always wanted to be in the center of everything that had to do with family. She was given drugs to deal with the fierce pain in her bones, and other drugs to cut down anxiety. They were moderately effective, but the liquid morphine had the side effect of making her hallucinate. Becoming aware of that, she said, "I don't care how much pain I have, I am not taking that drug any longer." And she didn't!

Dates blurred together for me as we continued the day-and-night vigil, with our total focus on Wanda. She was going downhill fast. It took awhile for it to sink in on her that she and I were about to part forever, as far as this mortal life is concerned. She had earlier confided to a nurse at the hospital, "I don't mind dying, but I just don't want to leave Arny." When she told me the same thing I was barely able to choke out, "Honey, you will never leave me. Your life has had such an impact on me, I will always carry you with me, because you have had such a part in making me who I am. I will never be the same as I was before I met you." Those talks seemed to bring her along toward the reality of death.

However, as it became even more of a reality to her, she started to ask specific questions about the death event. One day I got her outside in the wheelchair to push her around the block. The day was brilliant, and it felt good just to be outside with her. She finally asked quietly, "How will they come for me? How will I go?" By then I was able to say without blubbering, but still with tears restrained, "Your body is gradually pushing out your spirit. When it leaves your body, Jesus will be there to meet you." The answer seemed to satisfy her momentarily. On that same little outing a neighbor asked where we were going. When I told him Wanda was on her way to heaven, he said, "No, I mean where are you going now?" We repeated that she really was going to heaven very soon, perhaps within a week. That made him very uncomfortable and he looked away, not wanting to continue the conversation. He did not want to hear a word about death. Few non-Christians we met were prepared to respond when the subject of death came up.

Almost every day Wanda would have only a brief window of time when she was quite aware and able to communicate. The remaining time she would be sleeping, or hurting desperately and gasping for breath, making us wonder if the end was imminent. The eleventh of February seemed to start off as a bad day. She could hardly move. It turned out to be a day when she got more serious about saying good-bye to all of us again. With her short-term memory it needed to be done more than once. There was a period during this day in which I wondered if we could ever stir her, she was so unresponsive. Finally the hospice attendant came and Wanda was willing to take a shower, this after a lot of indecision. But the shower actually helped her regain some zest for living. I read her some of the beautiful notes, mostly emails, that had been sent to her from many places in the world. Then she had a very loving and tearful phone conversation with dearest old friend, Ellen Duren. Shortly after that there were a lot of tears, especially from Shenna and Sonja, as she said her good-byes to them. "Good-bye, my sweet Shenna! I will see you in heaven," were the words that at first caused Shenna to flee the room in tears. Then she came back for a hug and more tears, adding her own words that she looked forward to seeing Grandma in heaven. Nicole also was deeply touched by the good-byes.

A bit later Wanda perked up a bit, and was up for taking a ride with me in the car. That was perfect, since it was Friday, our traditional "date night." While driving she was very quiet with her thoughts seemingly running deeper than they had for a long time. Suddenly she spoke those thoughts very softly, "So we are not going together then, are we?" I nodded in agreement with her, barely able to whisper that it was true we would not go together. "It seems like we should be able to just wrap our arms around each other and go at the same time," she said. As mentioned earlier, over the years we had often talked of trying to figure out a way to go to heaven at the same time. I suggested we might drive up to Mount Lemmon just a few minutes away and sail off the highway into a gorge together. It was a poor attempt at humor. She did not comment on that proposal, certainly did not reject the idea. We went to a Sonic drive-thru and ordered a large chocolate malt to split between us, as we so often had done on date nights in the past. We both knew it was to be our last date. I took her to nearby Lincoln Park where we had played with our extended family many times in the past. It is just a small, inconspicuous little place with few recreational facilities. We sat on a picnic bench sipping our malt, snuggling up together in the cool breeze. In mid-February every plant and tree looked dead, including the grass. Overall it was a drab scene. Wanda saw it differently. She said, "It is the most beautiful park I have ever seen." I took another look around and decided it was indeed beautiful, but only because she was still with me. I pushed her wheelchair a bit on the limited sidewalk that runs on one side of the park, and we just looked around, saying little while my heart was bursting with pain, mixed with exquisite joy. This day would not come again. I brought her home and she immediately crashed into that other world of semiconscious pain.

It was nearing Valentine's Day, and I did not want to miss it with Wanda. She got up that morning and wanted to go back to bed immediately with no breakfast. Hoping to revive her spirits I brought out her heart-shaped box of chocolates and a lovely card I had bought for her. It was a particularly bad morning for her, but she perked up immediately, smiled, and responded gratefully to the gifts, even eating a couple of the chocolates.

The end drew near, and Wanda still seemed concerned about who was coming to get her. We marveled at the special thing God did for her to ease that anxiety. One day, when Camille, Cheryl's youngest, was over to the house, along with the other family members, Wanda had a special vision. With everyone surrounding her bed, Wanda suddenly asked Cheryl, "Who is that standing next to you?"

"That's Camille," Cheryl said.

"No, the person next to Camille."

"What does he look like?" asked Yvonne.

"It's not a 'he'!" she said tersely, as though Yvonne was being silly. "It's a woman."

"Does she have wings?" Yvonne asked excitedly.

When Wanda did not answer immediately, Cheryl asked, "Is she comforting, Mom?"

"Yes," and Wanda began to cry.

"Because you were wondering if someone would come to take you away?" asked Cheryl.

"Yes," and Wanda cried a bit harder.

"Why are you crying, Mom?"

"Because I'm the luckiest person in the world!"

In her world of pain and anxiety, I believe God gave her a good idea of who it was that was going to come and get her to take her to heaven. She asked no more about who was coming to get her or how she would die.

Wanda had a grateful attitude that characterized her throughout her last days. She never complained or showed anger that God was taking her away from the people she loved. She was content to be surrounded by family. One day, when she was very weak, and I feared she might be going in the next twenty-four hours, I asked, "Honey, is there anything at all that I can do for you?" With softest eyes and softer voice, she made her request with just one word, "Kevin?" She wanted to have her son beside her when she left this earth. I assured her that he was coming soon. She thanked each person who cared for her, no matter how small the task. She once became distraught when being physically lifted for toiletry needs, saying, "I just don't like causing my family so much trouble."

On Valentine's Day I recorded in my journal that it was definitely Wanda's hardest day. Even though I had previously given her an early Valentine and a box of chocolates, I spontaneously bought her another card, along with a very soft pink teddy bear. She truly loved it, and from then on to the end it was under her arm, in bed with her, or when she was walking around. Then Wanda got very romantic. It was after a shower and she felt a tiny bit better. We sat on the couch where she hugged on me and seemingly could not get enough kisses. It was as though it was her last fling at expressing her love. Emotionally she was back to her old self as she had been in prestroke days. We talked about how much we had loved each other over the years, and what a wonderful life we had experienced. I was quite overwhelmed, as she had not acted like this for many years.

On February 15 Wanda greeted grandson Kennie royally in the early morning. Kennie had helped on night watch a couple of times. Then our old friends, Bob and Barbara Chapman, visited us from Massachusetts. Wanda rose to the occasion of receiving them royally as guests, as usual going beyond herself. She greeted the Chapmans with her big smile. Her first words to Barbara were, "When you come to heaven I want you to play 'He Lives' for me on the organ. And you better play it good, cause it's for me." Barb sat beside her quietly for most of the time, as she and Bob just absorbed this God-given opportunity of closure with a lifelong friend. We had been through so many crises during Borneo days, and now here they were, able to be with her in her final crisis hour. I kept thinking how good God was in orchestrating everything perfectly, while we were down here, "playing it by ear," from our perspective.

I also sensed God's good plan regarding the timing of Kevin's arrival. He arrived late on the night of February 15. I picked him up at the Tucson Airport. I had feared he would miss seeing his mother, even as I had missed seeing mine. Though experiencing jet lag, he still took the opportunity of staying up all night with his mother. It was not clear whether or not she recognized him that night. The next day, her clouded vision cleared, and her face brightened as she focused on him. She said, "Oh, Kevin, you are here. I thought I'd never see you again." Now her world was complete. All four children were around her bedside, taking turns at loving on her, and caring for her every need. Wanda and I had often said our lives were most full when all of our children lived at home. Our empty nest years were good, too, but the richest era of our lives was when we had the house full of children. Wanda was blessed beyond measure at the tender hands of all four of her children.

On February 16 we did a lot of singing. Yvonne had already been singing over her mother, sometimes for an hour at a time, especially when she was restless. Now we all gathered around her bed to sing old hymns. Kevin got Leilani to set up her keyboard and computer in Indonesia, playing for a family congregated in America. For once the Skype computer program that allows us to see each other halfway around the world never froze up on us. From their home in Indonesia, Leilani played and led us all for long periods of time. With one voice we claimed the words of "Great is Thy Faithfulness," and many other precious old hymns. Breeana was there also to join in the singing. Breeana and Leilani were able to say their good-byes to "Mom" and she to them. Another time, Joshua and Dave from Cyprus also joined us via Skype in our living room. Joshua played the keyboard for us to sing. Both of them said their good-byes to Wanda and released her to go to heaven. We maximized Wanda's every waking moment that day, singing and sharing our love for each other.

The night of February 16 could only be described as extremely excruciating and long. Wanda's lungs were filled with fluid and she was fighting desperately for every breath. Cheryl especially begged God to release her mother from that body. The next morning the girls woke me up at 5:00 a.m. to tell me they thought it was their mother's last hours or minutes. Indeed, it seemed that every heaving breath would be her last. Pastor Ron Rushing came, and we began planning for a graveside service and memorial. Here is my journal from that last day of her life:

February 17, 2011: Wanda went peacefully at 10:50 this morning, with all of her children and myself gathered around her bed. God's timing was perfect.

Skype calls and telephone calls are going to many quarters of the world. She was dearly loved by everyone who knew her. We were just saying, as a family, she was the most guileless person we knew, and we knew her very up close. She was always thinking of others. Pastor Ron came about 10:00 this morning and quoted her some verses. We had all given her permission to go. Ron repeated that she was free to go and that she had lived a wonderful life. She showed some clear facial expression and gurgled, "OK." A few minutes later we were standing around her when she took her last breaths. Then she was gone. My heart was so squeezed by pain, and my voice so constricted I could barely whisper the words, "Free, free at last!" as I gave her face a few gentle strokes. The sense of loss was so very painful for the first fifteen minutes or so, I thought my heart would burst, and then there was the relief of picturing her in heaven, and out of that beat-up old body. I repeat what I have often said lately. In the old translation it was worded, "He doeth all things well." His timing was perfect. We will miss her terribly, and we will at the same time have the greatest of all comfort from the Comforter.

Kevin set up the computer so Leilani and Breeana could see Wanda in her death state. Somehow, seeing their grief-stricken faces and tears allowed both them and us to feel that they were deeply involved in this final transition. Missionary families often miss the opportunity to share in the grief process. This can leave a permanent hole in the heart for years. We also connected with David and Joshua in Cyprus by Skype so they could see Wanda's body immediately after death. These were important foundation stones for helping family feel connected and for future healing.

Leilani phoned the news to scores of Indonesian friends by text message, and received back as many messages as she sent. A flood of emails came also as a result of my letter to them. When Wanda's memorial service was held just three days later, three hundred and fifty people came to show their respect. Eight former Kalimantan missionaries came to the service, and the presidents of two large international mission agencies were there as well. All of my children spoke eloquently of their mother's life. Tennille Komulainen and Denyse Grippentrog also gave deeply touching testimonies of what Wanda's life had meant to them. Together, they painted a picture of who the real Wanda was. Each of them made it clear that her charisma and good works came out of an obedient life and a deep commitment to spend time with God each day. It was ultimately He who got the glory. I had been attending this church for almost eight years where the members thought of Wanda as "a nice little old lady." I had sometimes wanted to shout, "You have no idea who this woman is!" Now they knew, and many came up to offer their astonished comments, saying, "Why did I not try to get to know her better?" I felt so gratified that they could finally understand what an impact she had had on the world for the Lord Jesus.

The reader may wonder why I have spent so much time commenting on Wanda's last few weeks, in comparison with her many other years on earth. Undoubtedly it is in part because I am writing these pages just three months after her death, and it is still so vivid in my mind. But primarily I feel it is because she died so bravely, and so very sure of where she was going. Over the last fifteen years we had been obsessing about the goal of "finishing well." She completed her mission of finishing well. She died as she had lived, thinking of others. To me, that is the epitome of finishing well – thinking of others.

As I think back on Wanda's death, I am reminded of my old friend U.T. Simatupang whom I described in Part Three of this writing. The last time I was ever to see him was in January of 2010. That was Wanda's and my last visit to Indonesia. I was inside our Bethesda Hospital in Serukam, Kalimantan Barat when I heard he was out front, on his way into the city. I found him out there, near his old jalopy, headed into Singkawang for his bimonthly dialysis treatment. He greeted me warmly and smiled his old smile, but seemingly could not look directly into my eyes.

His complexion was ash gray, and his eyes hardly seemed to focus. His movements were slow and lethargic. It was easy to see he was not long for this world.

Seeing his pitiful condition, I tried to offer him some comforting words, saying that while my health seemed good, I knew I would soon be following him to heaven. He interrupted me, not wanting to hear my words of consolation, saying, *"O ya, Pak, tetapi kita masih bisa dipakai pada usia tua."* ("O yes, friend, but we can still be used in old age.") He then invited me to go to Dawar with him the next Sunday to preach. I was amazed he was still actively serving the Lord. Sure enough, he had been going on alternate Sundays on a very rough Jeep road, back up to Dawar where I had met him forty-five years earlier. The church had gone downhill a bit over the years, and he was helping them reorganize and move ahead again. His youngest son was his driver, and he carried his oxygen tank with him in case of an emergency.

I never saw Simatupang again. He passed away just a few months after the time of our meeting. But his words still ring in my ears, "O yes, friend, but we can still be used in old age." May it be true, O Lord. May it be true! Both for me and for all who read these words, for whatever years you and I have left on this earth. Let the *golden thread* still weave its way into our lives until we take our last breath. As I first said at age seventeen, "Lord, my greatest desire is to know Your will for my life, even now, and to *finish well*."

> *They will still bear fruit in old age,*
> *they will stay fresh and green,*
> *proclaiming, "The LORD is upright;*
> *He is my rock, and there is no*
> *wickedness in Him." (Psalm 92:14-15)*

CPSIA information can be obtained at www.ICGtesting.com
Printed in the USA
BVOW040214290612

293941BV00001B/3/P